Sibling Issues in Therapy

D1528276

Also by Avidan Milevsky

UNDERSTANDING ADOLESCENTS FOR HELPING PROFESSIONALS

WILL I EVER BE HAPPY AGAIN: A Jewish Approach to Helping Children Deal with the Loss of a Loved One

THE TRANSITORY NATURE OF PARENT, SIBLING, AND ROMANTIC PARTNER RELATIONSHIPS IN EMERGING ADULTHOOD

SIBLING RELATIONSHIPS IN CHILDHOOD AND ADOLESCENCE: Predictors and Outcomes

Sibling Issues in Therapy

Research and Practice with Children, Adolescents and Adults

Avidan Milevsky

Kutztown University of Pennsylvania, USA
Wellspring Counseling, Towson, MD, USA

First published 2016 by
PALGRAVE MACMILLAN

Palgrave Macmillan in the UK is an imprint of Macmillan Publishers Limited, registered in England, company number 785998, of Houndmills, Basingstoke, Hampshire RG21 6XS.

Palgrave Macmillan in the US is a division of St Martin's Press LLC, 175 Fifth Avenue, New York, NY 10010.

Palgrave Macmillan is the global academic imprint of the above companies and has companies and representatives throughout the world.

Palgrave® and Macmillan® are registered trademarks in the United States, the United Kingdom, Europe and other countries.

ISBN 978–1–137–52845–2 hardback
ISBN 978–1–137–52846–9 paperback

This book is printed on paper suitable for recycling and made from fully managed and sustained forest sources. Logging, pulping and manufacturing processes are expected to conform to the environmental regulations of the country of origin.

A catalogue record for this book is available from the British Library.

Library of Congress Cataloging-in-Publication Data
Milevsky, Avidan.
    Sibling issues in therapy : research and practice with children, adolescents and adults / Avidan Milevsky.
        pages   cm
    Summary: "Sibling matters underlie issues at the core of many clinical difficulties presented by adult clients. Recent studies show that individuals with a close sibling relationship are more emotionally mature, are happier, have positive psychological well-being, and have closer friendships. This book incorporates the latest research and clinical work in family dynamics to examine multiple angles of integrating sibling issues in therapy. Using theoretical perspectives, a wealth of empirical data, testing instruments, and case studies readers will experience an engaging and thorough examination of these issues, along with obtaining tools and techniques that can immediately be implemented in practice." — Provided by publisher.
    ISBN 978–1–137–52845–2 (hardback) —
    ISBN 978–1–137–52846–9 (paperback)
    1. Brothers and sisters—Psychological aspects.   2. Families—Psychological aspects.   3. Psychotherapy.   I. Title.
    BF723.S43M54 2015
    155.9′24—dc23   2015023387

To my wife Ilana . . .

Contents

Tables

Preface

We were sitting in the living room illuminated by a flickering memorial candle struggling to stay alive. The funeral-home director insisted that the candle would last for seven days. On a short wooden bench to my right were my two older brothers, Moshe and Yirmiya. My younger brother, Yonatan, was on a bench to my left. My kid sister, Devorah, aged seven, was in the other room with our mother. Her long-term plan was world travel, not widowhood at 46. Twenty-four hours prior we had spent a dreary afternoon burying our father. After a negotiation that lasted close to five years, he valiantly acquiesced to the wishes of the Angel of Death. He finally lost an argument.

We were in the midst of day two of the week-long mourning period known in our faith as the "week of Shiva." Being a well-regarded Talmudic scholar, our father gained many followers over the years, all of whom wanted to pay their last respects to the family of their revered rabbi.

Our house was inundated with people from around the globe offering their condolences to a family whose foundation had just been upended. On that day, as the visitors came and went, my brothers and I inconspicuously found our way to the backyard and began to kick around a soccer ball. Being from Uruguay, our father instilled in all of us a love for the game. His favorite childhood memory was when the Uruguayan national team beat Brazil in the 1950 World Cup final. Playing our father's game on that day seemed right. We found the outing uplifting and decided to take many such soccer breaks over the upcoming, dreadful few days.

Although many visitors coming to the house of mourning found it peculiar to see the sons of the great sage playing soccer outside instead of sitting in the living room lamenting, we continued with our newfound tradition throughout the week. In the backyard that week was the finest soccer ever played.

While many would attribute the healing power of those outings to the "beautiful game," I suggest that what was truly reassuring as we chased down the ball was something far greater than a game. What offered a sense of well-being during those games was the sibling bond. Although our world was turned upside down, those soccer games reminded us that our relationship with each other had not changed. Regardless of the turmoil in our midst, we were still there together offering each other a profound sense of stability and continuity.

Siblings are one of the most important influences in our life. In childhood, they are the context in which we learn about social interactions, conflict resolution, sharing, negotiations, and emotion management, all essential life lessons. In adulthood, siblings can be a profound source of support as we deal with life's challenges. On the other hand, destructive sibling relationships can make for a miserable childhood and a chaotic adulthood. Knowing how to harness the power of this fascinating relationship can offer a lifelong gift of support, warmth, and affection.

Considering the potency of the sibling bond, sibling issues often, overtly or covertly, permeate the content of psychotherapy. Clinicians working with clients of all types and ages will be well served by having an understanding of the role played by siblings throughout life, what impacts the sibling bond early in life, and how sibling issues impact adulthood well-being. This book offers researchers and clinicians a comprehensive understanding of sibling issues, including how to apply the knowledge in therapeutic interventions.

Acknowledgments

My interest in siblings developed many years ago working under the direction of Dr. Mary Levitt in the doctoral program in developmental psychology at Florida International University. I am grateful for her continued inspiration and support.

I am privileged to serve as a faculty member of Psychology at Kutztown University of Pennsylvania where I have been able to continue pursuing my research on families. The work on which this book is based was made possible by several grants from the university's Professional Development Committee and the Pennsylvania State System of Higher Education Faculty Professional Development Council. I would also like to thank my colleagues in the department for their continued support and for creating a collegial atmosphere conducive for personal growth.

Thank you to the staff and research assistants of the Center for Parenting Research at Kutztown University of Pennsylvania. Special thanks to Kristine Hernandez for her research and editorial assistance for this book. Additionally, I would like to acknowledge Melissa Schlechter, the longest serving member of our research team, who even after her graduation and current successful academic and clinical career continues to find the time to serve as a consultant for our various research projects.

I am fortunate to be working with Ken Zeigler, MSW, LCSW-C, Founder and Clinical Director of Wellspring Counseling in Towson, MD, and the other clinicians at the practice: Amy Price, Katie Kavalsky, and Kate Richa. Special thanks to Wellspring's Administrative Assistant Kris Bailey for her continuous help and support.

It has been a pleasure working with the team at Palgrave Macmillan during all phases of the publication process. Special thanks to Nicola Jones, Eleanor Christie, and Libby Forrest for their assistance throughout the project.

About the Author

Avidan Milevsky is Associate Professor of Developmental Psychology at Kutztown University of Pennsylvania and a psychotherapist at Wellspring Counseling in Towson, MD, where he specializes in sibling issues. He holds a Ph.D. in developmental psychology from Florida International University and a B.L.S. in behavioral sciences from Barry University. He is a prior visiting professor at the Hebrew University in Jerusalem.

He serves as Director of the Center for Parenting Research at Kutztown University of Pennsylvania. He teaches undergraduate and graduate courses in lifespan development and assessment. His clinical research has produced over 100 conference presentations and more than 20 papers including publications in the *Journal of Social and Personal Relationships*, *Social Development*, *Educational Psychology*, the *European Journal of Developmental Psychology*, *Child and Family Studies*, and the *Journal of Adult Development*. He is also a contributor to the *Encyclopedia of Adolescence*. His four books include *Sibling Relationships in Childhood and Adolescence: Predictors and Outcomes* and *Understanding Adolescents for the Helping Professional*.

He has lectured to audiences in the United States, Canada, South America, Europe, and the Middle East on various topics including family issues in therapy, parenting, and sibling relationships. He has been a guest expert on TV, radio, and the media about his work, including stories in the *Washington Post*, the *Wall Street Journal*, the *Associated Press*, *Real Simple*, and *Allure* magazine. Additionally, he is a columnist for *Psychology Today* and the *Huffington Post* on family issues.

He is currently consulting for the Pennsylvania State House's Children and Youth Committee in an effort to introduce legislation that would strengthen sibling visitation rights in family court and recognize the importance of sibling relationships on the emotional and psychological development of children and adolescents.

My brothers I seek...

Genesis, 37:16

Part I

The Foundation: The Role of Siblings in Developmental and Clinical Literature

1

The Significance of Siblings throughout Life

As the field of mental health matures, a consistent stream of cross-sectional and longitudinal research emanating from developmental and clinical psychology has highlighted distinct correlates between early life experiences and adult functioning. From as early as prenatal development and onward, numerous aspects of an individual's surroundings provide ingredients that coalesce with biological determinants to produce epigenesis. A long list of significant lifelong human features including physical health, food choices, intelligence, occupational status, political ideology, spirituality, sociability, and psychological well-being has been suggested to be influenced by early childhood environment.

One particularly fertile line of research on environmental influences and development has emphasized the importance of family interactions and atmosphere. Driven by the early theoretical models of Freud, Bowlby, Harlow, and Ainsworth, with their initial limited emphasis on the importance of early maternal interactions, subsequent theoretical and empirical work has offered an array of data highlighting the crucial role played by the entire family system in producing adaptive development in multiple domains (Bronfenbrenner, 1979; Furman & Buhrmester, 1985; Levitt, Guacci, & Coffman, 1993; Levitt, Guacci-Franco, & Levitt, 1993).

Introduction to siblings

Within this complex web of family connections, one particular relational category with enormous potential for both positive and negative consequences is the sibling relationship. Based on demographic statistics of Western countries, it is apparent that the large majority of individuals, over 90% in some regions, have a sibling (Cicirelli, 1982). Additionally, in comparison to all other family and extra-familial relationships, the sibling bond is the most long-lasting. Parent and child relationships are cut short by the passing of the preceding generation, spousal relationships only begin later in life and are often short-lived, and friendships are similarly transitory. On the other hand, the sibling bond is often formed early in life and can last a lifetime.

Beyond the prevalence and endurance of the sibling bond, a recent scientific focus in both developmental and clinical literature has begun to unravel the many ways in which brothers and sisters influence our life in magnificent ways. Childhood cognitive and social development, adolescent identity and delinquency, and adulthood well-being, adjustment, and successful aging are but a few examples of significant lifelong outcomes driven by overt or covert sibling forces (Cicirelli, 1980; Downey & Condron, 2004; Kramer & Kowal, 2005; Lewin & Sharp, 2009; Milevsky, 2011; Schulman, 1999). Although still in its infancy, a robust and emerging literature has emphasized the central role played by siblings throughout life.

Unfortunately, the power of this inimitable and complicated family connection has been untapped in clinical settings. Understanding the complexities of this bond and possessing the knowledge of how to unleash its potential in therapy can offer clinicians a powerful tool in their healing arsenal.

The neglected relationship

Regrettably, even with the growing developmental and clinical appreciation of the integral role played by siblings throughout life, multiple sectors of practice have failed to account for the significance of siblings. Among other fields, this neglect can be seen in education, disability and social services, and family law.

Education

Schools disregard the role of siblings in neglecting to devise ways for siblings to assist students with schoolwork. Schools have back-to-school nights for parents but little effort is made to include siblings in these evenings. These oversights are particularly startling considering the growing research on the impact siblings have on cognitive and educational domains (Downey & Condron, 2004; Smith, 1993).

Furthermore, when schools assess peer violence they often neglect the context of the sibling relationship as an antecedent of the aggression. Numerous studies have shown that childhood aggression is linked with sibling relational dynamics (Bank, Burraston, & Snyder, 2004; Downey & Condron, 2004). Schools can be served by integrating siblings into their broader efforts at minimizing peer victimization (Dusenbury & Falco, 1997).

Lastly, a lack of sibling sensitivity and a misunderstanding of sibling de-identification processes may lead schools to judge younger siblings based on expectations born from school experiences with older siblings (Seaver, 1973). Understanding sibling issues can help schools offer a non-constricting environment for all children.

Disability and social services

A combination of societal and legislative changes has made the lives of individuals with disabilities and their families more comfortable relative to the experiences of similar families throughout history. From education to industry, the accommodations and sensitivity offered to individuals with disabilities have created a less restrictive and more accessible environment. Families of individuals with disabilities have also gained attention and now have an array of services provided for their education and support. However, disability services often lag when it comes to attending to the unique issues faced by siblings of those with disabilities. Siblings often feel neglected by parents and service providers and report being in the dark about what is happening with their siblings (Abrams, 2009; Safer, 2002).

Social services offered for other problems, such as antisocial behavior and criminality, similarly fail to approach conceptualization and intervention using a broader sibling-based orientation. Long-term change resulting from intervention is less likely to succeed when the intervention targets only one sibling within a family. Intervention programs would be served by considering the role siblings play within the maladjusted system. Studies have shown that siblings influence each other's behavioral patterns in profound ways. For example, Klein, Alexander, and Parsons (1977) found that an intervention targeting children's antisocial behavior had an indirect effect on the criminality of their siblings even when the siblings did not participate in the intervention program. Similar findings were reported on interventions for antisocial behaviors in pre-school children (Brotman, Dawson-McClure, Gouley, McGuire, Burraston, & Bank, 2005). Siblings have a unique potential for influencing each other and ignoring this powerful force of change risks minimizing the likelihood that interventions will result in meaningful change.

Family law

Family law is an additional sector that unfortunately neglects the vital role played by siblings over the lifespan. Although varied by country, similar patterns can be found in international jurisprudence when it comes to this issue. For example, United States family law mainly focuses on two relationships: the bond between spouses and the bond between parent and child. The limited focus on marriage and parenthood in United States family law comes at the expense of considering how the law should regulate and protect other family relationships including the sibling bond.

This neglect can be seen in multiple areas. First, undocumented immigrants living in the United States and raising citizen children may be able to avoid deportation. This is not the case if the connection is through any other relationship, including siblinghood. Furthermore, employees may have the right to unpaid leave to care for an ill spouse, child, or parent. This is not the case when caring for any other family member, including siblings.

More significantly, and impacting families in more direct ways, United States family law governing sibling visitation in cases of family dissolution seldom considers the importance of the sibling bond. Siblings are often separated at adoption or placed separately after the divorce or death of their parents with no right to communicate. For example, only "reasonable effort" needs to be made to place siblings together when the children are up for adoption together. When separately placed siblings seek post-adoption contact and the adoptive parent objects, it may be unconstitutional to force contact under the Supreme Court's opinion in *Troxel v. Granville* (Hasday, 2012). In this case, the court held that a Washington State statute authorizing courts to "order visitation rights for any person when visitation may serve the best interest of the child" was "an unconstitutional infringement on [the mother's] fundamental right to make decisions concerning the care, custody, and control of her two daughters."

Similarly, in cases when split custody is decided post-divorce or when siblings are placed in different homes after parental death, the legal system frequently provides no help for siblings seeking visitation rights. This situation stands in stark contrast to United States family law relating to grandparents. In the United States, every state has some form of grandparent visitation law. Post-divorce, grandparents can petition the court for visitation rights with their grandchildren even when the custodial parent objects. This imbalanced representation is probably driven more by lobbying efforts and political sway of older Americans and less by what is in the best interests of children (Hasday, 2012). In fact, the United States Congress designated 1995 as the "Year of the Grandparent." Siblings, unfortunately, have limited advocacy and enjoy no such status.

In sum, numerous areas of practice with direct and indirect impacts on individuals and families have neglected the essential role played by siblings in the socialization of children and adolescents and in the offering of vital support functions throughout life. Hopefully, the emerging focus in developmental and clinical literature on siblings and the consistent stream of findings supporting the indispensable role played by siblings during all ages will influence educators, service providers, and policymakers to begin accounting for the unrepeatable position occupied by siblings during the course of life.

Siblings in clinical practice

As noted, the most long-lasting and enduring relationship an individual can develop is with a sibling. Considering the closeness in age between siblings and the fact that often siblings are born into a family early in the life of children, siblings can bond for a lifetime (Cicirelli, 1980, 1982). Researchers are beginning to appreciate the sibling link and its important role in psychological well-being throughout life. Studies are now showing that individuals with close sibling relationships are more emotionally mature, are happier, have enhanced psychological well-being, and have closer friendships than those without warm sibling relationships (Downey & Condron, 2004; Dunn, Brown, & Maguire, 1995; Dunn, Brown, Slomkowski, Telsa, & Youngblade, 1991; Kramer & Kowal, 2005; Milevsky, 2011;

Smith, 1993). Similarly, sibling problems are often an integral part of adulthood instability. Past sibling memories and current relational dynamics can often impede healthy psychological adjustment (Coles, 2003; Lewin & Sharp, 2009; Schulman, 1999).

Unfortunately, sibling issues are rarely discussed in therapy even though past and present sibling dynamics are an integral part of child and adult adjustment, personality, mental health, and well-being (Schulman, 1999). This is particularly disturbing considering the mounting evidence emanating from developmental and clinical psychology highlighting the unrepeatable and inimitable role played by siblings throughout life. In childhood, siblings are central socialization agents possessing the ability to offer considerable cognitive, social, and emotional provisions. On the other hand, hostility between siblings can have deeply damaging consequences for children and families. Beyond the negative effects of sibling hostility in childhood, unresolved past and current sibling issues infiltrate many aspects of adulthood well-being. Understanding how to integrate sibling issues into therapy holds considerable therapeutic potential for enhancing adult sibling relationships. More importantly, the integration of sibling issues in therapy can help in confronting other well-being issues that are seemingly unrelated to siblings but are, at the core, influenced by underlying sibling issues.

Clinical attention to sibling issues is scarce with the emphasis often being on how siblings play a role in brief family therapy interventions. Little attention has been given to broader sibling issues in therapy (Coles, 2007; Edward, 2013; Gnaulati, 2002; Kahn & Lewis, 1988; Lewis, 1995). Neglecting sibling therapy as a treatment modality on its own is baffling considering the powerful psychological issues that develop from the passion, longevity, and intensity of the sibling bond throughout life.

This limited attention to sibling issues in therapy may be driven by the centrality of parents in the Oedipus complex, which dominated traditional practice for many years (Edward, 2013). Coles (2007) suggested that the neglect of sibling issues in therapy might be driven by unconscious desires of therapists to rid themselves of their own siblings and be an only child. Irrespective of the reason for the neglect, therapists and researchers with an understanding of the integral role played by siblings throughout life can enhance their practice in profound and meaningful ways.

The current book

As an additional thrust in the growing effort to draw attention to sibling issues in general, and the unique benefits of integrating sibling issues in therapy in particular, this book uses the latest research and clinical work in sibling dynamics to examine multiple ways of integrating sibling issues in therapy. It explains how close sibling relationships develop and specifically looks at the ways practitioners can integrate sibling issues in therapy with various populations and in multiple settings. When sibling therapy is sought for cases of sibling aggression, the book highlights how to work with parents to create a home environment that fosters close sibling bonds. Parents can also influence sibling relationships by the way they intervene when their children fight. The book details the types of interventions that are most likely to be effective and produce a better understanding between siblings. Practitioners hoping to assist families in enhancing the sibling bond will gain immensely from understanding these factors.

For direct therapy with children and adolescents, the book reviews several situations where sibling integration may occur including working with siblings jointly in cases of divorce, trauma, and family dissolution.

In addition to the application of sibling issues in therapy with children and adolescents, the book examines how to integrate adult sibling issues in therapy. The book shows how past and present sibling issues lie at the core of many difficulties presented by adult clients. First, sibling discord in adulthood can propagate relational tensions resulting in significant individual and family disruption. Second, underlying past sibling dynamics can impact adult emotional and psychological well-being in dramatic ways. Tending to sibling issues in therapy can help minimize both overt sibling problems and other life difficulties tied to past sibling narratives. Having the tools for discovering, assessing, and integrating these issues in therapy will be immensely beneficial to practitioners looking to expand and enhance their effectiveness in providing meaningful interventions.

Using theoretical perspectives, a wealth of empirical data, testing instruments, and clinical examples, the book provides a hands-on and thorough examination of these issues and offers specific tools and techniques that can be used in practice.

In summary, the book helps practitioners appreciate the crucial role played by siblings in the therapeutic process, discover how sibling concerns are an integral part of childhood and adulthood psychotherapy, and learn how to use unique tools to integrate sibling relationship issues in therapy with clients of all ages. The book presents the latest, evidence-based, clinical work on effective integration of sibling issues in therapy with children, adolescents, and adults.

The book is intended for psychologists, therapists, counselors, marriage and family therapists, social workers, case managers, social service providers, and other mental health professionals working with individuals and families in multiple settings.

Book structure

As the developmental and clinical literature suggests, the sibling relationship is a powerful socialization agent with potential to impact an individual's life in significant ways. Hence, working with families on strengthening the sibling bond while children are young holds considerable therapeutic potential in limiting family hostility and cultivating a significant source of support. Furthermore, attending to sibling issues in clinical work with adults holds considerable promise considering the integral role played by siblings in early development and the potential for sibling support to be activated and relied upon as a source of comfort and care in later life. Hence, the current book provides an examination of the clinical potential of integrating sibling issues in therapy with parents, families, and adults.

Chapter overview

Part I, including the current and next chapters, offers a review of the integral role played by siblings throughout life. Chapter 1 provides an overview of the book and explains how the book can be used in practice. As a continuation of the current chapter, Chapter 2, "Siblings in Developmental and Clinical Research," provides a review of the research on the significant role played by siblings throughout life and the outcomes associated with sibling relationship quality. It includes literature on the importance of sibling relationships for multiple domains of functioning including cognitive, social, and emotional well-being in childhood, adolescence, and adulthood. The chapter further examines the theoretical and clinical literature on the importance of integrating sibling issues in therapy for individual and family well-being. The significance of siblings sheds light on how well-being difficulties may be driven by sibling-related issues. Once the literature on the many benefits of sibling relationship warmth unfolds, it becomes apparent how integrating siblings in therapy as a support tool can be extraordinarily helpful for clients of all ages.

Part II, which includes chapters 3 through 6, examines how clinicians can assist families in parenting siblings. Chapter 3, "Indirect Ways Parents Impact Sibling Bonds," highlights the benefit of working on creating closeness between siblings early in a family and presents several family-system dynamics that contribute to sibling relationship quality. Clinical applications of these dynamics are presented for use by clinicians working with families on creating the right home environment for sibling warmth.

Chapter 4, "Direct Ways Parents Impact Sibling Bonds," presents research-based direct ways in which parents can navigate the relationship between their children including minimizing favoritism, emphasizing de-identification, and properly intervening when siblings fight. As with Chapter 3, clinical applications of these tools are presented for use by clinicians working with families on enhancing the sibling bond.

Chapter 5, "Sibling Issues in Diverse Families," reviews the empirical and clinical literature on unique sibling relationship issues faced by single-parent and blended families and provides suggestions for clinicians working with these families. Similarly, Chapter 6, "Siblings of Children with Disabilities," reviews the empirical and clinical literature on the difficulties experienced by siblings of children with a disability and provides suggestions for clinicians working with these families to enhance the adjustment of the well siblings.

Part III, "Siblings in Therapy with Children, Adolescents, and Adults," examines the more direct role played by clinicians when working with siblings in therapy. Chapter 7, "Siblings in Child and Adolescent Individual Therapy," identifies the two primary situations where a therapist may work individually with child or adolescent siblings: to help bring peace to rivaling siblings and to trigger a source of compensatory support in cases of turmoil. The chapter elucidates a research-based therapeutic process and goals for each of these situations.

Chapter 8, "Siblings in Child and Adolescent Family Therapy," surveys how sibling work within a family context can help in the assessment and intervention of overall family hostility. Sibling issues in some situations are a cover for underlying family tensions and integrating siblings in family therapy in these instances can help direct spouses to focus on the real issues at hand.

Chapter 9, "Cognitive-Behavior Interventions for Adult Sibling Issues," examines the integration of sibling therapy with adults who present with antagonistic sibling dynamics. The chapter specifically provides cognitive-behavior techniques to be used in psychotherapy to enhance adult sibling relationship quality.

Finally, Chapter 10, "Brief Psychodynamic Interventions for Adult Sibling Issues," describes how the integration of siblings in therapy can be beneficial in confronting both overt sibling issues, where the sibling tension is the presenting problem, and covert sibling issues, where past sibling dynamics are interfering with other aspects of a client's current functioning. This "past sibling interference" is not initially seen as sibling-based. Therapy in this latter case entails working with clients to uncover core sibling tensions and how they are linked with the client's current disturbance.

Assessments

The field of family research offers a wide range of easily administered assessment tools that can be applied in practice. Although designed for research use, they can offer a quick way of measuring various aspects of family process and functioning in therapy. When applicable, the book highlights some of these measures that can be used as an aid in assessing family and sibling relational dynamics. The book offers an explanation of the way the measures can be applied in practice, including a description of the measures, administration process, and reference information.

Case studies

In order to further comprehend the application of the concepts, techniques, and tools covered, each chapter includes a case study emanating from the author's clinical practice. The cases describe a clinical account including a portrayal of the presenting problem, the conceptualization of the problem, and an intervention using the material from the chapter. Names and specific circumstances of the cases presented have been changed or amalgamated for confidentiality. The case studies offer clinicians a clear description of the way intervention with siblings can be used with individuals and families throughout the lifespan.

The combination of theoretical and empirical information, assessment tools, and the case studies offers an integrated understanding of the effectiveness of attending to sibling dynamics in therapy and provides a concrete plan of how to apply sibling work in multiple therapeutic settings.

Chapter summary

Sibling relationships are the most long-lasting relationship individuals develop throughout life. They offer unique socialization tasks in childhood and adolescence and provide inimitable support during adulthood and aging. Considering their sophisticated role in development and well-being, attending to sibling issues in therapy holds important diagnostic and intervention potentials. Unfortunately, sibling issues are often neglected in multiple sectors of practice including education, disability and social services, and family law. This book offers a systematic survey of the importance of siblings throughout life and provides concrete ways of integrating sibling issues in therapy with various populations and in multiple settings.

2
Siblings in Developmental and Clinical Research

The early years of the study of developmental and clinical psychology has traditionally focused on the maternal bond as the foundation of socialization. However, during the latter part of the twentieth century, numerous efforts have been made at expanding our understanding of the circle of childhood influences. This reexamination of socialization dynamics introduced several lines of research on the role of other support providers including fathers, grandparents, and siblings. As a result, a steady stream of research on the predictors and outcomes of sibling relationship quality emerged over the past several decades in developmental, clinical, and family literature.

The developmental significance of siblings

In most of the early, theoretical literature examining a child's social network and socialization, the focus has been on the mother–child dyad. The importance of mothers for a myriad of developmental outcomes can be seen in psychoanalytic theory (Freud, 1938), attachment literature (Ainsworth & Wittig, 1969; Ainsworth, Blehar, Waters, & Wall, 1978; Bowlby, 1969, 1973, 1977, 1980), and "social referencing" work (Feinman & Lewis, 1983), to name a few. However, over the past several decades, a number of neo-Ainsworth theorists have looked beyond the mother–child dyad, suggesting that as children develop, they are exposed to a vast network of individual relationships each possessing unique developmental importance (Levitt, 1991; Lewis, 1994; Stocker, 1994).

Beyond the importance of these dyadic relationships, the interaction and flow between relationships further contributes to developmental outcomes (Bronfenbrenner, 1979; Furman & Buhrmester, 1985; Levitt, Guacci, & Coffman, 1993; Levitt, Guacci-Franco, & Levitt, 1993). As the famed ecological theorist, Urie Bronfenbrenner, noted,

> Children need people in order to become human. It is primarily through observing, playing, and working with others older and younger than himself that a child discovers both what he can do and who he can become. Hence to relegate children to a world of their own is to deprive them of their humanity, and ourselves as well.
>
> (1972, Preface)

This expanded view of socialization has propagated multiple lines of research on various other members of a child's network, beyond the mother, including investigations on fatherhood (Day & Lamb, 2004; Lamb, 1986) and grandparents (Eisenberg, 2004). An additional beneficiary of this evolving understanding of what drives social development is the sibling bond. Although still in its infancy, a growing body of work has underscored the crucial role played by siblings in lifelong adaptive development (Dunn, 2000).

Siblings in developmental theory

The theoretical significance of siblings has been examined from multiple viewpoints. First, at the most basic level, sibling exchanges offer children the first microcosm of social interactions with a peer (Lockwood, Kitzmann, & Cohen, 2001). Siblings close in age, living together, and constantly competing for attention, resources, and space offer each other a great milieu to begin learning about the world. During the course of the day, children find themselves in countless basic social situations with their siblings that can offer them a training ground for working on cognitive, social, and emotional development. Children are socialized as they engage their siblings and learn about language interpretation, personal identification, family differentiation, emotional regulation, social engagement, problem solving, conflict resolution, and emotion management.

The importance of siblings has also been viewed in the context of a child's broader social relationships. In early theoretical models comparing childhood relationships with adults and peers, Piaget (1965) and Sullivan (1953) suggested that both adult and peer relationships offer children unique and separate provisions.

Relationships with adults offer children a model for comprehending the order and regularity of society. With limited comprehension of their surroundings, children view the world as chaotic and unorganized. However, by means of relationships with adults, who impose rules and regulations pertaining to acceptable and unacceptable behaviors and emotions, children are provided with a much-needed sense of structure in life. Children also learn through their relationships with adults that although they may not understand the motivation behind the rules imposed, they must nevertheless follow them to avoid confrontations with the adults (Sullivan, 1953).

In contrast, the nature of childhood peer relationships is one of shared ideas and conversation. Unlike the pre-constructed order and regularity presented by adults, peer interactions offer children the opportunity to express their own views and formulate new ones as they engage their peers. Peer interactions foster a sense of understanding and sensitivity in children (Youniss, 1980).

In defining this distinction between adult and peer relationships, Hinde (1979) characterized the structured and rule-governed adult interactions as *complementarity* and the shared connection of peer relationships as *direct reciprocity*. Based on this formulation, the uniqueness of the sibling relationship can be viewed as containing elements of both complementarity and direct reciprocity. Dunn (1983) theorized that siblings might serve as a model for the order emblematic of adult relationships in addition to offering children the sense of mutuality found in peer relationships. The merging of these two concepts serves children well as they embark on engaging a broader world that often contains a similar plurality.

Hence, the sibling bond possesses an unrepeatable potential that if harnessed can offer unique contributions to lifelong development.

Research on the significance of siblings

The theoretical advances in understanding the importance of siblings have spawned mounting empirical research on the significance of sibling relationships across the lifespan. The studies emanate from a diverse group of international researchers using a range of samples, data-collection methods, and analysis procedures. The findings point to a distinct set of advantages offered by sibling relationship quality which impact cognitive, social, and emotional development in childhood, adolescence, and adulthood.

Childhood

Children with a sibling relationship characterized by warmth and support are more likely to have better cognitive abilities (Smith, 1993), greater social intelligence (Downey & Condron, 2004), better emotional understanding (Dunn, Brown, Slomkowski, Telsa, & Youngblade, 1991), greater moral awareness (Dunn, Brown, & Maguire, 1995), and better psychological well-being (Kramer & Kowal, 2005) than children who do not have a close sibling relationship. In a commonly referenced study of 85 second-graders, Stocker (1994) found that participants with warmth in their sibling relationship scored higher on indices of self-esteem and lower on measures of loneliness than a comparison group of children without warm sibling relationships. More significantly, Pike, Coldwell, and Dunn (2005) found that sibling relationship quality accounted for better psychological adjustment in children even after controlling for parental relationship quality, suggesting a distinct ability of siblings to influence well-being.

In addition to the many benefits of sibling support in normative situations, a growing body of research has suggested that siblings may offer each other a buffer against the negative outcomes associated with heightened ecological risk (Sandler, 1980). The literature on ecological risk underlines the particular negative outcomes common in children experiencing a myriad of environmental disadvantages such as family distress, economic hardships, living in single-parent homes, foster-home placement, and neighborhood turmoil. A buffer under these challenging conditions would entail a protective factor that children possess that serves to shelter them from the expected negative outcomes (Rutter, 1990).

Accordingly, a series of studies suggest that sibling support may offer a buffer for children experiencing ecological risk. For example, in a longitudinal study by Vondra, Shaw, Swearingen, Cohen, and Owens (1999) on 204 children experiencing multiple ecological risks, including neighborhood and family difficulties, participants with a close sibling bond at three years old were found to have closer social relationships and better self-control by the time they were in first grade than those without a close sibling bond. Lockwood, Gaylord, Kitzmann, and Cohen (2002) studied 47 elementary school children under high family stress conditions and found that those with siblings showed significantly less aggressive-disruptive behavior than those without siblings. Siblings have also been found to offer buffering in several other difficult family conditions including parental marital hostility (Jenkins, 1992), parental divorce (Hetherington, 1989), and foster-care placement (Linares, Li, Shrout, Brody, & Pettit, 2007).

In a related risk condition, siblings have also been found to offer compensatory support in the absence of support from other members of the social network. Compensatory mechanisms are triggered when an individual relationship is not offering the adequate level of social support and, as a result, a child reaches out to a different member of the network to substitute for the missing support.

The potential for compensatory effects emanate from several theoretical frameworks. Most significantly, Weiss' (1974) social provisions theory offers a clear social mechanism that may trigger a compensatory process. The theory suggests that members of an individual's social network offer specific social provisions, or support functions, which include the six basic provisions of attachment, alliance, enhancement of worth, social integration, guidance, and opportunity for nurturance.

These six social functions are distinct and are offered by particular individuals. However, under specific conditions, these provisions can be obtained from multiple individuals. Hence, when a specific relationship is not delivering a needed provision, the receiver may compensate for the deficiency by turning to a different network member to provide the missing support function (Furman & Buhrmester, 1985).

Similarly, Takahashi (1990) suggests that interpersonal relationships, or "affective relationships," provide specific behaviors that satisfy vital emotional needs. These needs are met by multiple individuals but may be reassigned to other people over the course of development. This change may only occur once the new provider has been tested and proved to be an effective support provider. Compensatory support is hence triggered when an "affective relationship" is deficient in meeting a support need and is replaced by a more qualified provider of support.

Empirical research on compensatory processes has been applied to parent support compensating for the absence of peer support (Patterson, Cohn, & Kao, 1989) and parent support compensating in the absence of support from another parent (van Aken & Asendorpf, 1997). Studies on siblings have suggested that sibling support may offer compensation in the absence of parent or friend support.

In one of the earliest examinations of sibling compensatory effects, Bossard and Boll (1956) noted,

> [When] the parents are tired and weighed down with care and responsibilities, they may not have the time, inclination, energy, or affectional resources to satisfy the respective emotional needs of their children. In such cases, it is natural for children to turn to other persons; and often this means other siblings. (p. 156)

Subsequent work found that siblings may compensate in multiple ways for the absence of parental support, or as Kahn (1982) called it, "a vacuum of parental care." This phenomenon of siblings aiding each other when parents are absent has been seen in clinical populations (Bank & Kahn, 1982), in a laboratory situation of parents ignoring their children (Bryant & Crockenberg, 1980), and even in cases of older children responding with warmth to newborn siblings when their mothers were tired and depressed post-partum (Dunn & Kendrick, 1982).

Siblings have also been found to compensate for the lack of friend support. McElwain and Volling (2005) found that greater sibling relationship quality during free-play compensated for low relationship quality with friends in pre-school. Stocker (1994) reported sibling compensation in cases of low friend warmth in a sample of second-graders.

In a study of 200 sixth-graders, East and Rook (1992) found that friend-isolated children turn to siblings for support to compensate for the lack of friendships. Similarly, Milevsky and Levitt (2005) found sibling compensation for the lack of friend support in a multi-ethnic sample of 695 students in grade six and eight.

Hence, beyond the cognitive, social, and emotional advantages of closeness between siblings in normative situations, siblings may serve a unique role during difficult times, offering a buffer against multiple environmental risks, and serving a compensatory role during times of support deficiencies. This buffering and compensatory potential of sibling support is expanded on in future chapters as it contains a potent tool to be used by clinicians when designing family intervention plans in cases of atypical support environments.

The power of siblings can also be seen in studies examining the destructive potential of this bond. Studies exploring negative sibling bonds have shown an association between sibling hostility and future disruptive and aggressive behaviors (Bank, Burraston, & Snyder, 2004; Garcia, Shaw, Winslow, & Yaggi, 2000; Volling, 2003). Other studies have examined the destructive outcomes associated with sibling rivalry (Stocker & Dunn, 1990) and sibling perceptions of parental favoritism (Boer, 1990). Although these studies emphasize the dark side of sibling relationships, they highlight the potency of this bond and its potential for both promise and destruction in childhood.

Adolescence

The adolescent years are marked by a social transition entailing a slow separation from family in favor of greater friend engagement. With these changes come modifications to the sibling bond, including spending less time together and being less intimate (Cole & Kerns, 2001). However, even with these social shifts, adolescent siblings continue to be attached and the benefits of a close sibling bond are significant for cognitive, social, and emotional outcomes (Updegraff, McHale, & Crouter, 2002).

Milevsky and Levitt (2005) reported that greater sibling support in adolescents was linked with more positive school attitudes. Using hierarchical linear modeling, Richmond, Stocker, and Rienks (2005) found that, as adolescence unfolded, improvements in sibling relationship quality were linked with decreases in depressive symptomology. Similarly, Yeh and Lempers (2004) reported an association between sibling relationship quality and lower depression, lower loneliness, and higher self-esteem in a three-year longitudinal study of 374 early adolescents. This study is particularly consequential considering the natural difficulties experienced during the transitory early adolescent years. Sibling support during adolescence has also been shown to be associated with lower levels of externalizing and internalizing problems (Branje, van Lieshout, Van Aken, & Haselager, 2004; Buist, Dekovic, & Gerris, 2011). In a qualitative study of the sibling bond, Milevsky, Schlechter, Klem, Edelman, Kiphorn, and Anrico (2007) had 272 high-school students complete a narrative about their sibling relationships. The majority of the responses, which were analyzed using thematic analyses, were positive, including a participant who noted, "My siblings and I get along great. Sure we argue from time to time, but we love each other very much."

As in childhood, during the adolescent years, siblings continue to offer both buffering and compensatory support. In a study on the buffering effects of sibling support in a multi-ethnic sample of 695 adolescents experiencing ecological risk, Milevsky and Levitt (2005) found that sister support was related positively to school adaptation. Using structural equation latent growth curve modeling, East and Khoo (2005) found, in a sample of 227 Latino and African American families experiencing ecological risk, that sibling warmth predicted lower drug use and less risky sexual behaviors for adolescent girls over a five-year period.

Studies on the compensatory patterns of sibling support in adolescents have also forwarded promising results. In a study with 300 high-school students in Israel, Seginer (1998) found that adolescents with low peer acceptance but with high sibling warmth were as satisfied with their emotional support as adolescents with high peer acceptance.

Empirical research supporting the ability of sibling support to offer significant benefits to adolescents in normative and high-risk circumstances holds considerable clinical potential considering the turmoil often emblematic of the adolescent years. Tapping into the capacity of siblings to offer much-needed support during a time of change, uncertainty, and shifting social alliances can serve as an important tool in clinical interventions with adolescents.

Adulthood

During the transition to adulthood, the sibling relationship matures as the span of the relationship lengthens and the unique sibling and family historical narrative broadens. Furthermore, the connection between siblings transitions from an imbalanced older sibling–younger sibling dynamic to a more balanced and egalitarian dyad with greater abilities in negotiation (Dew, Llewellyn, & Balandin, 2004; Laursen, Finkelstein, & Betts, 2001). The sibling relationship during this time is also more independent and voluntary and is less governed by parental choreographies (Stewart, Kozak, Tingley, Goddard, Blake, & Cassel, 2001).

Although the challenges and schedules of adult life often limit the ability of siblings to see each other frequently, as they did during the childhood and adolescent years, studies have indicated that, nonetheless, adult siblings feel a sense of emotional closeness with their siblings (Cicirelli, 1991; Milevsky, Thudium, & Guldin, 2014; Scharf, Shulman, & Avigad-Spitz, 2005). Sibling relationship warmth in adulthood continues to be linked with well-being, including higher self-esteem and life satisfaction. Sibling closeness in adulthood has also been found to be inversely related to loneliness and depression (Milevsky, 2005, Milevsky & Heerwagen, 2013; Waldinger, Vaillant, & Orav, 2007).

An interesting added benefit to sibling support in adulthood that surpasses the impact of sibling support in childhood and adolescence is the more significant influence of sibling compensation in cases of low friend support. Studies on compensatory support have differentiated between partial compensation and complete compensation. Partial compensation refers to when the sibling support that is being relied upon as compensation is offering some benefit to the receiver but is not as effective as the original lost support. Complete compensation, on the other hand, refers to when the substitute support is such that it produces the same benefits as what would have been present if the original lost support were intact.

Sibling support in cases of diminished friend support in childhood and adolescence has been found to offer partial compensation (East & Rook, 1992; Milevsky & Levitt, 2005). However, Milevsky (2005) investigated the potential of sibling support to offer complete compensation for a lack of friend support in adulthood. Using a sample of 305 young adults, he examined social support and adjustment using a number of support and well-being indices. Based on scores of the support measures, the sample was divided into four groups: high friend–high sibling support, high friend–low sibling support, low friend–high sibling support, and low friend–low sibling support groups. Using orthogonal, a priori contrasts comparing the high friend–high sibling support group and the low friend–high sibling support group, the authors found that low support by friends was completely compensated for by sibling support for self-esteem, depression, and life satisfaction. Hence, unlike in childhood and adolescence, siblings may offer complete compensation for low levels of friend support in adulthood.

An additional unique dimension of sibling relationships in adulthood is that adult siblings often need to partner with each other as they offer assistance to their aging parents. This partnership often leads to an increase in the level of intimacy between the siblings as they support each other during this demanding time (Blasinsky, 1998).

Interestingly, the benefits to psychological well-being associated with sibling relationship quality in adulthood have not been found to be a function of frequency of contact with siblings (McGhee, 1985; Van Volkom, 2006). This finding highlights the importance of sibling relationship quality as opposed to quantity in adulthood. Hence, just the knowledge that the sibling is available for support or counsel when needed is, in and of itself, beneficial for adults. As discussed at length in Chapter 9, the realization that a close sibling bond is possible even without a considerable time commitment can be a central element of cognitive-behavior interventions when therapists work with sibling relationship mending in adulthood.

Older adulthood

As adults mature and begin transitioning into the older adult years, their sibling relationships shift in several ways. First, at this advanced point in life, the relationship with a sibling has been in existence for many years, often being the longest relationship older adults have. Furthermore, as their schedules open up, due to retirement and family changes, siblings become closer and spend more time with each other. As parents die and children move out of the house, siblings increasingly depend on each other for help, including instrumental help or assistance when ill (Cicirelli, 1991; Moyer, 1992).

In some cases, siblings depend on each other as their lone source of support (Cicirelli, 1991). This dependency is particularly distinct for older adults who have never married or have no children (Moyer, 1992). Studies have also investigated how older adults depend on each other in times of crisis such as the death of a spouse. O'Bryant (1988) reported on the unique contribution and healing potential of sibling support during widowhood.

Beyond support, older adult siblings offer each other advice, companionship, and feelings of self-worth (Cicirelli, 1991; Gold, 1987).

Older adults with a warm sibling bond have been found to age more successfully. Cicirelli (1989) reported that older adult siblings who reach out to each other often report feeling more in control of their lives. Hence, as the sunset of life ascends, siblings remain the consistent relationship that links a reassuring present with the memories of the past.

In summary, a growing body of empirical work suggests that as individuals develop, they gain unique and unrepeatable provisions from having a close sibling bond. In childhood and adolescence, sibling relationship quality has been found to be associated with positive cognitive, social, and emotional outcomes. In adulthood, siblings offer each other support and validation. Furthermore, as adults transition into older adulthood, siblings continue to be relied upon for companionship, advice, and warmth.

Siblings in clinical and family theory

In addition to the developmental literature on the significance of siblings, theoretical models and clinical research have contributed to our understanding of the significance of attending to sibling issues in therapy. Both psychoanalytic and family-systems theories offer a clear foundation for understanding the importance of sibling interactions on personality development, symptom conceptualization, and therapeutic intervention.

Psychoanalytic theory

Although the majority of psychoanalytic theoretical work emphasized the maternal relationship as being the main source of socialization, multiple references can be found throughout early psychoanalytic thought stressing the importance of siblings. As discussed in Chapter 10, Freud's writings include frequent references about the lifelong significance of siblings on the psyche (Kivowitz, 1995; Sherwin-White, 2007). For example, sibling-related forces have been suggested by Freud to influence sexual development, love partnerships, social dynamics, emotional development, competitiveness, and intellectual inquisitiveness (Freud, 1955). These essential components of the human experience encompass lifelong and therapeutic implications. Furthermore, Adler's work on birth order continued to highlight the essential nature of the sibling bond. The potential of siblings as support providers can been seen, as well, in the work of

Anna Freud, who highlighted the role played by siblings in the lives of survivors of concentration camps after the Holocaust (Freud & Dann, 1951).

The neo-analytic work of self-psychology is further theoretical support for the importance of siblings in self-development and for the therapeutic relevance of siblings. According to self-psychology, the development of a healthy adult personality is contingent upon the stable availability of important others in childhood who offer specific "selfobject" needs (Kohut, 1971). These needs include the need to feel valued, the need to feel one with a dominant "selfobject," and the need to feel a sense of togetherness with others (Banai, Mikulincer, & Shaver, 2005). When these needs are not met by parents, children may turn to siblings to provide "selfobject" needs (Kahn, 1988; Wittenberg, 2009).

However, siblings may be ill-equipped to offer "selfobject" needs due to their immaturity and their own developmental process. A sibling may fulfill these needs in an inadequate manner, resulting in a sense of bitterness from the receiving sibling, or the sibling may take on an exhausting amount of responsibilities, resulting in a denial of their own needs and feelings of resentment. These feelings of bitterness or resentment may impact other areas of the sibling's functioning (Agger, 1988; Rosner, 1985; Schulman, 1999).

Hence, early sibling dynamics have a lasting impact on the development of the adult psyche and personality. An exploration of these sibling issues in therapy can provide relief for both contentious sibling relationships and other sibling-linked psychological disturbances.

Family-systems models

Theories emanating from family-systems models provide an additional, clear basis for actively confronting sibling issues in psychotherapeutic interventions. Specifically, Bowen's family-systems theory, Minuchin's structural family therapy, and Satir's experiential therapy all offer an understanding of the sibling role within the overall family system.

Family-systems theory

Bowen (1974) has written extensively about the essential elements of healthy families with siblings playing a vital role in the process. First, Bowen described the important process of *differentiation*, which refers to the ability of members of a family to separate their thinking and emotions from the family. Individuals with a low sense of differentiation become fused with others and are incapable of thinking and acting independently. These low-differentiated individuals rely heavily on the thoughts and opinions of family members, depend on them for approval, and try to please family members by conforming to their standards (Kerr & Bowen, 1988). This emotional dependency creates greater reactivity in the family relationships. A lack of differentiation can occur between siblings, creating an unhealthy dependency that may trigger negative emotional reactions.

On the other hand, high family differentiation is linked with a sense of independence of thought and action. As Donley and Likins (2010) explain, "In families with higher levels of differentiation, relationships are calmer and individuals are more autonomous and thus less sensitive and reactive to each other" (p. 393).

An additional essential element of healthy family dynamics is the avoidance of the formation of relationship triangles (Bowen, 1974). Referred to as *triangulation*, this unhealthy family process occurs when a family dyad is experiencing some tension. Instead of discussing the tension openly and trying to resolve it, a member of the dyad reaches out to a third family member to try to reduce the tension. This is accomplished by either using the triangulated family member as a means to influence the rivaling family member or by creating a unit with the triangulated member to the exclusion of the family member with which the tension exists. This unhealthy maneuver serves to aggravate the family hostilities. Siblings are often used in these triangles by parents or by other siblings in the family. Triangles fashioned early in childhood can endure and have long-term family and sibling consequences.

Emotional cutoffs can further impact families in unhealthy ways (Bowen, 1993). This occurs when family members are in conflict and incapable of resolving their dispute. The tension is magnified to a degree where the family members disconnect from one another. The cutoff may ease tensions in the short term, but the natural emotional connection between family members and the interconnectivity between the quarreling dyad and other family members serve to further the tensions and contaminate other relationships over time. Siblings may be a victim of cutoffs or may be drawn into the unhealthy mix when cutoffs occur with other family members.

These unhealthy dynamics may have multigenerational consequences, impacting parents and siblings, which, in turn, impact the
next generation of relationships between the grandchildren, aunts,
uncles, and cousins (Donley & Likins, 2010). Hence, siblings play
a significant role in these destructive family dynamics and confronting these issues in therapy with siblings can have considerable,
multigenerational consequences.

Structural family therapy

One of the most significant elements of healthy family dynamics,
according to structural family therapy, is the existence of clear family boundaries (Minuchin, 1974). According to this theory, adaptive
families need to establish three distinct units with clearly demarcated boundaries: the parent unit, the sibling unit, and the overall
family unit. The parent unit is the supervisory and administrative
center of the family operating without intrusion by children. Children understand that their parents are a unit and that there are
topics of conversation and decisions shared by the parent unit that
are off limits to the children in the family. Similarly, the sibling
unit has definitive boundaries with exchanges and conversations
that are limited to the children in the family without parent intrusion. The third unit is the family unit, which contains a family
identity and culture, distinct from other families, that promotes
a sense of definition and uniqueness to the family (Minuchin,
1981).

The existence of these units, and the establishment of healthy
family boundaries, helps children develop a strong sense of balance
between belongingness and personal identity. As Minuchin (1974)
wrote, "In all cultures, the family imprints its members with selfhood.
Human experience of identity has two elements; a sense of belonging
and a sense of being separate. The laboratory in which these ingredients are mixed and dispensed is the family, the matrix of identity"
(p. 47).

Unfastened family boundaries may create family enmeshment,
when family members are overly close and dependent on one
another, or family disengagement, when a sense of detachment
permeates the family. Early family enmeshment can lead to difficulties in developing close social relationships outside the family
and, similar to Bowen's concept of enmeshment (Bowen, 1974),

may be a breeding ground for triangulation. On the other hand, family disengagement can lead to an insufficient sense of support and guidance as children mature into adulthood.

Sibling dynamics play a decisive role in the establishment of family boundaries. Feeble family boundaries can have a profound impact on siblings as parents invade the bond and meddle with the establishment of the sibling unit. On the other hand, a strong sibling bond can foster robust boundaries across the entire family. Considering the importance of family boundaries, working with siblings therapeutically is an essential component of meaningful individual and family intervention.

Experiential therapy

Finally, the work of Satir (1964) and her emphasis on open communication is an additional family therapy model that highlights the way sibling dynamics are an integral component of well-being. A cornerstone of a healthy family environment is the ability of family members to discuss issues without restrictions. When members of a family have a low sense of self-esteem, they may develop difficulties in expressing themselves and communicating openly. Family issues or concerns that are not discussed openly continue to brew under the surface, contributing to family resentment and bitterness.

Alternatively, adaptive families create a culture of congruence, or authenticity, between thought, emotion, and action which leads to open communication. Healthy families encourage their members to be "straight" with each other and say what is on their mind (Satir & Baldwin, 1983). Part of this congruence is the ability to communicate about the present, disallowing past experiences to cloud open sharing and receiving about the present.

Working with families on enhancing open communication entails improving self-esteem, encouraging personal choice, and promoting responsibility over personal growth. These important dimensions of family and personal health impact siblings and can be promoted by integrating siblings into family and individual therapy.

Integrating siblings in therapy

Based on the aggregate of the theoretical and empirical research on the lifelong significance of siblings, an emerging clinical literature has promoted the integration of sibling issues into therapy with children, families, and adults.

Sibling therapeutic integration with children and adolescents

Considering the many positive outcomes associated with sibling relationship quality in childhood and adolescence, working with parents early in the life of the family on enhancing the sibling bond can offer lifelong cognitive, social, and emotional benefits. When parents emphasize and value the sibling bond of their children and have the necessary tools to navigate their relationship, they are providing their children with a source of support with lifelong dividends. With the right training and information, therapists can play a crucial role in helping families create sibling intimacy. Clinical studies utilizing various approaches to family intervention have shown that integrating sibling issues in therapy with families can minimize sibling aggression and enhance sibling relationship quality (Arnold, Levine, & Patterson, 1975; O'Leary, O'Leary, & Becker, 1973; Olson & Roberts, 1987; Smith & Ross, 2007).

The applied importance of working with families on sibling issues can further be seen by the numerous studies that show the negative clinical outcomes associated with destructive sibling dynamics. For example, studies have shown that children and adolescents with older siblings who engage in drug use, risky sexual behaviors, or delinquency are more likely to engage in such behaviors themselves in comparison to those without delinquent older siblings (East & Khoo, 2005; Khoo & Muthén, 2000; Pomery, Gibbons, Gerrard, Cleveland, Brody, & Wills, 2005; Rowe & Gulley, 1992; Snyder, Bank, & Burraston, 2005; Whiteman, Jensen, & Maggs, 2013, 2014). This elevated sibling-based risk has been shown to be significant even after factoring in genetic relatedness (Rende, Slomkowski, Lloyd-Richardson, & Niaura, 2005). Other studies have shown that sibling aggression in childhood and adolescence is linked with college dating violence and conflict in adulthood (Noland, Liller, McDermott, Coulter, & Seraphine, 2004; Shalash, Wood, & Parker, 2013). Therefore, encouraging parents to attend to sibling dynamics and their correlates can offer advantages to children and adolescents in areas outside sibling relationship quality.

Furthermore, working with siblings in therapy directly can offer other therapeutic advantages beyond relationship enhancement. The ability of sibling support to offer significant benefits to children and adolescents under high-risk conditions holds considerable clinical potential. On a simple level, studies have indicated that children in family therapy are more at ease and feel more secure when their sibling is with them in the session (Strickland-Clark, Campbell, & Dallos, 2000). More importantly, tapping into the potential of siblings to offer support during times of turmoil can provide clinicians a natural ally in working with children and adolescents who have experienced hardship.

Family benefits of sibling therapeutic integration

Beyond the individual benefits to children and adolescents of clinically attending to sibling issues, benefits to overall family functioning can also be gained with therapeutic attention to sibling issues. Aggression between siblings is common and occurs more often than aggression in any other type of relationship (Straus, Gelles, & Steinmetz, 1980; Wiehe, 2000). Sibling conflict is so common that when it happens it is often taken for granted. Sibling aggression impacts the well-being of the entire family. It is a major stress to families and has been reported to be one of the greatest childrearing concerns cited by parents (Milevsky, Thudium, Milevsky, & Roth, 2013; Perozynski & Kramer, 1999).

In some cases, sibling problems in a family are a symptom of greater family and marital systematic difficulties. However, in many cases, sibling aggression may be a function of a lack of sibling parenting knowledge. Training parents in specific prevention and intervention tools can assist in enhancing the sibling bond, minimizing aggression, and creating family peace.

Enhancing the bond early has lifelong family benefits. First, a close sibling unit helps foster healthy family boundaries overall (Namysłowska & Siewierska, 2010). Clearly demarcated boundaries are an essential ingredient of healthy families (Minuchin, 1981). Furthermore, a close childhood sibling bond has been shown to carry into adulthood, offering unique familial tasks throughout life. In adolescence, siblings can offer each other individuation from parents through modeling, shared secrets, and boundary formation, enhancing overall family functioning. In adulthood and older adulthood, siblings can offer shared responsibility and negotiation over aging parent care, further impacting the entire family (Blasinsky, 1998; Hequembourg & Brallier, 2005).

Of particular note is the advantage to families of attending to sibling issues in cases where the family is dealing with non-normative circumstances such as single-parent families, blended families, and families with children with special needs. In these situations, sibling dynamics create unique challenges that impact the entire family. Awareness of these unique challenges and confronting them when working with families can have considerable family-wide benefits.

Siblings in therapy with adults

Having a sibling mind-frame in therapy and mastering effective techniques in dealing therapeutically with adults and siblings can be instrumental in three clinical contexts. First, clients may enter therapy with the expressed goal of repairing their strained sibling relationship. Naturally, in such a case, knowledge about working with adults and siblings in therapy can be instrumental in helping clients achieve their goal (Lesser, 1978). More significantly, a sibling-sensitive therapist may notice in the course of treatment that sibling issues are creating tumult in a client's life. In this case, the need to focus on siblings in therapy may be introduced by the therapist.

In both the former and latter situation, there are numerous benefits of expensing efforts at repairing the sibling bond. First, the minimization of sibling hostilities can, in and of itself, offer needed relief. As detailed by the review of the developmental research, siblings can serve as an exceptional source of support for adults. Adults with close sibling relationships report greater well-being and life satisfaction (Cicirelli, 1991; Milevsky, 2005, 2013). More prominently, considering the societal changes currently being experienced by adults, including the vast number of aging baby boomers and changes in family composition, the likelihood of older adults living alone is increasing. Being sensitive to, and having the necessary tools for, therapeutically confronting sibling issues in therapy with adults can offer clients an essential source of support as they transition into their older adult years (Weisner, 1982). Another reason for discussing sibling issues in therapy with adults is the destructive outcomes for the entire family of sibling disconnect, including the damaging ways families cope with parental death when sibling disharmony exists and the intergenerational transmission of negative sibling dynamics (Schulman, 1999).

The third situation where a sibling orientation can be therapeutically valuable is when broader presenting problems are viewed via the prism of past and present sibling dynamics and tensions. Drawing from the reviewed clinical and family theory literature, underlying sibling-linked dynamics oftentimes play a significant part in broader well-being disturbances. Issues such as relationship difficulties, mood disturbances, self-esteem issues, and occupational uncertainties are frequently linked to sinister sibling forces (Wittenberg, 2009). Allowing for an exploration of past and present sibling issues in therapy can unearth fundamental sibling-related dynamics that may be at the core of the broader tensions. This exploration can, in turn, assist in symptom minimization (Coles, 2003; Lewin & Sharp, 2009; Schulman, 1999).

Case study: "Never good enough"

Frank, a married 57-year-old with two grown children, entered therapy to deal with depressive moods and marital discord. Frank reported that his wife, Anna, was very critical of him and, regardless of what he did, she found ways to point out his flaws. He thought that his depression was a result of being married to a spouse who was constantly minimizing him, which made him feel worthless. Frank's feelings of worthlessness were exhibited in multiple areas of his life. Although Frank was a successful attorney, he constantly noted that he felt that he was "never good enough" and that he could be doing better at work. Furthermore, Anna would often tell him that his devotion to his work took a toll on her and the children over the years. Even though Frank seemed to have a close relationship with his children, Anna's admonishments made Frank believe that he was an inadequate father.

Therapy transitioned into an examination of Frank's sibling relationships. Initially Frank was ambivalent about this exploration and questioned its relevance. This resistance was seen by the therapist as a confirmation that Frank may be dealing with underlying sibling tensions relevant to the presenting problem. After acknowledging and facing the resistance, Frank spoke about his family of origin and described his relationship with his two older brothers. He described his father as detached and cold and his mother as a devoted and warm wife and mother. Although he was not very close with his brothers, Frank had a particularly competitive relationship with his second brother, Dan, who was four years older than he was. This rivalry began in childhood and continued throughout their adult years. Dan dealt with the competition by belittling Frank throughout their childhood and teen years, constantly remarking about Frank's inferior intellect and failures. For example, during college when Frank told his brother about his intentions of enrolling in law school, Dan responded that it would be a waste of time because he would never graduate.

The exploration of past sibling dynamics helped Frank appreciate how these unresolved feelings about his brother impacted his present circumstance. Frank understood how his intense emotional reactions, resulting from his wife's negativity, were triggered by his underlying and unresolved feelings of sibling inferiority. Once Frank acknowledged the link between his presenting problems and his past sibling narrative, a more direct investigation of his past and present sibling relationship occurred. This more overt sibling relationship intervention helped Frank develop the comfort to reach out to Dan and attempt to repair the bond with him. Furthermore, the sibling intervention helped minimize his depressive moods and his negative reactions to his wife's disapproval.

Chapter summary

A consistent stream of developmental and clinical research has detailed the integral role played by siblings throughout life. The developmental focus on siblings has been driven by a reevaluation of socialization dynamics and its focus on understanding the role played by multiple support providers in development, including siblings. Empirical research based on this renewed attention has found that sibling relationship quality is associated with many positive outcomes for children, adolescents, and adults. Beyond the developmental significance of siblings, clinically focusing on sibling issues in therapy has been shown to enhance sibling closeness in childhood and adolescence and has been suggested as improving psychotherapy outcomes for adults. Understanding how to integrate siblings in therapy in assessment, conceptualization, and treatment can offer clinicians a valuable tool for use with individual and family interventions.

Part II

Siblings at Home: Helping Families Parent Siblings

3
Indirect Ways Parents Impact Sibling Bonds

The foundation for healthy sibling relationships begins early in life. Closeness between siblings in adulthood is driven by the way they engaged each other in childhood. Hence, the childhood years are a crucial building stage for solidifying the sibling bond. With a correct mix of ingredients, siblings can emerge from their childhood years with a sibling bond that will serve them well as they enter the adolescent years and transition into adulthood. Consequently, efforts at creating closeness between siblings in childhood are well worth it considering the importance of sibling relationship warmth throughout life. Clinicians are often called upon to help parents in these efforts.

Part II examines ways in which clinicians can assist families in creating intimacy between siblings in childhood. This chapter and Chapter 4 will detail the indirect and direct ways parents impact sibling bonds, whereas chapters 5 and 6 examine sibling dynamics in diverse families.

Constellation variables

Studies on the predictors of sibling relationship warmth have suggested several interacting variables that may impact the sibling bond. One fertile area of research on this topic focuses on constellation variables, or structural variables, which emphasizes the way gender, age, and birth order impact sibling outcomes.

The study of constellation variables and siblings has been applied to many different outcomes, beyond sibling relationship quality, including more than 2,000 studies on how birth order influences sibling differences in intelligence, personality, and well-being (Healey & Ellis, 2007; Sulloway, 2007; Wichman, Rodgers, & MacCallum, 2006). In fact, in one of the earliest evaluations of constellation variables and sibling outcomes, Francis Galton suggested a link between birth order and achievement based on his analysis of the disproportionate number of first-born members of the Royal Society (Sulloway, 2007).

Constellation variables have also been implicated in determining sibling relationship quality. Numerous studies have highlighted specific structural variables that may predict sibling relationships including gender, age, and family size (Buhrmester, 1992; Furman & Lanthier, 1996; Minnett, Vandell, & Santrock, 1983).

Sibling gender

The gender composition of sibling dyads has been shown to impact their relationship. Sibling dyads of boys have been suggested to be more negative and aggressive than girl sibling dyads (Hetherington, 1988). On the other hand, the relationship between sisters has been found to be more supportive and intimate than the relationship between brothers (Buhrmester, 1992).

In adolescence, sister dyads report higher reciprocal advice than brother or mixed-sex dyads. Females also report being more influenced by siblings, receiving more support from siblings, and being more satisfied with their sibling relationships than males (Tucker, Barber, & Eccles, 1997). Similarly, Milevsky and Levitt (2005) found in their study on sibling relationships in a sample of 272 students in grades 9 and 11 that females reported higher sibling support than males. Interestingly, when gender and grade were analyzed together, an interaction indicated that in grade 9, males and females had similar levels of support, but by grade 11, the gender gap became drastic, with females reporting significantly more support than males. Dunn and Kendrick (1982) found that same-sex dyads reported lower levels of sibling conflict than did mixed-sex dyads.

Hence, gender has been found to impact sibling relationship quality. Across childhood and adolescence, sisters seem to have warmer and less combative relationships than do brothers and mixed-sex sibling dyads report higher conflict in their relationships than do same-sex dyads. Interestingly, Kim, McHale, Osgood, and Crouter (2006) found that although mixed-sex sibling dyads displayed lower levels of intimacy in comparison to same-sex dyads, mixed-sex dyads exhibited an increase in intimacy during middle adolescence. A similar increase during middle adolescence was not found in same-sex sibling dyad intimacy. The authors suggested that this increase may be driven by siblings reaching out to their opposite sex brother or sister for dating advice and support as they begin expressing interest in romantic partnerships.

An additional less known but fascinating gender-linked family feature that has been found to influence sibling relationship quality is family gender-tilting (Falconer & Ross, 1988). Families with a male tilt are families with more males in the home, whereas families with a female tilt are those with more females in the home. Studies have indicated that families with a male tilt report higher levels of family hostility and lower levels of family satisfaction than female-tilted families (Falconer & Ross, 1988; Falconer, Wilson, & Falconer, 1990).

Sibling age

Research on age and sibling relationships examines three age-related determinants. First, studies assess changes in the sibling relationship as children mature. Second, studies examine sibling relationship quality based on age differences between the sibling dyad. A third related age-based family dynamic with interesting sibling relationship consequences is birth order.

Developmental changes in sibling relationship quality have been studied in childhood and adolescence. Overall, studies indicate that sibling relationship quality is consistent throughout childhood. However, once children transition to the adolescent years, sibling intimacy has been found to decrease (Buhrmester, 1992; Buhrmester & Furman, 1990; Parker & Asher, 1993). This decrease in sibling relationship intimacy is in line with broader shifts in an adolescent's social network which include greater emphasis on friendships and less of a focus on family.

In terms of research on sibling age gap and closeness, studies have indicated that in childhood, siblings closer in age may serve as playmates and are hence more likely to be close. However, siblings farther apart in age may be less close possibly due to the older sibling finding the younger one annoying. On the other hand, during the adolescent years, the opposite may be true. Closely spaced siblings may develop greater conflict during the adolescent years as they each work on carving out their own identity. Having a sibling close in age may trigger comparisons which may serve as an impediment to identity formation. This in turn may trigger sibling rivalry and hostility (McHale, Updegraff, Helms-Erikson, & Crouter, 2001; Milevsky & Levitt, 2005).

Studies on birth order and sibling relationships have consistently found that older siblings in the family often take on a semi-parental role with younger siblings by offering them support, advice, education, and mentorship. Consequently, younger siblings admire and venerate their older siblings (Buhrmester & Furman, 1990; Dunn & Kendrick, 1982).

Perlmutter (1988) suggested, based on clinical observations, that families often subscribe to mythical narratives about birth order and personality which then influence sibling exchanges. For example, families may subscribe to the myth of first-born children being idiosyncratic, middle children being guilty, and latter-born children being pleasing. These arbitrary labels may impact expectations and perceptions which are then followed during family interactions.

Finally, research examining both birth order and gender has found that the least intimate sibling dyad is the older brother–younger sister pair (Dunn, Slomkowski, & Beardsall, 1994).

Family size

Family size is an additional variable found to impact sibling relationship quality. Paradoxically, studies comparing sibling dynamics in large and small families suggest advantages for each type of family situation.

Rosenberg (1982) maintained that in comparison to small families, large families contain a more diversified and uniform power structure which reduces conflict. When a family has many children, additional effort needs to be applied to the daily functioning of the home. In such cases, all of the siblings in the family have specific tasks and roles which in turn help to diversify the family power structure. On the other hand, smaller families may rely exclusively on older siblings for assistance, producing power inequality and feelings of jealousy and hostility from younger siblings (Newman, 1991, 1996; Wagner, Schubert, & Schubert, 1985).

Other advantages of large families, vis-à-vis sibling relationships, include the greater likelihood of the existence of a group orientation which fosters a sense of sibling cohesion (Bossard & Boll, 1956), the availability of more siblings to interact with (Riggio, 2006), and the potential of the formation of sibling subgroups (Furman & Buhrmester, 1985). In fact, in a comparison between large and small families, Bat-Chava and Martin (2002) found more positive sibling relationships in the larger families.

On the other hand, several studies have highlighted numerous ways in which smaller families nurture better relationships between siblings in comparison to larger families. In smaller families, siblings may communicate more often with each other than siblings from large families (Newman, 1991). Goodwin and Roscoe (1990) noted that in smaller families, there may be less competition and conflict over resources in contrast to larger families where resources may be scarce.

The research findings pointing to both advantages and disadvantages in families of all sizes can be used by clinicians when counseling families on sibling relationship improvement. For example, parents of larger sibling groups can be encouraged to schedule individual time with each child to minimize the perception of limited parental resources. In smaller families, parents can be counseled in ways to diversify family responsibilities by delegating duties to all siblings in the family. A sense of group cohesion can be established in smaller families by fostering relationships with extended family members such as cousins (Milevsky, 2011).

Broader family and ecological factors

Outside the reviewed structural variables, several other broader variables have been shown to impact sibling relationship quality. For example, in families experiencing economic hardship, the sibling relationships of the children may be impacted deleteriously (Duncan & Yeung, 1995; Milevsky, 2005; Zukow, 2002). Furthermore, in a sample of adolescents, Milevsky (2005) found that nonreligious participants scored lower on sibling support and warmth than religious participants.

In summary, family constellation variables such as the gender and age of the sibling dyad and size of family have been shown to impact sibling relationship quality. Additionally, broader factors such as economics and religiosity have also been shown to correlate with sibling relational dynamics.

Family processes and sibling relationships

Although family constellation and broader factors have been shown to impact sibling bonds to some degree, more recent studies suggest that internal family processes are stronger predictors of sibling relationship quality than cursory constellation variables (MacKinnon, 1989; Milevsky, 2011). Supporting this assertion is a multilevel analysis of numerous family relationships concurrently by Jenkins, Dunn, O'Connor, Rasbash, and Behnke (2005), which found similarities in sibling relationship quality within families with multiple sibling dyads. This finding highlights the importance of examining processes within families that may be contributing to sibling relationship formation.

Research on family processes and sibling dynamics can be classified into two general categories of influences: indirect and direct (Milevsky, 2011). Indirect influences refer to ways in which the general family atmosphere or parent behaviors serve as a model for children in their sibling interactions (Parke & O'Neil, 1999). These indirect mechanisms include marital relationship modeling, overall family positive engagement, and parenting styles. The current chapter surveys these effects and examines how to integrate them in practice with families.

Direct influences refer to ways in which parents actively manage and direct the sibling relationships of their children. These direct processes include encouraging healthy sibling de-identification, avoiding parental favoritism, and sibling dispute intervention. Chapter 4 covers these direct influences in detail.

Working with families on sibling discord prevention and intervention necessitates a systematic focus on minimizing the negative aspects of the relationship and enhancing the positive using both indirect and direct interventions.

Marital relationship modeling

One way parents impact their children's sibling relationship is via the model they offer in their marital relationship. The connection between marital and sibling relationships is substantiated by multiple findings including developmental and clinical research on marital dynamics and divorce.

Divorce, hostility, and siblings

Parental divorce has deleterious impacts on offspring in multiple ways. Studies show that children and adolescents who experience parental divorce show greater levels of aggression and hostility, difficulties developing friendships, lower academic achievement, diminished psychological well-being, and higher drug abuse in comparison to children and adolescents who did not experience parental divorce (Amato & Keith, 1991; Hetherington, 1989; Wallerstein & Kelly, 1980). These negative impacts can be seen years later when these children reach adulthood and have lower education, lower occupational status, lower income, and are more likely to have relationship difficulties than adults whose parents did not divorce (Amato, 1996; Powell & Parcel, 1997; Ross & Mirowsky, 1999).

Sibling relationships have also been found to be a victim of parental divorce. Studies indicate that children of divorced parents show greater levels of aggression and lower levels of warmth with their siblings than children from non-divorced families (Hetherington, 1989; MacKinnon, 1989). Similar patterns of divorce and negative sibling dynamics can be found in studies with adolescents (Noller, Feeney, Sheehan, Rogers, & Darlington, 2008) and have also been seen to carry into adulthood (Milevsky, 2004; Riggio, 2001).

Multiple factors may be serving as mediators in the relationship between divorce and sibling hostility. For example, the disruption to family life and daily routine, common in divorce situations, may be contributing to the negativity between siblings. However, studies indicate that one of the processes that may explain why divorce impacts the sibling bond destructively may be the accompanying harmful marital communication observed by the children.

Marital hostility has been found to be associated with aggression between child and adolescent siblings (Erel, Margoline, & John, 1998; Stocker & Youngblade, 1999). In fact, studies assessing both parental marital hostility and divorce have found that compared to divorce, martial hostility was found to be a stronger predictor of sibling conflict (Milevsky, 2004; Panish & Sticker, 2001). Hence, an important determining factor in producing negativity between siblings in cases of divorce is the marital conflict observed by the children in the family. Conversely, positivity in the sibling relationship can be attributed to healthy marital connections (Furman & Giberson, 1995).

Marital dynamics and siblings in therapy

Integrating marriage issues in therapeutic work with sibling conflict can be used as both prevention and intervention. Young parents can be introduced to the link between marital features and sibling relationships before the marital or sibling conflict is present as a means of preventing sibling difficulties from developing. Focusing on the marital relationship can also be used as intervention once conflict is present.

The focus of treatment in both these cases is the marriage, with the goals being improving marital communication and relationship enhancement. The resulting healthy marital communication and connection is then used by the children in the family as a model for proper interactions with siblings.

An exhaustive review of marriage counseling is beyond the scope of this book. Many effective treatments exist including emotion-based, cognitive-behavior, and communication approaches (Dattilio, 1993; Gottman & Levenson, 2002; Johnson, 2008). The focus here is on an element of the martial relationship that offers a clear model for children in their sibling interactions: proper communication.

Modeling open communication

The method in which parents talk and interact with each other serves as a model for children as they engage their siblings. Couples can be classified into one of three general types of communicators: open communicators, fighters, or avoiders (Gottman & Krokoff, 1989). Open communication, as opposed to fighting, involves several interactional characteristics. First, communicators avoid bringing up difficult topics of conversion at the wrong time. An open exchange of ideas is more likely to occur if both partners are relaxed and open to talking. Confronting a partner as they walk through the front door after a long and stressful day at work may not be the right time to bring up their annoying habits.

Open communication also involves focusing on a specific problem during difficult conversations. Focusing on a specific problem can help the couple identify the issue at hand and work toward a solution to the difficulty. A statement such as "when you said that you needed your own space this morning it really hurt my feelings" is more effective in promoting a conversation intended to reach a satisfying conclusion than simply declaring "you always ignore me" or "you never pay attention to me."

Communicators make efforts at understanding the grievance of their spouse by asking questions about the complaint in a calm manner. They also make sure to acknowledge the feelings of their partner and are open about their own feelings. Finally, communicators share responsibility for the difficulties the couple is experiencing.

Fighters, on the other hand, bring up difficult topics at the wrong time, focus on general problems, become defensive and do not inquire about the true grievance of their spouse, do not acknowledge feelings, and do not share responsibility for the problems. Conversely, the third type of communication includes avoiding any communication that may involve difficult topics.

These styles of communication are observed by children and replicated in their sibling interactions. When siblings engage each other, they may openly communicate about their concerns or they may interact with each other in a harsh and hostile manner. They may also choose to ignore each other and avoid talking about matters that are upsetting to each other.

Once parents appreciate how their communication styles impact the manner of engagement employed by their children with each other, parents can assess their communication styles in therapy and discuss areas of improvement. Assessing family communication can be accomplished using the Family Problem Solving Communication Index (McCubbin, Thompson, & McCubbin, 1996). This ten-item measure is particularly useful for objectively assessing how the parental style of communication permeates the entire family system. The measure begins with the statement "When our family struggles with problems or conflicts which upset us, I would describe my family in the following way..." and includes options such as "we yell and scream at each other," "we are respectful of each other's feelings," "we talk things through till we reach a solution," "we work hard to be sure family members were not hurt emotionally or physically," and "we walk away from conflicts without much satisfaction." The scale aggregate produces two subscale scores based on the family's propensity toward *inflammatory communication* and *affirming communication*. Families scoring high on *inflammatory communication* are equivalent to the fighting style of communication and those scoring high on *affirming communication* can be categorized as open communicators. Those scoring low on both subscales are deemed avoiders.

Discussing the link between marital communication and sibling relationships coupled with the completion of the Family Problem Solving Communication Index can be used as an integral component of working with parents on enhancing the relationship that exists between their children.

Family positive engagement

In addition to the indirect way marital communication impacts the sibling bond, more intentional parenting behaviors within the family can also indirectly influence how siblings relate to each other. As an extension of ecological and systems approaches to the study of families, reviewed in Chapter 2, research has examined the way general parent–child interactions contribute to sibling relationship development in childhood and adolescence (Dunn, Deater-Deckard, Pickering, Golding, & the ALSPAC Study Team, 1999; Feinberg, McHale, Crouter, & Cumsille, 2003). The proposed connection between the way parents relate to children and the way children relate to each other is based on classic *attachment theory*.

Attachment theory and siblings

John Bowlby developed the initial formulation of attachment theory during his work in British orphanages in the aftermath of World War Two. He noticed that although the orphanages were providing children with appropriate food and shelter, many children in these orphanages developed psychological difficulties. Bowlby suggested that while these children were given their basic physiological provisions, they lacked a basic human need: physical closeness. Children need to be touched, children need to be caressed, and children need to be cuddled.

The need for closeness is driven by evolutionary forces. The only way a child can survive in a chaotic and dangerous world is if he or she develops an attachment with a protective attachment figure. Attachment to a protecting caregiver maximizes the offspring's probability of survival. In the original theory, it was the mother who served as the protector of her offspring. Through physical and emotional connections between a mother and her offspring, an infant develops a sense of security in the world. This connection is developed during infancy by engaging in attachment behaviors such as when the mother and baby caress, hug, and cuddle. The formation of this attachment to a primary caregiver is a vital development task of infancy (Bowlby, 1969).

Attachment must be solidified for children to feel a sense of security as they explore their surroundings. Caregivers serve as a "secure base" for infants from which they can draw confidence to explore the world. As the confidence in exploration grows, the need to retreat to the security of the caregiver diminishes (Ainsworth & Wittig, 1969). Hence, the task of infancy, and the mark of a secure attachment, is the development of a balance between proximity to the caregiver and exploration.

The development of a secure attachment is contingent upon maternal behaviors toward infants. According to Ainsworth, Blehar, Waters, and Wall (1978), when mothers consistently respond to their infants' distress with warmth, understanding, acceptance, and cooperation, the infants will internalize a sense of security over time and develop a secure attachment.

On the other hand, mothers who are rejecting of their infants and become irritated when their infants are in distress produce offspring with an insecure attachment. These mothers are also found to be emotionally rigid and display aversion to close bodily contact with their infants. Hence, early dynamics between mothers and their infants determine the development of infant attachment patterns.

The importance of early attachment formation is further magnified considering that according to the theory, the type of attachment developed in infancy serves as a model for all future relationships. Securely attached infants generalize their frame of mind to include feelings of security in relationships as a whole. On the other hand, infants with insecure attachments proceed to generalize this sense of insecurity in all their future relationships. Hence, early attachment serves as an "internal working model" for all future relationships.

This model is an internal schema of relationship expectations, perceptions, rules, and beliefs that is established in infancy and becomes imprinted over time (Bowlby, 1977). Once the model is established, it becomes resistant to change. New information inconsistent with the schema is disregarded. For example, if an infant develops a secure attachment after repeated warm interactions with a mother, later instances of aloofness are disregarded and the child retains security as their default orientation. Studies indicate that barring any severe trauma or damaging life circumstances, attachment classifications remain stable throughout adolescence and adulthood (Sroufe, Egeland, & Kreutzer, 1990).

Considering that the mother established archetype of relationships serves as a model for all future relationships, it would be expected that maternal and sibling relationships would follow similar patterns. According to the theory, the internal working model established during infancy would be generalized to other relationships including the sibling relationship. Hence, congruity between parent and sibling relationships should be expected, with securely attached individuals projected to develop warmth in their sibling relationships as well.

Supporting attachment theory, research has confirmed the congruous expectation in both positive and negative situations (Criss & Shaw, 2005; Ingoldsby, Shaw, Owens, & Winslow, 1999). For example, Brody, Stoneman, and McCoy (1992) found that families exhibiting positive functioning and harmony were more likely to have children who engaged each other positively and in non-conflicting ways than families exhibiting disharmony. Conversely, Teti and Ablard (1989) found that children with insecure maternal attachments exhibited hostility with their siblings. Similar negative congruity between maternal and sibling relationships were found throughout childhood, adolescence, and emerging adulthood by Feinberg, Reiss, Neiderhiser, and Hetherington (2005), Margolin, Christensen, and John (1996), and Scharf, Shulman, and Avigad-Spitz (2005). In fact, the importance of exploring the link between tense sibling relationships and early maladaptive parent interactions has been suggested by Bank (1988) as an integral component of clinical work.

Assessment and application with families

The manner in which attachment forces permeate the entire family relational system is referred to as the *cross-system contagion* model (Criss & Shaw, 2005). The nature of interpersonal interactions established by parents tends to spread throughout the entire family system. Positive parental interactions can offer positive contagion throughout the family. Alternatively, destructive family-wide contagion can occur as a result of negativity in the parental interactions.

Considering the cross-system contagion model, working with families on creating a home environment of warmth, closeness, and comfort can serve as an important addition to sibling relationship enhancement. Parents can be encouraged to integrate specific activities and projects at home to enhance the family's sense of positive engagement, cohesion, mutual interest, pride, loyalty, shared experiences, collective memories, and mutual knowledge.

Positive family engagement is more likely to occur with parents who enjoy the process of childrearing and who are willing to foster a home atmosphere conducive to family warmth and cohesion. Hence, psychotherapeutic work on positive family engagement can begin with assessing parental attitudes and feelings about the parenting experience. This evaluation can be done using a clinical interview inquiring about the parents' own experiences with their parents growing up, their early parenting narrative, and their current parenting experience including their enjoyments and stresses with their children.

Additionally, the Parenting Experience Scale (Milevsky & Rodriguez, 2015) can be used to assess enjoyment experienced by parents in their interactions with their children. This measure, developed by the author, includes 14 items scored on a one-to-five Likert-style scale asking about specific thoughts, feelings, and behaviors parents have relating to their children. Sample items include: "I often surprise my child(ren) with something positive," "When I have free time, I like to spend it with my child(ren)," and "I sometimes regret having my child(ren)." See Table 3.1 for the complete measure. After reversing the scores for items three, four, and ten, higher scores indicate greater parental enjoyment. Completing and discussing the results of this scale can help clinicians identify aspects of childrearing that parents enjoy and evaluate areas that need to be amended in creating an overall sense of positive family engagement.

Clinicians can work with parents on designing a positive engagement plan while taking into account the family's style, resources, and schedules. Suggestions of areas of focus and activities can include scheduling one-on-one time with each child, encouraging family conversations, and scheduling family dinners and game nights. When engaged in family activities, parents should minimize the use

Table 3.1   The Parenting Experience Scale

When parenting my child(ren) . . .	SD	D	IB	A	SA
1. I often surprise my child(ren) with something positive.	1	2	3	4	5
2. When I have free time, I like to spend it with my child(ren).	1	2	3	4	5
3. My child(ren) and I often disagree.	1	2	3	4	5
4. I feel like spending time with my child(ren) is an obligation.	1	2	3	4	5
5. I feel satisfied with the job I have done as a parent so far.	1	2	3	4	5
6. I look forward to moments of play with my child(ren).	1	2	3	4	5
7. I am proud of my child(ren) regardless of their accomplishments or failures.	1	2	3	4	5
8. I find myself laughing with my child(ren).	1	2	3	4	5
9. I am affectionate with my child(ren).	1	2	3	4	5
10. I sometimes regret having my child(ren).	1	2	3	4	5
11. I comfort my child(ren) when they are down.	1	2	3	4	5
12. Most nights I sit down for dinner with my child(ren).	1	2	3	4	5
13. Coming home from work, I am excited to see my child(ren).	1	2	3	4	5
14. I often tell my child(ren) I love them.	1	2	3	4	5

Note: Please indicate the extent to which you disagree or agree with the following statements regarding your parenting by placing a circle around your response.
1. Strongly Disagree 2. Disagree 3. In-between 4. Agree 5. Strongly Agree.

of distracting electronic devices and should encourage their children to act similarly. In order for the children in the family to feel a sense of ownership over the activities and commitment to their success, the family engagement plan can include creative activities conceived of jointly with the children.

Enhancing a sense of family pride, loyalty, and shared experiences can be accomplished by making use of family photos. Parents can print hard copies of digital photos and create family albums which are then placed in the living area of the house. Children sitting together and viewing the albums creates an atmosphere of reminiscing about past family events, triggering a sense of family togetherness.

Case study: "Ignoring each other and wanting to kill each other"

Kevin, a recently divorced 36-year-old single father, entered therapy for assistance with multiple difficulties he was experiencing with his three children, aged four, six, and nine. Of particular concern for him was the antagonistic relationship that existed between his nine-year-old daughter Leah and his six-year-old son Brandon. As Kevin described it, his two older children would vacillate between "ignoring each other and wanting to kill each other."

Therapeutic intervention included helping Kevin come to terms with the hardships he was experiencing and helping him adjust to life without his wife. Beyond the emphasis on the divorce, several sessions were devoted to enhancing the relationship between his children. The therapist inquired about the way he communicated with his ex-wife, Pam, about their divorce and parenting arrangements. Kevin described how difficult he found it to talk with "her" and noted that he either tried to avoid Pam or got into brash arguments with her.

The therapist helped Kevin find the corollary between his method of interaction with his ex-wife and the way his children engaged each other. Concrete steps were discussed to try to help Kevin develop healthier ways of interacting with Pam. In a subsequent session, Kevin recounted a conversation he had with Pam about the relationship between their two older children. Pam was also troubled by the relationship between the children. Kevin brought up the conversation he had with the therapist on the matter and Pam was willing to entertain the link between the way she interacted with Kevin and the way the children engaged each other. They agreed to develop a plan of communication that involved more open conversation and less antagonistic exchanges.

Additionally, Kevin described the tension that existed in his home due to the stress of the divorce and some financial difficulties he was having. Kevin was encouraged to create a warmer home environment by discussing with his children ways of integrating into their schedule activities that would enhance positive family engagement. Kevin and his children decided in collaboration that one of the things they could do together as a family would be to move the furniture in their living room on Sunday nights and have family soccer night in the open space. This activity turned out to be the highlight of the week for the children and helped create a sense of family cohesion. The games were eventually moved to the playroom once a picture frame came crashing down after an impressive kick by Brandon. They also devised a plan including opening a tent in the house and having a night of indoor camping. After bath time and pajamas, the family would go into the tent, eat marshmallows, tell stories, and then sleep in the tent. The objective of these activities was to create a sense of family positive engagement and cohesion.

Kevin appreciated the progress in therapy and was able to think about a few other things he could do to develop better communication with his ex-wife and create a more positive home environment. Over time, Kevin reported that he noticed that his children were spending more time together and getting into less fights. In a subsequent email to the therapist, Kevin wrote, "Thanks for your suggestions. Balancing fatherhood and parenthood is not always easy but it is making a big difference in my kids' lives. I am having lots more fun with my kids and we have even been able to keep all picture frames intact."

Parenting styles

Extending the link between attachment, home environment, and siblings, an additional important way parents indirectly support or hinder their children's sibling relationships includes parenting styles. Referring to specific parental behaviors employed by parents in their childrearing, researchers on parenting styles have explored multiple outcomes associated with style classification in childhood and adolescents, including sibling relationships.

Parenting styles classification

Originated by the work of Baumrind (1971), the traditional parenting classification included three distinct styles common in families. Authoritative parenting included parent behaviors marked by a combination of warmth, support, conclusive discipline, and stability. The authoritarian style was distinguished by a pattern of parenting interactions that included detachment, punitive discipline, and unpredictability. The third style, the permissive type, was discernible by a combination of warmth and diminished supervision.

More recent classifications of parenting styles, based on Baumrind's original three types, utilize four types based on levels of behavior on two overarching parenting constructs: responsiveness and demand-ingness. Parental responsiveness includes behaviors that display a sense of love, acceptance, involvement, and closeness. Parental demandingness includes supervision and monitoring of children's behaviors and activities.

Authoritative parents are those who show considerable respon-siveness toward their children in combination with high demands. Authoritarian parents are those who exhibit high levels of demand-ingness but show low levels of responsiveness. Indulgent parents show high levels of responsiveness but are low on parenting demands. The fourth classification includes the neglectful parents who exhibit low behaviors on both responsiveness and demanding-ness (Steinberg, Lamborn, Darling, Mounts, & Dornbusch, 1994).

Parenting styles and outcomes

An impressive literature points to many advantages of authoritative parenting for children and adolescents. In childhood, authorita-tive parenting has been linked with secure attachments, greater independence, and better academic outcomes (Karavasilis, Doyle, & Markiewicz, 2003; Kauffman, Gaston, Santa Lucia, Salcedo, Rendina-Gobioff, & Gadd, 2000). In adolescence, authoritative parenting has been shown to be associated with psychological adjustment and aca-demic achievement (Gonzalez, Holbein, & Quilter, 2002; Milevsky, Schlechter, Netter, & Keehn, 2007; Weiss & Schwarz, 1996).

Parenting styles and sibling relationships

Parenting styles have also been shown to be associated with sibling relationships. Studies have found that parents employing patterns of childrearing that include warmth, support, and consistent discipline were more likely to have children with closeness in their sibling rela-tionships than children of parents not employing authoritative-type parenting (Brody, Stoneman, & Burke, 1987; Dunn, Deater-Deckard, Pickering, Golding, & the ALSPAC Study Team, 1999).

A similar alignment has been reported in studies on parenting and adolescents as well (Feinberg, McHale, Crouter, & Cumsille, 2003). However, a common limitation of parenting style research in general is that when studies use the common "active" consent procedures, requiring parental written consent prior to the study, the final sample surveyed is often disproportionately low in participants of neglectful parents. This occurs due to the fact that, by definition, neglectful parents are less likely to respond to requests by researchers regarding their child's participation.

In order to counter this methodological difficulty, Milevsky, Schlechter, and Machlev (2011) studied the association between parenting styles and sibling relationship quality in adolescence using a unique approach. In order to assess all four categories of parenting, including neglectful, a "passive" consent procedure was used after approval by the authors' institutional review board. In this method, parents were informed in advance about the objectives of the study and were offered an opportunity to decline their child's participation. From over 300 parents contacted via post mail, only one declined participation. Students whose parents did not decline were approached in school about participation. The use of this method has been approved in prior work by the United States Department of Education (see Steinberg, Lamborn, Darling, Mounts, & Dornbusch, 1994). In addition to the parental "passive" consent, student participants completed informed assent. An additional advantage of the Milevsky, Schlechter, and Machlev (2011) study was its assessment of both maternal and paternal styles separately using the Authoritative Parenting Measure (Steinberg, Lamborn, Darling, Mounts, & Dornbusch, 1994). Results indicated that adolescents with authoritative parents scored higher on sibling support and closeness than adolescents with authoritarian and neglectful parents. Interestingly, these outcomes were found for both maternal and paternal parenting styles, highlighting the crucial role played by fathers in the link between parenting and sibling dynamics as well.

Assessment and application with families

Working with families on improving parenting styles necessitates an open discussion with parents about their current style of childrearing and its impact on their children's functioning. Similar to the process of creating positive family engagement, psychotherapeutic work can begin with an evaluation and assessment of parenting styles. This assessment can be done with a clinical interview, including an inquiry into the couple's own experiences with their parents growing up, their early parenting narrative, and their current parenting methods.

Additionally, research on families offers multiple measures of parenting styles that can be amalgamated and used in clinical settings.

Although scores on these measures are primarily used as norm-referenced criteria by comparing individual scores with other participants' scores to develop descriptors or associations, scores on these measures can be used by comparing them with commonly found scores in studies on parenting and by identifying extremes. Completion of these measures can also be used as a means to discuss the particulars of specific parenting styles by reviewing the individual items on the measure. These measures can be given to children to complete about their parents in general or about each of their parents separately. The measure can also be reframed for appropriate use with parents.

A widely used measure of parenting styles is the Authoritative Parenting Measure (Steinberg, Lamborn, Darling, Mounts, & Dornbusch, 1994), including three subscales appropriate for use with older children and adolescents. For parenting styles assessment, the acceptance/involvement and the strictness/supervision subscales are used. Sample items on the acceptance/involvement subscale, which correspond to the aforementioned responsiveness construct, include "I can count on my mother/father to help me out if I have some kind of problem" and "When my mother/father wants me to do something, she/he explains why." Responses to each of the nine items on the acceptance/involvement subscale are scored on a one-to-five Likert-style scale, with higher scores indicating higher acceptance/involvement. Sample items on the strictness/supervision subscale, which corresponds to demandingness, include "How much does your mother/father try to know where you go at night?" and "How much does your mother/father really know what you do with your free time?" This set of items is scored on a one-to-three Likert-style scale. Additionally, the strictness/supervision subscale includes the items "In a typical week, what is the latest you can stay out on school nights?" and "In a typical week, what is the latest you can stay out on weekends?" These two items are scored on a one-to-seven Likert-style scale. After combining both sets of items in the strictness/supervision subscale, totaling eight items, higher scores indicate higher strictness/supervision.

The scores are then used to place participants into one of four parenting style categories. Authoritative parents would be those whose children score high on both acceptance/involvement and strictness/supervision. Authoritarian parents are those whose children score low on acceptance/involvement and high on strictness/supervision. Permissive parents are those whose children score high on acceptance/involvement but low on strictness/supervision. And neglectful parents are those whose children score low on both acceptance/involvement and strictness/supervision. This categorization can be done separately for maternal and paternal styles in cases where the children complete the scale twice, for both mothers and fathers.

Once the classifications are established, clinicians can engage parents in a discussion about their current style of childrearing and how it impacts their children's sibling relationships. The specific items on the measure can be used as a guide for particular areas of improvement. The clinical setting can also be used for an open discussion between parents about differences they have in their parenting. Studies indicate that parents often engage in different patterns of parenting (Milevsky, Schlechter, Klem, & Kehl, 2008). Highlighting these differences in therapy can help parents minimize parenting mixed messages and develop a congruity of practice which will serve the family in multiple beneficial ways. The importance of parenting message congruity is further examined in Chapter 8.

Chapter summary

Parents play a significant role in fostering positive sibling relationships. Several indirect mechanisms have been shown to impact sibling relationship quality. First, marital relationships have been shown to impact the quality of the relationship that exists between siblings. Children are more likely to develop antagonistic sibling dynamics in hostile homes. Clinicians working with families should consider examining the marital relationship when attempting to minimize sibling hostility. Additionally, the overall home atmosphere created by parents and the parenting styles they employ have also been shown to impact the sibling connection. Therapeutic work with families should focus on these factors when engaging in prevention and intervention for sibling relationship improvement.

4
Direct Ways Parents Impact Sibling Bonds

In addition to the indirect ways parents impact their children's bond via marital relationship modeling, overall family positive engagement, and parenting styles, parents also influence their children in more direct ways. These direct influences refer to the ways parents actively manage and direct the sibling relationships of their children.

Parents can actively shape the relationship between their children from early in life. For example, Dunn and Kendrick (1982) found that mothers who encouraged their young children to help with a newborn sibling and talked to the young children about their new sibling's needs were more likely to have children who displayed friendliness toward the new sibling than mothers who did not include their young children in the newborn's care.

As children develop, the direct paths that parents can follow to enhance the sibling relationships of their children include encouraging healthy sibling de-identification, avoiding parental favoritism, and understanding sibling dispute intervention. Sibling relationship enhancement requires a systematic focus on minimizing the negative aspects of the relationship and improving the positive using both indirect and direct methods.

Sibling differences

When siblings are similar to each other in personality, interests, and hobbies, they are more likely to fight. The comparisons that are often made between siblings who are alike can produce competition, tension, and rivalry. For example, siblings with similar personalities may trigger people to make comparisons between the two, resulting in elevated sibling competition and antagonism. Siblings interested in similar types of toys are more likely to be jealous of each other's possessions. Siblings involved in similar athletics may experience elevated levels of sibling hostility due to comparisons made in their abilities. On the other hand, sibling dissimilarity reduces comparisons, rivalry, and jealousy, which produce a more peaceful sibling relationship atmosphere.

Sibling non-shared environments

Even with the genetic and home environment similarities shared by siblings, studies have found that siblings often diverge in many aspects of their interests, well-being, and personality (Conley, 2004; Dunn & Plomin, 1990). These differences have been attributed to several factors. For example, beyond their shared experiences, siblings each have considerable aspects of their lives which are not shared. Aspects of their non-shared environment may include personal friendships, diverging peer and teacher interactions, or particular illnesses or accidents occurring to only one sibling, prompting them to develop differing life tracks (Dunn & McGuire, 1994; Rowe, Woulbroun, & Gulley, 1994).

Another way in which siblings may have divergent experiences in life may include parental differential treatment or the way parents react in dissimilar ways to different siblings in the family (Shanahan, Mchale, Crouter, & Osgood, 2008). Hence, several aspects of siblings' environment are not shared, which may account for differences found between siblings.

Sibling de-identification

Beyond the impact of the non-shared environment in producing differences between siblings, there is an additional, more active, and intentional process that may account for sibling differences. Understanding this force, and knowing how to navigate it correctly, can be a powerful tool used by parents in sibling relationship enhancement.

Referred to in developmental psychology as sibling de-identification, the process that produces sibling differences may be actively initiated by children, intentionally or unintentionally, by choosing a path that is different than the one charted by their siblings (Feinberg & Hetherington, 2000; Teti, 2002). From a young age, children may seek an identity that is different than the one held by their siblings.

Several theoretical models offer frameworks to understand the motives behind the need for children to de-identify. Psychoanalytic thought, based on the sibling work of Alfred Adler, suggests that de-identification is orchestrated by children as an attempt to minimize sibling rivalry. By being different, each sibling is able to enhance their self-worth, without minimizing the sibling, which results in less sibling competition and rivalry (Ansbacher & Ansbacher, 1956). Neo-analytic work, based on Erik Erikson's ideas of identity development, suggests that de-identification from siblings is an integral ingredient of healthy identity development. This may account for the particularly salient sibling differentiation that is found during the adolescent years, a time of heightened identity exploration (McHale, Updegraff, Helms-Erikson, & Crouter, 2001). Other theories place de-identification within the structure of self-concept. The need to de-identify may be fueled by self-esteem needs. Minimizing the importance of an older sibling's accomplishments and choosing to get involved in other activities helps younger siblings build their sense of self (Bossard & Boll, 1956; Tesser, 1980).

Accordingly, researchers have found de-identification mechanisms in studies on sibling differences in parental relationships, gender roles, personality, and school achievement (Feinberg, McHale, Crouter, & Cumsille, 2003; McHale, Updegraff, Helms-Erikson, & Crouter, 2001). Several other findings emanating from research on de-identification help support the theoretical foundation and clarify the process of de-identification. For example, Grotevant (1978) found that girls with older sisters were more likely to choose male stereotypical interests than did girls with older brothers. The girls with older sisters may have attempted to de-identify by choosing traditional male interests as a way to stand apart from their older sisters. Feinberg, Reiss, Neiderhiser, and Hetherington (2005) found greater levels of de-identification in homes reporting elevated levels of marital conflict. In situations of family conflict, children may need to stand out in greater ways to receive needed attention.

Sibling modeling

An additional line of empirical studies on de-identification examines the interaction between de-identification processes, modeling, and family constellation variables. Researchers have attempted to reconcile competing expectations regarding sibling differentiation (Whiteman, McHale, & Crouter, 2007). As reviewed, based on de-identification forces, it would be expected that younger siblings choose different paths than the ones pursued by older siblings. However, based on social learning and modeling theory (Bandura, 1962; Bandura & Huston, 1961; Bandura, Ross, & Ross, 1963), it would be expected that older siblings would serve as a model for shaping the thoughts, interests, and behaviors of younger siblings, resulting in younger siblings following paths similar to the ones followed by older siblings (Mischel, 1966). Modeling dynamics would be particularly salient with siblings considering evidence emanating from social learning theory that modeling forces are most present when the model is more powerful than the learner is, is similar to the learner, and is nurturing to the learner, all characteristics common in sibling relationships.

Supporting the modeling expectation, studies have in fact found similarities between siblings in vast areas of personality and behaviors (Bank, Patterson, & Reid, 1996; Cox, DuRant, Emans, & Woods, 1995; East, 1998; Slomkowski, Rende, Conger, Simons, & Conger, 2001; Slomkowski, Rende, Novak, Lloyd-Richardson, & Niaura, 2005; Tucker, Updegraff, McHale, & Crouter, 1999). Hence, modeling is expected to increase similarities between siblings, contrary to the de-identification expectation.

Studies reconciling these competing hypotheses help clarify the complexity of sibling family processes. This is particularly important when considering how research findings on sibling de-identification can be applied in clinical practice.

Unifying sibling de-identification and modeling is accomplished by examining how these two seemingly opposing forces play out within the context of sibling constellations. Schachter, Shore, Feldman-Rotman, Marquis, and Campbell (1976) examined de-identification and modeling in adolescents by comparing sibling dyads who were different than each other by sibling position (i.e. siblings who were *first pairs*, firstborn and second-born, siblings who were *second pairs*, second-born and third-born, and siblings who were *jump pairs*, firstborn and third-born) and different than each other by sex and age-spacing.

First-pair siblings were found to have the strongest de-identification followed by second-pair siblings. Jump-pair siblings were found to have the weakest de-identification (i.e. they were most similar). First-pair siblings were most de-identified when they were of the same sex, which lends support to the psychoanalytic approach to de-identification. First-pair siblings were initially the only two siblings in the home and over the years have spent a considerable amount of time together, a combination of factors that is likely to increase rivalry. The sense of rivalry is further amplified in cases of similarity of sex between the siblings where interests are often similar. The confluence of these factors, which results in elevated levels of rivalry in first-pair, same-sex siblings, produces a need to minimize the potential conflict via de-identification. Hence, de-identification may be particularly prominent in first-pair, same-sex siblings. On the other hand, modeling forces may be more likely to be at play in other sibling constellation situations.

Sibling de-identification in practice

Although de-identification is an active process undertaken by children, parents may play a role in its development as well (Saudino, McGuire, Hetherington, Reiss, & Plomin, 1995). In a longitudinal study, Schachter, Gilutz, Shore, and Adler (1978) found remarkable similarities between parent reports of de-identification of their children and reports of de-identification of the children themselves when they were adolescents. This finding may indicate that parents actually orchestrate de-identification between their children from an early age in order to minimize potential sibling rivalry. By overtly and covertly highlighting differences between children when they are young, parents begin shaping their offspring's personal identities, producing a process analogous to a de-identification self-fulfilling prophecy. Over time, this molding helps to reinforce the children's natural disposition, solidifying their identities as they reach the adolescent years. Their distinctive identities help each of the children in the family, in turn, feel a sense of personal uniqueness, resulting in less sibling comparisons and diminished sibling rivalry and hostility.

The potential of parents in playing an active role in shaping the identities of their children in an effort to minimize sibling comparisons holds both promise and the potential for complications. When done appropriately, parents have the ability to craft a niche for each of their children based on their unique potentials. Doing so can enhance their personal sense of esteem and help in minimizing future rivalries. In practice, parents of young children can be educated about sibling de-identification and be encouraged to identify their children's unique potential. Parents should highlight each of their children's individuality and stress how each of their personal intelligences, personalities, interests, and talents are all exceptional and virtuous.

Unfortunately, parent-driven de-identification has the potential of producing several unintended negative consequences such as when parents classify divergence between children as demonstrating a difference between superiority and inferiority. Healthy de-identification involves each sibling in the family feeling a sense of self-esteem from their unique family position.

However, if the sense perceived by some in the family is that their sibling is "the good one" at some task and they are the inferior one, the result will include negativity and sibling tensions. In fact, Cornell and Grossberg (1986) found that when children perceive being less gifted than their older sibling, based on messages received from parents, they experience diminished self-esteem. Similarly, Neaves and Crouch (1990) found that when de-identification was perceived by a child as an expression of inferiority in reaction to an older sibling's superior intellectual abilities, the child experienced negative self-esteem.

Hence, it is crucial for parents to actively shape their children to de-identify in ways that magnify their unique potential as opposed to de-identifying children based on meaningless arbitrary differences or based on superiority/inferiority. For example, Tesser (1980) cautioned that when an older child excels in academics, a younger sibling might attempt to de-identify by minimizing the importance of academics. In such cases, it is important for parents to minimize the academic comparison and accentuate positive aspects of the younger child's persona.

By working with parents at crafting healthy sibling de-identification within their children, clinicians can play an important role in helping families enhance sibling relationships.

Parental favoritism

Treating all children in a family equally is a common tenet in many Western families (Kowal, Krull, & Kramer, 2006). However, equality of treatment is often difficult to accomplish considering differences between ages and needs of children in a family. When children perceive that they are being treated unfairly by their parents, in comparison to their siblings, they often experience a minimization of personal well-being and it often leads to sibling discord. Hence, understanding the process and impact of parental favoritism can be an important addendum to sibling relationship enrichment in practice.

Parental differential treatment

Referred to in the literature as *parental differential treatment*, studies have indicated that parents do in fact treat children differently or, more directly, display favoritism toward a specific child in the family (Shebloski, Conger, & Widaman, 2005; Tejerina-Allen, Wagner, & Cohen, 1994). Both parents and children note the existence of parental differential treatment and agreement often exists within family members concerning its presence (Brody, Copeland, Sutton, Richardson, & Guyer, 1998; Kowal, Kramer, Krull, & Crick, 2002). This family agreement indicates that parental favoritism is more than just a child's own perception of the phenomenon; it actually exists. Disparity in treatment can be expressed by parents in several ways such as by showing more affection and support to a specific sibling, responding more harshly to a specific sibling, or providing more privileges to a specific sibling.

Studies have shown that children who perceive parental differential treatment report greater levels of depression and maladjustment in comparison to those not reporting perceived favoritism (Kowal & Kramer, 1997). These negative associations have been shown to last into adulthood (Finzi-Dottan & Cohen, 2010; Jensen, Whiteman, Fingerman, & Birditt, 2013; Pillemer, Suitor, Pardo, & Henderson, 2010).

Sibling relationship quality is an additional victim of parental differential treatment. Children and adolescents who report feeling that their parents favor their siblings over them show higher levels of sibling hostility and lower levels of sibling intimacy in comparison to those not reporting parental differential treatment (Kowal & Kramer, 1997; Scholte, Engels, de Kemp, Harakeh, & Overbeek, 2007). Similar to the findings on the link between parental differential treatment and diminished personal well-being, the impact of parental favoritism on sibling relationship quality has also been found to last into adulthood. Adults recalling parental differential treatment in childhood report lower levels of sibling closeness in adulthood in comparison to others (Jensen, Whiteman, Fingerman, & Birditt, 2013; Suitor, Sechrist, & Pillemer, 2007; Suitor, Sechrist, Plikuhn, Pardo, Gilligan, & Pillemer, 2009).

Parental differential treatment in practice

In order to help parents improve the relationship that exists between their children, issues of parental differential treatment must be confronted in practice. Some degree of differential treatment is unavoidable considering the unique needs of children based on their disposition or age (Jensen, Whiteman, Fingerman, & Birditt, 2013). However, in some cases, parents may favor one of their children in subtle ways or may react to one of their children in privileged ways without awareness. This dissimilar treatment directed toward a specific child may be driven by difficult behaviors exhibited by the child, such as a child entering the adolescent years and beginning to exhibit some common adolescent belligerency. In other cases, the differential treatment may be based on more obscured forces such as when the child triggers a transference reaction by the parent. If one of the children in a family reminds a father of his mother-in-law, it may be hard for the father to hold back reacting to that child differently than the way he reacts to the child that reminds him of himself. Openly discussing these issues in session with both parents can help in exposing the existence of differential treatment which can then be used as a way of developing a plan to minimize its occurrence.

Even in cases when parents are aware of the pitfalls of parental favoritism, the need for a careful assessment of differential treatment issues with parents is important considering that often parents respond to issues of parental differential treatment in counterproductive ways. Parents often deal with favoritism issues using a reactionary hyper-awareness of equality of treatment at all costs. In these cases, parents make every effort to offer each of their children equality of time, resources, and support.

This hyper-awareness of equality at all costs may be driven by natural occurrences common in today's Western families. The prevalence of smaller families, with fewer children, closer in age, has resulted in what is known as *high-access siblings* with common friends, school, activities, bedroom, and clothes (Bank & Kahn, 1982). This elevated level of access between siblings is a natural breeding ground for scrim-mages over sharing, turf wars, and personal-space issues, all of which can lead to feelings of having less than siblings. Hence, the smallest indication of inequality between siblings is responded to harshly by children.

Parents may also feed this awareness with a mentality of equality at all costs, further creating the potential for feelings of mistreatment with minor inequalities. Parents react in destructive hypersensitive ways for several reasons. First, the dangers of parental differential treatment are often discussed openly and are well known in soci-ety. Parents may also have past childhood experiences of being slighted by parents and as a result are vigilant about not repeating the mistakes of their parents.

Unfortunately, equality at all costs is a standard that is impossible for parents to achieve (Felson, 1983). Insisting on the illusion that children can truly be given everything equally results in resentful children who are perpetually jealous of each other.

The answer to issues of parental differential treatment is not a reac-tionary family regulation of absolute equality. Like any other family issue, feelings of parental differential treatment by children need to be confronted with open discussions with the children about their thoughts and feelings about its existence. When a child comments that it is not fair when their sibling receives an extra resource, parents should respond by asking the child to elaborate on the concern.

Clinicians should encourage parents to allow their children to expand on the thoughts and feelings associated with their perceived injustice. The child's protest is often emanating from a more sys-tematic sense of being less valued or loved that the "fortunate" sibling. Allowing for children to express themselves can help uncover these feelings, providing a sense of being attended to, and offering an opportunity to confront these feelings of jealousy. Parents can confront feelings of "you love him more than you love me" openly.

Children should be given an opportunity to offer an alternate explanation to why their sibling received the extra provision to counter the explanation they prescribed to it involving the parents loving the sibling more. For example, when a child complains that his brother got a new backpack for school and he did not, the child can explore the reason for this seeming injustice, including that the sibling's old backpack was tattered and his was not. Confronting feelings of being less loved and highlighting individual needs can help parents confront issues of differential treatment effectively. Finally, as noted in the previous section, highlighting de-identification can help minimize sibling comparisons and magnify individual uniqueness. By appreciating each child in the family and stressing their unique character and needs, differential treatment can be viewed in the context of individual needs as opposed to parental favoritism.

Sibling dispute intervention

One of the greatest childrearing stressors reported by mothers and fathers is when their children fight (Milevsky, Thudium, Milevsky, & Roth, 2013; Perozynski & Kramer, 1999). Unfortunately, sibling fighting is extremely prevalent. Straus, Gelles, and Steinmetz (1980) reported that over 80% of families they interviewed had instances of sibling aggression. In fact, studies indicate that sibling violence is more common than any other relational conflict (Straus, Gelles, & Steinmetz, 1980; Wiehe, 2000).

In addition to sibling aggression being troublesome to parents, sibling aggression in childhood has been found to be linked with many negative outcomes in childhood and beyond. Sibling hostility has been found to be associated with future aggressive behaviors, psychological problems, and emotional difficulties (Garcia, Shaw, Winslow, & Yaggi, 2000; Volling, 2003). Studies have even suggested that childhood sibling aggression is linked with delinquency in adolescence and interpersonal problems in adulthood (Bank, Burraston, & Snyder, 2004; Noland, Liller, McDermott, Coulter, & Seraphine, 2004). Hence, efforts at minimizing sibling aggression in childhood have the potential of offering multiple long-term advantages.

Sibling aggression may be driven by multiple internal and external factors (Felson, 1983). However, working with parents on appropriate intervention strategies can help minimize the fighting which can directly impact the type of relationship that exists between siblings (Chengappa, Stokes, Costello, Norman, Travers, & McNeil, 2013).

Sibling dispute intervention in theory and research
The theoretical literature offers two distinct and seemingly contradictory suggestions regarding parent involvement in sibling disputes.

Adlerian theory would posit that siblings fight in order to draw attention from parents (Dreikurs, 1964). Based on this premise, it would be unadvisable for parents to intervene when their children fight as this may reinforce the attention-seeking fighting. On the other hand, based on the importance of parent modeling and the role of parents in facilitating social interactions (Bhavnagri & Parke, 1991; Ladd & Golter, 1988), it would be sensible for parents to intervene in sibling disputes as a way for them to offer important lessons to their children in conflict resolution and perspective taking.

Empirical research on sibling dispute intervention shows that once age is taken into account, both of the noted theoretical propositions may coexist. When children are young, they have yet to develop proficiencies in social relationship management. Sibling disputes produce an opportune time for parents to offer children much-needed basic lessons in interpersonal interactions, conflict resolution, problem solving, and social engagement (Buist, 2010; Garcia, Shaw, Winslow, & Yaggi, 2000). For example, a sibling fight as a result of jealousy over a toy can offer children an opportunity to experience and understand the concepts of possessions and ownership. A child may use the interaction as a way of comprehending that "I have some things but other things may not be mine." This can, in turn, promote the vital process of individuation and separation (Edward, 2013; Jacobson, 1964). Furthermore, when a child is not able to possess an object or quality that his or her sibling holds, it can help promote an understanding of the difference between desires and what can be obtained in reality, "thereby helping to transform early feelings of omnipotence into a more reality-based view of the self" (Edward, 2013, p. 78). Those early sibling fights can also help children appreciate that mixed feelings are possible as the child may love and hate a sibling at the same time.

Hence, when done correctly, parents can use sibling fighting as a teachable moment. The proficiencies learned from parents about proper social exchanges during sibling disputes can then be applied by children in future sibling altercations leading to greater understanding and connectedness between the siblings. In fact, several studies with children have indicated that parental intervention in childhood sibling disputes is linked with closer sibling relationships (Perlman & Ross, 1997; Ross, Filyer, Lollis, Perlman, & Martin, 1994).

An important qualification that needs to be made in the link between intervention and positive sibling relationship outcomes in childhood is the method of involvement used by parents during the intervention. Studies indicate that parents tend to react to sibling fighting in one of three methods of response. The first method is *non-involvement*, which entails ignoring the problem or telling the siblings to deal with the problem themselves. *Coaching* includes a child-centered approach entailing mediating the fight and helping each sibling to recognize the perspective of the other sibling. Coaching also involves helping the siblings find a compromise and resolution. The third method, *intervention*, is when parents intervene by punishing the siblings and eliminating the problem.

Effective parent involvement in sibling disputes necessitates coaching. The only way parents can teach siblings about conflict resolution, problem solving, and social engagement during fights is by coaching children through the process of resolution. Studies showing an association between parental intervention and sibling closeness entail interventions that include coaching-type techniques. For example, in a study with pre-school children, Kramer, Perozynski, and Chung (1999) found that when parents engaged in child-centered strategies of coaching during sibling conflict, their children were more likely to have closer relationships with each other in comparison to children whose parents did not utilize coaching.

On the other hand, as children mature and enter their pre-adolescent and adolescent years, parents may need to reconsider their intervention strategies. Studies indicate that as children transition into their adolescent years, they may find parental coaching during sibling disputes as intrusive and counter-productive. As the developmental process of adolescent individuation and identity unfolds, parents need to step back and allow adolescents to face their sibling disputes on their own. For example, McHale, Updegraff, Tucker, and Crouter (2000) studied the intervention styles of mothers and fathers in 185 families. Parents reported on the way they would react to hypothetical situations of sibling fighting. Mothers and fathers were provided a measure of sibling dispute intervention which categorized parental reactions into three intervention styles: non-involvement, coaching, and intervention. Sibling intimacy and negativity were assessed using personal interviews. Results indicated that direct intervention by either mothers or fathers was associated with less intimacy and more negativity between the siblings. Non-involvement by mothers was also found to be associated with higher sibling intimacy. However, based on follow-up analyses, the authors noted that in some cases parents may choose not to intervene when they know that the siblings who are fighting usually have a good relationship and will deal with the problem themselves. This shows that intervention type may in some cases be based on child characteristics.

Similarly, Milevsky, Schlechter, and Machlev (2011) surveyed 272 students in high school about the way their parents react when they fight with their siblings. The survey also assessed sibling relationship quality. The analysis included a unique person-centered approach to capture the combination of ways parents may react to sibling disputes. Considering that parents react to fighting using a variety of involvement methods, the analysis assessed patterns of common groupings of intervention methods by examining clusters of involvement styles. After finding different cluster solutions based on gender, separate analyses were conducted for males and females. These clusters were then compared on sibling relationship quality.

For boys, mothers were found to either intervene or coach, but were not likely to have an exclusive style of not getting involved. For the female participants, mothers had some coaching peppered throughout the three patterns and were more likely to have a distinct pattern of not getting involved with girls compared to boys. This, once again, may indicate that intervention type may in some cases be based on child characteristics, in this case, gender. Mothers may choose not to get involved when they know that their fighting daughters usually have a good relationship and will deal with the problem themselves.

For fathers, on the other hand, the three patterns of intervention found were similar for both males and females. One group reported high levels of coaching, some intervention, and low levels of non-involvement. Group two noted low levels on all the involvement styles, indicating a pattern of paternal detachment. Group three was distinct, with high non-involvement, including some intervention, and little coaching. One minor shift was found based on gender. For group two, the detached cluster, males reported somewhat more father intervention that females did. This result is consistent with other work that has shown that fathers may feel an added sense of responsibility for parenting their sons (Harris & Morgan, 1991).

After identifying these distinct gender-based patterns of interventions, the authors examined the link between parental involvement clusters and sibling relationship quality. Results indicated that girls in the high mother-coaching cluster were found to report higher sibling warmth than girls in the other mother clusters. Furthermore, boys in the high father-coaching cluster were found to report higher sibling warmth than boys in the other father clusters.

Although the finding that coaching in adolescence was related to sibling warmth is in conflict with previous work on the deleterious impact of coaching in adolescents, a cautious examination of the findings may highlight an important element of dispute intervention overall. The results showed that coaching was linked with sibling warmth only for females and maternal coaching, and for males and paternal coaching. As noted, parents may select an intervention type based on characteristics of the children. Parents may choose to engage in coaching only when they know that their children will be receptive to the coaching. The findings of Milevsky, Schlechter, and Machlev (2011) may indicate that females are more receptive to mother coaching and males may be more receptive to father coaching. Hence, the impact on sibling relationship quality may be a function of matching intervention type with the unique characteristics of the adolescents involved.

In summary, research on sibling dispute intervention has shown that the manner in which parents intervene may be linked with sibling relationship quality. However, interventions must take into account the precise method used and the developmental stage of children. In childhood, proper coaching is found to be associated with sibling closeness and warmth. Lacking experience in conflict-resolution strategies, children may need parents to walk them through sibling fights. With proper coaching, children can learn how to engage their siblings more effectively, resulting in closer relationships. However, as children mature and develop advanced social competencies, parents should approach intervention in sibling disputes more cautiously. During the teenage years, it is imperative to consider the distinct characteristics of the adolescents when determining whether and how to intervene when siblings fight. In adolescents, blind coaching may lead to greater sibling disputes and hence should be used only when the siblings are receptive to the mediation.

Sibling dispute-intervention assessment and practice

When attempting to resolve sibling relationship disputes, clinicians may be called upon to work with parents on their sibling parenting or may actually work directly with children on the conflict resolution. Continuing the parenting approach assumed throughout this chapter, the current discussion focuses on working with parents on sibling relationship enhancement.

However, in some cases, therapists may determine that the sibling discord is driven by a broader problem involving the parents having a profound lack of basic parenting skills (Chengappa, Stokes, Costello, Norman, Travers, & McNeil, 2013). In such cases, parents may need basic parenting training which may include the therapist working with the parents and directly with the children on appropriate parenting modeling and sibling relationship management. Chapter 7 expands on this latter case, where clinicians work in this more systematic and direct way on sibling issues. The current review targets parents who possess appropriate parenting practices but lack more specific sibling-based parenting techniques.

Therapy with the parents can commence with an assessment of the way parents react to sibling disputes using the Sibling Conflict Intervention Style Measure (McHale, Updegraff, Tucker, & Crouter, 2000; Milevsky, Schlechter, & Machlev, 2011). This measure asks parents to answer how likely they are to respond in various ways to sibling fighting. The seven items, scored on a one-to-five Likert-style scale, are combined to produce the most common style. The items "ignore the problem," "tell children to work out the problem themselves," and "ask spouse to handle the problem" are averaged to derive the non-involvement score. The items "give them advice" and "explain the siblings' feelings to each other" are averaged to derive the coaching score. And the items, "step in and solve the problem" and "punish them for fighting" are averaged to derive the intervention score. Once common patterns are identified, the therapist can discuss with the parents the merits of their methods and the level of agreement between the parents in their approach.

Interestingly, the three approaches to dispute intervention are found to be similar to the three styles of family communication discussed in the previous chapter. Non-involvement is akin to avoiding conflict, coaching is similar to open communication, and intervention parallels fighting. Identifying the link between the parent's style of overall communication and their method of sibling dispute intervention can help parents appreciate the systematic nature of the family difficulties and confront change in a holistic fashion.

Considering the age-based distinct patterns of association between parental sibling dispute intervention and sibling relationship quality, it is important for clinicians working with parents to tailor their intervention based on the age of the children. When parents seek assistance with sibling fighting, clinicians should emphasize coaching techniques when the siblings in question are younger and highlight a more cautious approach when the siblings are older.

Coaching during childhood

When counseling parents of young children with sibling dispute intervention, the first thing to keep in mind is that often children misbehave simply because they are tired or hungry. Parents should monitor when their children are most likely to engage in fights. When the culprit can be identified as exhaustion or hunger, any type of intervention would be ineffective. In such cases, responding to the children's basic needs should be the method of reaction.

When sibling fighting is not a reaction to exhaustion or hunger, parents can use the fight as an opportunity to enhance the sibling bond by educating children about appropriate conflict resolution. When fights occur, parents should first avoid asking the children the common, ineffective question of "Who started it?" This question has rarely produced a definitive answer and knowing the wrongdoer is not the objective of the intervention. The objective is to engage the children in conflict-resolution strategies.

Parents should be encouraged to begin by offering the children a "cool-down" period. When children are extremely upset about the problem, they are physiologically unprepared for a peaceful perspective-taking discussion. After a few moments of deep breathing and relaxation, parents can inquire about what happened.

The decision about which of the children should begin recounting what occurred first is an important one. Several factors should be taken into account. First, does one of the children suspect that the parent favors the other over him or her? Allowing the insecure sibling to begin can help in avoiding having to deal with issues of parental favoritism at this point. Another consideration is the impulsivity of the children. The child more likely to lose interest in the upcoming exchange should be allowed to go first. However, if favoritism or impulsivity is not a problem, the younger child should go first as the older sibling is at a natural advantage in these types of exchanges due to their superior language abilities (Gnaulati, 2002).

Parents should begin by asking the chosen child "What happened?" and allow the child to express the emotions involved in the incident in addition to recounting the actual event (Faber & Mazlish, 2012). As the description of the event ensues, parents should prevent the other sibling from interfering. In cases where the other sibling does interfere, they should be told that they will have their turn to recount their version of the event. Children are more likely to believe that their turn will come when their parents follow this turn-taking regularly and consistently. Once the first child is done telling their version of the event, they should be asked, "Is there anything else you want to say about what happened before your brother/sister tells me what happened?" Once they are done, parents should allow the other child to tell their story, making sure the first sibling does not interrupt during the second recounting.

Ultimately, the objective of this process is not to reach a conclusion about what occurred. The goal is teaching the siblings how conflict resolution is embarked on. Allowing both sides to explain what happened teaches the siblings that others may have a different take on events, promoting their perspective taking in a real-life situation.

An integral part of this perspective taking should be about the emotional perspective of each sibling (Faber & Mazlish, 2012). It is crucial not only for each child to understand that their sibling may have a different story about what happened but also that their actions caused a particular emotion to be triggered in their sibling. Understanding the emotions of others is an important extension of perspective taking and is a crucial part of developing lifelong, healthy relationships (Salovey & Mayer, 1990). Parents can accomplish this by pointing out to each of their children the emotional effect they had on their sibling during the fight. It should combine both a realization that their action created the emotion in their sibling and the naming and identification of the emotion. For example, parents can state, "When you grabbed the toy away from your sister, she became very sad. Look how she is crying; she is very sad." Through this process, children learn that their actions can have emotional effects on others, they learn about the names of different emotions, and they learn what various emotions look like.

Once the perspectives of the siblings are examined, including the emotional consequences of their behaviors, an additional important lesson in conflict resolution is taking personal ownership of some of the things that happened during the fight. For example, parents can turn to each of their children and ask, "When you hit your brother when he took the car away from you, what else could you have done instead?" or "When you called your sister a baby after she started to cry when her toy broke, what else could you have said instead?" When children respond with a more socially acceptable course of action such as, "I could have asked him to give it back to me," or "I could have come to you and told you he took it away from me," or "I could have said to her not to cry," or "I could have said to her that I will fix her toy for her," parents should respond with an enthusiastic acknowledgement that this alternative would have been a much better way of responding. By showing children that they could have responded differently, parents are teaching them about personal ownership of their actions using language and concepts they can grasp on their level.

Once parents have helped their children find alternate words and actions, they can proceed with apologies. However, instead of demanding an insincere immediate apology, parents should encourage their children to offer an honest apology by saying, "I want you to think about what you did to your brother and when you feel sorry for what you did tell him you are sorry."

Most importantly, parents need to understand that change in the sibling relationship will occur over time. Proper coaching will not produce immediate change. Therapists need to stress the importance of consistency in parenting when parents are discouraged after a week of attempting these techniques. The objective is to create better sibling dynamics in the long run.

Caution's involvement as children mature

As noted in the literature, as children mature and enter the transition into adolescence, parent interventions need to be approached more cautiously (Felson, 1983). Assuming that parents offered children coaching during childhood, adolescence is a time for siblings to apply the social skills learned during past sibling exchanges. Parents should set some limitations on the volume of the sibling exchanges and institute prohibitions against physical violence, but they should be encouraged to direct their adolescent children to work out their fights themselves. When the sibling fighting does cross over the limitations set forth by parents, they should intervene in a calm fashion. Parents should not respond to the sibling fighting with aggression.

However, in cases where adolescent siblings were not coached during childhood and hence may not have the skills necessary for proper sibling exchanges, a more active parent role may be required. The involvement should be undertaken thoughtfully in a manner that the adolescents are more likely to accept and in a manner that matches intervention type with the unique characteristics of the siblings. Furthermore, engaging in sibling dispute intervention with adolescents may be more effective for girls when presented by mothers and for boys when presented by fathers.

A final note on adolescent sibling aggression is the need to monitor social and cyber aggression between siblings. Especially during the adolescent years, aggression may be expressed indirectly via social manipulation or via the internet (David-Ferdon & Hertz, 2007). Social aggression may occur when siblings try to alienate one another in the sibling group or even among their friends. Cyber aggression may occur with siblings posting insulting or hurtful posts on social network websites about one another or by monitoring the online activities of a sibling to use this information as a way of controlling them. Therapists should make parents aware of these potentials and encourage them to monitor their presence at home.

Case study: "They fight about the stupidest things"

Alina, a 33-year-old single mother, attended a parenting workshop at a local synagogue led by a therapist. Noticing that some of the suggestions offered about siblings could be helpful for the issues she was having with her children, she reached out to the workshop leader and made an appointment for individual therapy.

During the first session, Alina complained about the constant tension that existed between her three boys, eight-year-old Simi, six-year-old Moe, and three-year-old Judah. She described how the brothers were constantly bickering about the smallest things throughout the day. As she put it, "They fight about the stupidest things."

The fights would start before the boys even got out of bed in the morning about who would use the bathroom first. They would continue to fight at breakfast about where they should sit and about who got to look at the back of the cereal box. The boys would push each other off the chair they wanted to sit on and would grab the box of cereal that their brother was in the middle of looking at. After school, things would get even worse as the combativeness escalated into physical fights.

When asked about how she responded to the fights between her children, Alina sighed and said that she was just too tired to deal with it. Working two jobs and still recovering from her difficult divorce, she had little mental energy to do anything about the fighting. Either she would ignore the fights, or, when the children would get really loud or violent, she would yell at them or punish them with limited privileges. Alina reported that yelling seemed to work but hated it when her children started to cry after she had yelled, and she wanted to find more effective ways of working with her children.

Intervention included some basic stress-reduction techniques to help Alina deal with being overwhelmed by her daily routine. The therapist also explained to Alina how her children may not have the tools necessary to navigate the exchanges with each other and how she could play an important role in teaching her children about proper social engagement. She was encouraged to take on a more active role during the fights by allowing her children to express their frustrations and by coaching them during the fights.

Alina was given specific coaching suggestions to be used when her children fought, including allowing each of the children to describe what happened without interruption and pointing out to them how their actions impacted their siblings. The therapist also encouraged Alina to discuss with her children other ways of reacting during the altercations, followed by praising them when they generated appropriate alternatives.

The following week Alina reported that she had tried applying the advice but found it a bit difficult to engage in every time her children fought, especially when she was drained. The therapist expressed to Alina the importance of consistency in applying coaching and that the objective was to create better sibling dynamics over time. Additionally, the therapist reminded Alina to incorporate stress-reduction techniques into her schedule.

The combination of helping Alina minimize her overall stress together with guiding her in applying coaching created a more pleasant family atmosphere and a minimization of sibling tensions.

Chapter summary

Parents play a direct role in fostering positive sibling relationships at home. First, parents can encourage their children to develop healthy sibling de-identification, resulting in fewer sibling comparisons and competitions. Parents can also be cognizant of avoiding parental favoritism, further minimizing sibling rivalry. Finally, knowing how to intervene correctly during sibling disputes is an additional integral way parents can craft the relationship that exists between their children. Therapeutic work with parents should focus on these direct factors when engaging in prevention and intervention for sibling relationship enhancement.

5
Sibling Issues in Diverse Families

Continuing with material about how therapists can help families with sibling issues, the current and next chapter cover unique sibling relational dynamics common in diverse families. The current chapter examines several clinically important sibling facets in ethnic minority groups, families experiencing divorce, single-parent families, and blended families. Chapter 6 examines unique issues confronted by siblings of children with disabilities. As with the previous chapters, the current and next chapter offer suggestions for clinicians working with these types of families on how to integrate an emphasis on these sibling issues in clinical practice.

Siblings, ethnicity, and practice

Although the sibling dynamics in non-Western families have similar interactions and issues found in Western families, a growing body of research has highlighted several ways in which sibling bonds in minority group families contain numerous distinctive features (Avioli, 1989; Rabain-Jamin, Maynard, & Greenfield, 2003; Schneider, Smith, Poisson, & Kwan, 1997; Zukow, 1989).

First, large families, common in non-Western groups, often contain sibling clusters with large age gaps between the siblings. Additionally, considering the various daily functioning needs of the many children in large families, parents may not have the time or the physical and emotional resources to tend to all the demands. Hence, with the combination of the large sibling age gaps and the limited resources of the parents, older siblings in non-Western families are depended on for the care of younger siblings (Maynard, 2002; Weisner, 1989; Zukow, 1995).

Relatedly, in larger families, parents may find it difficult financially to sustain daily existence. This may require parents to work extra hours at multiple jobs, relegating family responsibilities to older siblings. This dependence is further amplified in collectivistic cultures that emphasize family interdependence and stress a sense of family closeness and familism (Romero, Robinson, Farish-Haydel, Mendoza, & Killen, 2004). This type of interdependence creates a family power structure that includes older siblings having some sense of control over younger siblings.

In immigrant families, children with superior local language skills may be given greater power as they serve as a broker between the parents and the larger culture (Falicov, 1998). In these families, the elevated sibling status is openly encouraged and respected by the parents and by the younger siblings.

Hence, in non-Western or immigrant families, sibling dynamics may contain features of both peer interactions and parental interactions. This twofold blend includes elements of both *direct reciprocity* and *complementarity* between siblings, as described in Chapter 2 (Hinde, 1979). These features of interdependence create a milieu of diminished competition and sibling rivalry which stands in contrast to Western and more individualistic families where emphasis is placed on autonomy and personal accomplishment (Weisner, 1993).

For example, several studies have compared the sibling interactions of Hispanic and European-American families (DeRosier & Kupersmidt, 1991; Updegraff, McHale, Whiteman, Thayer, & Delgado, 2005). Siblings in Hispanic families were found to spend more time in shared activities, have higher levels of companionship, and be more satisfied with their siblings in comparison to siblings in European-American families.

Multiple areas of clinical practice necessitate a keen sensitivity to culture (Sue, 1990). This need is particularly important when working on sibling issues with non-Western or immigrant families. Culturally diverse families contain discrete and particular sibling dynamics that clinicians need to be sensitive to.

For example, when working with children from non-Western or immigrant families, communication with the family about the treatment may involve reaching out to older siblings. In fact, consent for treatment of a minor may be provided by older siblings. Beyond the legal ramifications of such arrangements, clinicians may need to tailor the information they provide an older sibling about treatment considering the sibling's unique familial role.

Furthermore, several of the ways that parents impact the sibling relationship covered in the previous chapters may not be relevant in families with a significant power difference between siblings. For example, when an older sibling in the family holds a semi-parental role over younger siblings, issues of parental favoritism may be overwhelmed by the clear elevated role that the older sibling enjoys in the family. Additionally, when an older sibling is elevated within a family, disputes between siblings may include features of parent–child conflict. Therapeutic intervention in such cases may entail classic parent–child communication techniques and relies less on parent involvement.

Divorce, single-parenting, and blended families

The sibling dynamics in divorced, single-parent, and blended families contain several unique characteristics that may produce negativity and family turmoil beyond the norm. In addition to the indirect and direct techniques covered in the previous chapters, parents in these diverse families looking to create closeness between their children need to tend to several other factors playing a role in the sibling dynamics of their children.

Close to half of marriages in Western society end in divorce (Faber, 2004). After divorce, about 65% of women and 75% of men remarry (Dupuis, 2007). Furthermore, the majority of remarriages include entering the new marriage with children from previous marriages (Adler-Baeder & Higginbotham, 2004). Hence, issues of divorce, single-parenting, and blended families are very common, and considering that sibling difficulties are frequently found in these families, having the clinical tools for working with unique sibling issues is infinitely important.

Parent divorce and siblings

As detailed in Chapter 3, parent divorce has been found to be linked with negativity in the sibling relationship. Children, adolescents, and adults of divorced parents have been found to have greater levels of sibling aggression and lower levels of sibling warmth in comparison to offspring of non-divorced parents (Hetherington, 1989; MacKinnon, 1989; Milevsky, 2004; Noller, Feeney, Sheehan, Rogers, & Darlington, 2008; Riggio, 2001).

Several clinically relevant factors may explain the link between divorce and sibling antagonism. First, the natural disruption to family life and daily routine common during the divorce process may account for some of the tension between siblings. Additionally, the hostility between the divorcing parents may serve as a model of relationships that is recreated by siblings in their interactions with each other (Erel, Margoline, & John, 1998; Milevsky, 2004; Panish & Sticker, 2001). Parents may also be preoccupied with the divorce, which can result in the children feeling neglected (Wallerstein, Lewis, & Blakeslee, 2002). These feelings, in turn, are displaced on siblings with acts of aggression.

Single-parenting and family dynamics

Post-divorce, children may experience a period of being raised by single parents. Beyond the past disruption, negative modeling, and parental neglect, family dynamics can entail unhealthy boundary issues as well, leading to *parentification* and *triangulation*. Both of these dynamics have direct impacts on the sibling relationship of children.

Parentification

When children are called upon to perform parental family tasks that are inappropriate for their child role, they are elevated to parent status and experience *parentification* (Boszormenyi-Nagy & Spark, 1973). Children may experience parentification in cases of an inability of parents to perform parental roles or are relegated to this elevated status by parents as a means to offer companionship and support to overburdened or lonely parents. Children experiencing parentification often need to suppress their own developmental needs in order to fulfill their parent role (Carroll & Robinson, 2000; Jurkovic, 1997). This unhealthy family dynamic compels parentified children to lose their place in the family. Research on parentification indicates that girls are at a particular risk of taking on parentified roles (Byng-Hall, 2008; Jurkovic, 1997).

Children are incapable of truly assuming a complete parental role. Hence, parentified children often experience a sense of distress due to this inability (Byng-Hall, 2008). The anxiety, coupled with social isolation and the limitation of child experiences, results in parentified children experiencing negative outcomes. Studies have indicated that parentified children suffer from externalizing problems, attention difficulties, and diminished social understanding (Jones & Wells, 1996; Jurkovic, 1997). In addition to these difficulties, during the adolescent years, parentification may create an expectation by the child of premature independence, creating child–parent tensions. Parentification has even been linked with long-term difficulties in adulthood including elevated depression, unhealthy parenting, and trust issues (Chase, Deming, & Wells, 1998; Hooper, Marotta, & Lanthier, 2008; Nuttall, Valentino, & Borkowski, 2012).

Parentification can occur in many family situations, including in families with children with disabilities, as discussed in the next chapter. In single-parent homes, regardless of divorce status, parentification may occur as children serve as a surrogate spouse to offer comfort and support to the single parent (Byng-Hall, 2008; Jurkovic, Thirkield, & Morrell, 2001). In addition to the destructive, individual outcomes associated with parentification, family functioning and sibling dynamics are also disturbed. Parentified children often lack sibling reciprocity due to their elevated family status which limits the social competencies offered by horizontal sibling interactions. Furthermore, over-involvement with parents and under-involvement with siblings can lead to isolation. This may also result in the parentified children being the target of sibling jealousy from the non-elevated siblings (Byng-Hall, 2008; Lewis, 1988).

Triangulation

When single-parenting involves divorce, an additional, unhealthy family dynamic with consequences for the sibling relationship is the existence of *triangulation* (Bowen, 1974, 1993; Goldenberg & Goldenberg, 2012). This family process occurs when family members with a strained relationship use their relationship with a third family member as a means to gain access to or influence the family member with whom they have the strained relationship. This process results in the third family member being pulled into the conflict, creating an unhealthy triangle which magnifies the family turmoil.

In situations of divorce, one or more of the children in the family may be used by a parent to gain access to or influence an ex-spouse

(Abbey & Dallos, 2004; Wallerstein, Lewis, & Blakeslee, 2002). This boundary violation is a variation of parentification and places the child in an unhealthy position as the mediator between parents. When this type of triangulating occurs, it results in resentment by the triangulated child and furthers the detachment and family aggression. Beyond the destructive individual outcomes, triangulation impacts the sibling dynamic as well. The triangulated child is elevated by the mediator status, resulting in being a target of sibling jealousy from the non-elevated siblings.

Blended families with siblings

Blended families contain several characteristics that have direct impacts on the sibling relationships of both the biological siblings and the step-siblings in the new family. The biological siblings may continue to be impacted, albeit somewhat differently, by parentification and triangulation. When parentification occurred during single-parenthood, a reorganization needs to transpire after remarriage. Now that the parent has a new spouse, the parentified child's "parent services" are no longer needed as the parentified child is replaced by the step-parent.

As a result, the demoted, parentified child may respond with misbehavior and with continued efforts at exerting control over the family and the siblings. In some cases, the parentified child may take on the role of protector of his or her biological parent and siblings, producing tensions with the step-family.

Furthermore, triangulation issues can continue to impact blended families as parents attempt to use the children as tools for gaining access and influence over their former spouse. This process may be magnified as the newly married couple is seen as a threat to an insecure former spouse not enjoying the same level of renewal.

In addition to the issues faced by biological siblings, step-siblinghood in blended families can produce multiple, difficult dynamics, impacting the family and siblings (Visher & Visher, 2003). First, although remarried parents have the time to develop a relationship and a blending plan before the blending takes place, children are often left in the dark about the process and feel thrown into a new family with little input (Gonzales, 2009). As a result, step-siblings may see each other as strangers, which creates step-sibling tension and obstructs the family blending process.

Furthermore, in an attempt to find favor with new step-children, step-parents may interact with step-children in overly warm or even permissive ways, triggering feelings of jealousy from the step-parent's biological children. This dynamic may further the resentment between the step-siblings, impeding the progression of family blending.

Hence, family blending may involve multiple components that have the potential for producing difficulties between the biological siblings and the step-siblings. Clinical work with blended families attending to these sibling issues holds promise in both minimizing the sibling tensions and promoting overall family functioning (Visher & Visher, 2003; Walsh, 1992).

Intervention with divorced, single-parent, and blended families

The coalescing of the above factors in families experiencing divorce, single-parenthood, or blending can result in destructive sibling relationships. Hence, clinical work with divorced, single-parent, or blended families should entail an examination of some or all of the above enumerated issues including parental hostility, boundary blurring, and step-sibling blending. Clinical intervention for these issues can help in enhancing the sibling bond, creating an overall sense of improved family functioning.

Minimizing hostility

In cases of divorce, depending on the availability and will of both parents, intervention can include work with the divorced couple focusing on communication and partnership in parenting. This joint work can help create a workable relationship that will serve as a model for the children's sibling relationship.

The need to establish a manageable relationship with an ex-spouse will further serve several other areas of family functioning beyond the sibling bond. Considering that ex-spouses with children will need to interact in some way or another for many years, establishing ground rules early can help the family in multiple ways (Martin-Uzzi & Duval-Tsioles, 2013). Issues of school, family events, parenting, daily arrangements, and remarriages are just a few issues that would be served well with a workable relationship between ex-spouses (Visher & Visher, 2003). In fact, Dowling and Gorell-Barnes

(2000) have indicated that one of the most important elements for children for successful adjustment to parental divorce is open communication between the divorced parents.

Establishing a working relationship with an ex-spouse can also help in promoting healthy boundaries within the two families (Adler-Baeder & Higginbotham, 2004). However, if creating a relationship with an ex-spouse is difficult and emotionally tolling, therapeutic work should focus on internal boundary formation. The establishment of healthy family boundaries can help in minimizing parentification and triangulation.

Reconfiguration of parentification

Clinicians working with divorced, single-parent, or blended families should assess the presence of parentification and discuss the findings with the parents. Signs of childhood parentification that can be observed in therapy include parents looking to a child for their opinion on sensitive matters or parents seeking the support and encouragement of a child during difficult discussions. Indications from child behaviors that parentification may be present include a child inserting themselves into adult conversations or a child observing parent exchanges penetratingly and attempting to instruct or control the parents (Byng-Hall, 2008).

Parentification can also be evaluated using established assessment tools. Although the majority of parentification assessments are designed as tools for retrospective examination of past parentification, the available tools can be tailored for administration to parents or can be used as a base to develop clinical assessment questions. A common parentification measure that can be used is the Parentification Inventory (Hooper & Doehler, 2012), which is a self-report measure with 22 items scored on a one-to-five Likert-style scale. The questions consist of three dimensions: parent-focused parentification, sibling-focused parentification, and perceived benefit from parentification. An item on the parent-focused parentification includes, "I was expected to comfort my parents when they were sad or having emotional difficulties." The sibling-focused parentification includes the item, "I was responsible for making sure that my siblings went to bed every night." And the perceived benefit from parentification subscale includes the item, "I really enjoyed my role in the family."

In addition to raising awareness of the negative outcomes of parentification, clinicians can help divorced parents by encouraging them to seek out substitute sources of support such as family and friends. As noted, lonely, divorced, or single parents may have parentified a child for support-providing reasons. Helping these parents discover other sources of support can minimize the need for parentification.

Clinical work with blended families necessitates a focus on parentification features as well. In cases of remarriage, parentified children who are no longer needed for serving the parent role may react in negative ways to their demotion. They may react to the threat by misbehaving or by exerting control over siblings which can further ignite the sibling and family tensions. Clinical intervention may include helping the family with transitioning the parentified children back to a child role. Parentified children have been accustomed to and worked hard on their elevated role. Now that the parent has remarried, the parentified child might not give up the role easily nor without acknowledgement. Work with the new couple can include parenting training that encourages them to create with their children a family constitution or a child job description that defines everyone's new role in the blended family.

Furthermore, the parent who created the parentification may need some assistance in setting new limits on their children (Coale, 1999). This can include a positive parenting "in vivo exposure" where the parent creates a situation that triggers inappropriate demands by the child and the parent needs to exert their authority over the child. For example, this can be done with a trip to a toy store and the parent declaring "no" to the children's purchase demands.

Together with helping parents redefine their children's role, clinicians can work directly with the children in challenging parentification and rediscovering their child family role (Byng-Hall, 2008; Coale, 1999). Issues of parentification may surface as part of a discussion about family roles. Ideally, this discussion should occur with the children and parents together. This joint talk, and the uncovering of the children's feelings toward their parent role, can trigger the parents to contemplate the issue and understand their children's distress. Talking about it openly can also initiate a family discussion that may continue back at home.

Clinicians can trigger a parentified child by asking him or her questions that would make the role-blurring explicit such as, "How can you also be a parent and also be a child in this family?" or "How can you also be the man of the house and the child of the house?" This can be followed by trying to prescribe healthy roles for the children by asking them, "How can you make your mother happy as her child?"

In some cases, parentified children may have a hard time talking about their parent role openly with their parents out of fear or a sense of loyalty to the parents. In order to ease the parentified child into an open discussion about the issue, therapists may want to begin with a separate meeting with the child alone to prepare for the joint parent meetings (Byng-Hall, 2008).

Parentified children may need a slow transition into their new child role. This can be done by setting up with the family a system where children take on different roles on alternate days to ease the transition into their new role. Children can be told that on weekends they can still be "mom's partner" but during the week they need to act like children in the house and follow the "child job description" provided by the parents (Coale, 1999).

Parents can independently, or with the direct involvement of the clinician, generate rituals or tasks that highlight the new healthy roles prescribed to the children. For example, a graduation ceremony and award giving can be planned where the previously parentified child is commended for a job well done taking care of the family but is now "graduated" and transitioned into a child role. These efforts ultimately create equilibrium between the children in the family, resulting in healthier sibling interactions.

Redrawing the boundaries

Working with the family on establishing healthy boundaries lies at the core of challenging both parentification and triangulation. Triangulation efforts by ex-spouses can impact the sibling relationship and the broader family environment. It is important to discuss with remarried couples the importance of avoiding triangulation by an ex-spouse and how the establishment of healthy boundaries will protect the marriage and the children. Beyond the broader family benefits, working with couples on healthy boundary formation can foster a sense of matrimonial alliance (Martin-Uzzi & Duval-Tsioles,

2013; Visher & Visher, 2003). Furthermore, clinicians can work with siblings directly to create a sense of a sibling unit. Establishing a boundary around the siblings, by having them come together in therapy, can trigger an overall sense of family boundaries.

Additionally, in cases of divorce or remarriage, siblings often are the holders of past family "secrets" including the family narrative of hostility and what led up to the divorce. This burden is an inappropriate responsibility for children that further blurs the family boundaries. Siblings addressing these "secrets" in session together can release the children from the family triangle creating much-needed relief, boundary establishment, and sibling closeness.

Blending the families and siblings

Clinicians working on the sibling relationships of blended families need to focus on the family blending process and create a sense of sibling cohesion. Family blending can be encouraged by bringing the family together in session and working with parents on creating new family customs and activities (Adler-Baeder & Higginbotham, 2004; Purswell & Dillman-Taylor, 2013). Furthermore, step-sibling blending can be accomplished by bringing the siblings together in therapy, without the parents, feeding a sense of sibling unity and boundary formation. Step-sibling cohesion is an integral part of blended family success (Visher & Visher, 2003; Walsh, 1992).

The natural alliance that may exist in blended families between each parent and their biological children needs to be renegotiated by creating new boundary lines along the parent–sibling divide (Walsh, 1992). Working separately with the parent unit and the sibling unit can help nurture this new boundary mark. Establishing healthy boundaries in blended families will serve the family system overall and will bring the step-sibling circle together.

Long-term family intervention

Clinical work with divorced, single-parent, or blended families should include a focus on relationship modeling, boundaries, and family blending. By minimizing ex-spouse hostility, avoiding parentification and triangulation, and working on blending the step-sibling system, sibling relationships can be solidified and enhanced.

Furthermore, together with highlighting these issues, therapists should maintain contact with willing families to offer continuous support for potential ongoing common sibling pitfalls. Families may need ongoing guidance in managing the sibling relationship and can offer feedback to the therapist on how the interventions are impacting home behaviors.

As the family lifecycles shift, issues of hostility and boundary violations may resurface, necessitating ongoing clinical intervention. Birthdays, graduations, and weddings may require communication between ex-spouses about preparation for the celebrations, which can trigger conflict and boundary infringements.

More broadly, continuous engagement with clinicians can assist parents balance their own needs and the needs of their children. Working on the sibling issues in these families can serve as the "hook" to bring parents into therapy for individual or joint work. Ultimately, changes in the sibling bond may impact the entire family system. Divorce, single-parenting, or remarriage is often accompanied by emotional turmoil for the entire family. As the sibling bond is strengthened, it can give parents room to recover their own emotional resources.

Case study: "I hated being her therapist"

Laura, a 48-year-old recently remarried divorcée, came to therapy for advice on how to handle the sibling relationships of her newly blended family. She came to the first therapy session with her new husband, Carl, a 55-year-old widower. Laura and Carl were married for about three months and reported having significant difficulties across the sibling units in the family. Laura's three biological children, 16-year-old David, 13-year-old Hanna, and ten-year-old Jake, experienced a constant state of tension. David seemed to be exhibiting particularly problematic behaviors that impacted his relationship with his mother and new step-father, Carl, in addition to his relationship with his biological and step-siblings. The parents reported how David resisted any parenting and treated his siblings harshly. David also was disruptive throughout the family and blocked and challenged any parenting efforts across the family. Laura noted that David was especially hard to deal with after spending time or talking with his father, her ex-husband, Jim.

Carl's two children, 14-year-old Daniel and ten-year-old Ben, developed a close and protective relationship with each other. Carl described how during the time of his first wife's illness he had to spend a countless amount of time in hospitals and at treatments, during which his boys took care of each other. After the death of their mother, which occurred ten months prior to the first therapy session, Daniel and Ben continued to bond over their grief. Although they were both ambivalent about their father's quick courtship and remarriage, they took to their new step-mother and had been very warm toward Laura, a fact that delighted Laura. In fact, as Laura described her new relationship with Carl's two children, she became very emotional as she noted, "We have such a beautiful relationship. Ben even hugged me last week and did not let go of me as we stood there hugging each other for 20 minutes."

Carl's two children were open to developing a relationship with Laura's children. However, Laura's children, particularly David and Jake, were openly antagonistic toward Daniel and Ben. David was particularly punitive with Carl's two children, and would often pick on them, and was even physically abusive toward them.

Sessions proceeded with several meetings with Laura and her children and then Carl and his children. These sessions were interspersed with time spent in session with the parent and children together in addition to individual time with the therapist and children alone. The meetings included discussions about the past and about the current new family.

Of particular note was the session with Laura's children. Hanna and Jake seemed to resent David and ignored him during many exchanges. David described how he was in charge of many things in the house during the three-year period between the divorce and remarriage of his mother. At one point when he was talking about how his mother cried often during that time, David said, "I hated being her therapist." David said that he had nothing to do with his new step-father or step-brothers and was considering going to live with his father. In one heated exchange about his new step-family, he yelled out, "I hate the word step." The younger siblings indicated that they detested how close their mother was becoming with Carl's children. Jake noted, "We are her children; not them."

After several meetings with the children, the therapist engaged both Laura and Carl by highlighting several common themes found in blended families that seemed to be present in their new family, including issues of parentification, triangulation, and blending problems.

Both Laura and Carl were initially resistant to the prospect that the difficulties the siblings were experiencing were driven by systematic issues. They wanted the therapist to work directly with the boys on David's anger issues and on the grief that Carl's children were experiencing as a result of the death of their mother. Laura declared that once these things had been dealt with, the sibling issues would be resolved. When the therapist stressed the importance of parenting and family work in order to face the sibling issues systematical and meaningfully, Laura and Carl severed the therapeutic relationship.

After several weeks, Laura reached out to the therapists in response to a particularly hurtful exchange with David. She agreed to come in for a session with Carl so they could begin talking about the broader family issues.

First, the therapist encouraged Laura and Carl to begin thinking about ways to develop a sense of family in the newly blended group. This was accomplished by incorporating into their life specific, new family rituals and customs. Sessions proceeded with examining the role played by David in Laura's life during her single-parenthood. After being introduced to the concept of parentification, Laura acknowledged that she might have depended on David for things that were beyond his childhood role. The therapist explained how after the remarriage, David was replaced by Carl as the man of the house and was responding with exerting his authority over the entire house to protect his elevated status. The past parentification of David resulted in jealousy from Hanna and Jake and was now producing conflict throughout the family system.

In order to redefine David's new role in the family, the therapist encouraged Laura and Carl to acknowledge David's role and open a discussion with him about creating a revised family job description. This process was done with the assistance of the therapist, including working together on creating a new family role comprised of some parent and some child aspects. After this work, Laura and Carl took David out for dinner in "honor" of his new family position.

Along with the work on parentification, the therapist encouraged Laura and Carl to create other appropriate boundaries in the family in an effort to redraw the family lines. Instead of the family operating along the fault lines of Laura's family and Carl's family, boundary work was initiated to begin creating a family that operated along the parent–sibling line. For example, Laura and Carl initiated new house rules about not entering the parent's room without permission.

Potential triangulation by Laura's ex-husband Jim was also explored. In addition to Laura noting that David seemed to be especially belligerent after interactions with his biological father, in a session with the children, David revealed that his father often tried to acquire information about his mother from him. Laura was encouraged to initiate a discussion with her ex-husband about this issue. At Laura's request, the therapist reached out to Jim and facilitated a conversation between Laura and Jim about co-parenting.

An additional vital feature of intervention included focusing on blending the siblings. First, the therapist examined with Laura how her biological children perceived the close bond she had developed with Carl's children. The existence of jealousy between her children and Carl's children over Laura's affection and its impediment to step-sibling blending was also discussed. Laura and the therapist developed a plan which included reassuring her children that her relationship with Carl's children would not in any way minimize her love and affection toward them. This included having open conversations with her children about their apprehensions and making efforts to spend quality time with them.

Step-sibling blending was further accomplished with bringing all the children together in session without the parents. The therapist utilized this time to hear from each of the children about their concerns, which included themes of loss and competition. This process helped the children realize that they shared many of the same anxieties about their new family. Sessions also included playing board games together, which showed the children that they could enjoy each other's company. This helped in promoting a sense of sibling togetherness and intimacy.

During a process and therapeutic relationship that lasted over a year, the step-siblings developed a supportive relationship. The step-sibling alliance helped create an overall sense of family well-being and contributed to the establishment of healthy family boundaries. The marital bond between Laura and Carl was also strengthened as a result of the sibling unification and overall minimization of family hostility.

Chapter summary

Diverse families contain unique and multi-layered sibling dynamics. Awareness of these dynamics can help clinicians offer meaningful sibling-related interventions when working with an array of family types. Sibling relationships in non-Western families contain several unique characteristics, including differences in sibling responsibilities and power structure. Clinical practice necessitates an understanding of these culture-specific sibling dynamics and how they impact family intervention. In families experiencing divorce, single-parenthood, or blending, issues of hostility, boundary blurring, and family unification can impact sibling dynamics in several ways. Clinical intervention attending to these issues can help in enhancing the sibling connection and creating an overall sense of family functioning.

6
Siblings of Children with Disabilities

A combination of societal and legislative changes have made the lives of individuals with disabilities and their families more comfortable in comparison to the way things were throughout history. In vast areas of society, the accommodations and sensitivity offered to individuals with disabilities have created a less restrictive and more accessible environment to people with an array of challenges. Families of individuals with disabilities have also gained attention and now have a collection of services provided for their education and support.

However, as noted in the beginning of the book, there is one member of the overall family system who has been neglected as part of the broader efforts in disability services: the sibling of a child with disabilities. This chapter reviews the empirical and clinical literature on the unique difficulties experienced by siblings of children with disabilities and examines the factors associated with personal variations in the expression of these problems. The chapter concludes with suggestions for clinicians working with these families on enhancing the sibling relationship and adjustment of the well siblings.

Unique experiences of siblings

Siblings of children with disabilities experience a combination of emotional, relational, familial, and societal peculiarities that can produce tension affecting the sibling and their family (Meyer & Vadasy, 2008). Awareness of these difficulties and having the knowledge and tools for proper intervention can help those working in disability services serve their clients in significant ways. Even for those not working directly in disability services, issues of siblings with disabilities often surface as a concern in broader clinical settings. Possessing the necessary tools to address these issues can enhance therapeutic goals in systematic and meaningful ways.

Siblings may develop multiple difficulties

Studies have indicated that siblings of children with disabilities are at greater risk than children without siblings with disabilities of developing both externalizing and internalizing problems (Hasting, 2003; Petalas, Hastings, Nash, Lloyd, & Dowey, 2009; Rossiter & Sharpe, 2001; Verte, Roeyers, & Busse, 2003). Externalizing problems are difficulties impacting the external world of children such as behavior problems, delinquency, and social issues. Internalizing problems are difficulties which impact the internal world of children such as depression and anxiety (Achenbach & Edelbrock, 1983; Dishion & Stormshak, 2007).

Although both types of difficulties have been reported by the literature, internalizing problems are particularly prevalent in siblings of children with disabilities as it may be an attempt by siblings to hide their problems in an effort to be well behaved, or protect their already overburdened parents (Giallo, Gavidia-Payne, Minett, & Kapoor, 2012). Beyond externalizing and internalizing problems, other issues that these siblings may face are a lack of engagement in extracurricular activities and academic issues. These latter issues may be a result of the limited time and money that parents have to expend on activities or tutoring considering the medical expenses they endure on behalf of their child with the disability (Giallo & Gavidia-Payne, 2006).

Siblings develop parenting tendencies and independence

Considering the attention given to the child with the disability, siblings may neglect their own issues (Abrams, 2009; Giallo, Gavidia-Payne, Minett, & Kapoor, 2012). In some cases, siblings experience *parentification* where they are expected to have many responsibilities for themselves and their sibling to assist overburdened parents. These siblings develop duties similar to those of parents, leading to them overlooking their own need to act like children (Meyer & Vadasy, 2008). Although this sense of responsibility exhibited by these siblings may be seen as positive to parents, it may actually be a precursor to emotional distress.

Siblings may feel neglected by parents

The family focus on the child with the disability may take away from the attention needed by the well siblings (Abrams, 2009; Safer, 2002). Time spent on medical and therapy appointments for the child with the disability limits the amount of time parents can spend with the other siblings in the family, which can result in feelings of neglect by the other siblings (Gallo, Breitmayer, Knafl, & Zoeller, 1991). Furthermore, parents may spend a great deal of emotional energy on the child with the disability, leaving little emotional energy to support the other siblings in the family.

Siblings feel in the dark from parents and service providers

Siblings may have similar questions about the sibling with the disability as do parents, but have little information or resources available to them (Meyer & Vadasy, 2008). As a result, although they know that something is wrong with their sibling, they often lack information about the true nature of their sibling's problem. During doctor visits, they are often left in the waiting room wondering what is happening with their sibling.

Parents may want to keep well siblings away from the treatment environment or may want to protect the privacy of the sibling with the disability, leaving the well sibling feeling in the dark about what is going on with their sibling (Abrams, 2009; Safer, 2002). They may have many unanswered questions about their sibling including whether the disability can be transmitted and what will occur in the future. With little or no information, siblings may develop their own ideas about what is happening, often including imaginative elements that are much worse than the reality.

Siblings experience mixed emotions

Siblings may experience a range of emotions about their situation (Meyer & Vadasy, 2008). They may feel guilt wondering if they caused the disability of their sibling or they may feel guilt about why the disability did not happen to them. They may feel fear about the health of their sibling or about what may happen to their sibling in the future. Siblings may also experience resentment, anger, or jealousy toward their sibling due to the attention and resources expensed on their sibling (Safer, 2002).

An additional common feeling is embarrassment as a result of the behaviors and appearance of their sibling (Meyer & Vadasy, 2008).

In some cases, the embarrassment may be so great that they disassociate from the sibling with the disability. They may claim to be an only child or may not invite friends over so that they do not have to answer questions about their sibling.

The situation provides opportunities for siblings

Beyond what is known as the pathogenic perspective, which highlights the difficulties associated with having a sibling with a disability, several studies have focused on how the difficult circumstance may offer some opportunities for siblings (Abrams, 2009; Safer, 2002). Siblings of children with disabilities often develop certain positive characteristics such as self-control, cooperation, empathy, tolerance, altruism, maturity, and responsibility as a result of dealing with their family situation (Burke, 2010; Meyer & Vadasy, 2008). In some cases, these siblings use others' attitudes about special needs as a test for screening friends and mates. Their involvement with their sibling may even lead them to choose future occupations in the helping professions (Marks, Matson, & Barraza, 2005).

The sibling bond entails typical and unique aspects

The relationship between the well sibling and the sibling with the disability entails both typical elements found in normative sibling bonds and dimensions unique to the disability circumstance. Common feelings of sibling jealousy, rivalry, and competition may exist between the siblings, leading to animosity and even physical altercations. However, with these typical elements, siblings of children with disabilities may feel that they serve the role of a leader, teacher, manager, or model of proper social behavior and general skills (Safer, 2002). This, in turn, may lead them to develop loyalty and a protective attitude toward their sibling. An additional unique aspect of the relationship is the hard time they may experience in understanding, communicating, and playing with their sibling.

Variations in sibling problems

As noted, several studies have consistently highlighted the unique circumstances experienced by siblings of children with disabilities. However, particularly in reference to the externalizing and internalizing difficulties experienced by siblings of children with disabilities, the existing literature is plagued with some inconsistent findings (Ross & Cuskelly, 2006; Wood, Sherman, Hamiwka, Blackman, & Wirrell, 2008). These inconsistencies have been suggested to be a function of the different sources of information used in different studies to assess the difficulties or may be driven by variations in the occurrence of these problems based on personal factors.

Variations based on source

Studies using sibling self-reports show lower levels of difficulties in comparison to studies using parental reports (Guite, Lobato, Kao, & Plante, 2004). This discrepancy may be a function of siblings denying their hardships to protect their already overtaxed parents. It may also be driven by the parents magnifying their children's problems due to their own stress (Giallo, Gavidia-Payne, Minett, & Kapoor, 2012).

Furthermore, studies using parental reports to assess difficulties show lower levels of difficulties in comparison to studies using outcome measures assessed by mental health professionals. This divergence may potentially be based on parental lack of awareness of what is happening in the life of their non-disabled child due to their over-involvement with their child with the disability. Hence, when clinicians assess these difficulties in siblings of children with disabilities, it is important to examine multiple sources to gage how siblings are truly coping.

Variations based on personal factors

More important and relevant to practice and intervention, an additional reason for the discrepancies in outcomes between studies may highlight the variations in the occurrence of these problems based on situational, child, and family factors. By examining these variations, clinicians can be informed about the factors moderating the negative outcomes which can shed light on how these variables can be packaged and used as intervention tools.

Situational factors that have been shown to impact outcome include gender, sibling position, twinning, and size of family (Giallo & Gavidia-Payne, 2006). Older sisters are particularly prone to difficulties, in comparison to other gender and family position combinations, due to the common dynamic of older sisters taking on a large share of responsibilities for the sibling with the disability.

Having an older sibling with a disability may also be harder for a younger sibling, in comparison to the opposite, considering that having to care for an older sibling may be counter to the family role norm of older siblings tending to younger ones. Furthermore, having a twin with a disability may be more difficult for the well sibling considering the magnified "survivor's guilt" prevalent in twin situations. Moreover, having other well siblings in the family may offer protection to siblings by providing them a normative sibling dynamic that can be used as a source of support and common experience (Macks & Reeve, 2007).

A final situational factor that has been shown to impact sibling outcome is disability type (Floyd & Gallagher, 1997). When the sibling's disability is visible, it may cause the well sibling to experience an abundant sense of embarrassment. Moreover, disabilities that entail social and communication difficulties may also be linked with hardships considering the strain that this may create in the sibling relational dynamics.

Child factors that have been linked with variations in the experience of difficulties include how the siblings perceive the stress in their life and the methods they employ in coping (Harmer Cox, Marshell, Mandlesco, & Olsen, 2003). Family factors that have been shown to impact outcomes include family support, levels of parental stress, family conflict styles, family cohesion, and family communication (Giallo & Gavidia-Payne, 2006).

Intervention recommendations

Although the reviewed situational factors linked with sibling outcome variations are fixed aspects of the disability situation, the child and family factors examined are by nature aspects of the family circumstance that can be attended to and improved in a therapeutic milieu. The recommendations suggested here include both family and child aspects that can provide educational, emotional, and social support.

Engage entire family

Studies supporting the interconnection between personal factors and the way siblings of children with disabilities cope highlight the importance of integrating the entire family system in intervention for well-sibling adjustment and for sibling relationship enhancement. Numerous overall family environment and parent characteristics can be examined and therapeutically improved as clinicians work with all family members and reconnect family members to each other (Davis & Gavidia-Payne, 2009).

Parent perceptions

Parents can be engaged in a discussion about the way they have reacted to their child's disability and assess the way their reactions have impacted their children. For example, the manner in which the parents perceive and react to their family difficulties serves as a model for the entire family (Giallo & Gavidia-Payne, 2006). Parents can reevaluate their perceptions and redefine the tragedy of their situation as a challenge. Therapists can also work with parents on coping and stress reduction using classic cognitive-behavior or meditative techniques that can then serve as a family model.

Parent communication

Assessing and improving parental communication can also be an effective family-based intervention. Beyond a clinical evaluation of communication styles, the Family Problem Solving Communication Index (McCubbin, McCubbin, Thompson, Han, & Allen, 1997; McCubbin, Thompson, & McCubbin, 1996) is an excellent tool to assess the manner in which parents engage each other during conflict. Items in this ten-item measure include, "We talk things through till we reach a solution," "We work to be calm and talk things through," and "We yell and scream at each other." The items are scored on two dimensions: *inflammatory communication* and *affirming communication*. See Chapter 3 for an elaboration on this valuable assessment.

Studies on communication have emphasized the many family advantages to affirming communication, which is referred to in other contexts as open communication (Gottman & Krokoff, 1989). Emphasizing the importance of open communication can help in improving shared decision-making and problem solving. Family-wide open communication can assist in coping with the stress and adversity that accompany having a child with disabilities. Furthermore, this openness can be used as the parents reach common ground relating to parenting decisions about balancing the needs of their child with the disability and the needs of their well children.

Family routines

Having regular and predictable roles and activities surrounding mealtime, bedtime, leisure, hobbies, family, and play is an essential element of healthy families (Evans & Rodger, 2008; Fiese, Hooker, Kotary, & Schwagler, 1993). These family routines are particularly important for families with a child with special needs (Giallo & Gavidia-Payne, 2006). Considering the natural difficulties and sometimes chaotic environment that may develop in these families, having set family routines helps promote a sense of family stability, security, identity, belonging, cohesion, and positive experiences.

Working with families to develop consistent routines can help create a healthier family structure, impacting all family members including the well siblings (Werner DeGrace, 2004). Clinicians can begin working on one aspect of a family routine and then proceed from there. Bedtime routines may be an effective place to start. Bedtime unfolds naturally in a predictable manner and is usually performed one-on-one. These two facets of bedtime may serve the idiosyncratic behaviors common in children with special needs, creating a perfect mixture that can assist in the implementation of bedtime routines (Larson, 2006; Marquenie, Rodger, Mangohig, & Cronin, 2011).

The achievements with creating bedtime routines can then be used to face the more challenging task of developing dinnertime routines. Studies that have examined hardships in families with children with disabilities have reported that the large majority of parents note dinnertime problems (Marquenie, Rodger, Mangohig, & Cronin, 2011). Considering the peculiarities that children with special needs may have surrounding food consumption, parents are often permissive with them about their food desires, which often triggers resentfulness from the other children in the family. The tension often leads to dinnertime being centered on the child with the disability, creating a non-meaningful and unpleasant experience. Hence, working with parents to develop family routines surrounding dinnertime can be an effective way to continue setting in place a plan for creating broader family routines.

Provide early and ongoing support

Working with siblings of children with special needs necessitates creating an environment of support established early in the life of the sibling and offered consistently. This context of support should cater to the sibling's emotional, social, and academic needs.

Emotional needs

Siblings need to feel that talking about their feelings surrounding their situation is permitted and encouraged. Parents should avoid unwritten rules about not talking about the child with the disability. Parents should actively schedule one-on-one time with the siblings so their emotions and needs are attended to. When siblings ask questions about what is happening, they should be responded to openly.

Siblings may express both negative and positive aspects of life as a sibling of a child with a disability. Clinicians working with families can use the Sibling Daily Hassles and Uplifts Scale (Giallo & Gavidia-Payne, 2006), an effective instrument to help siblings capture their multilayered positive and negative feelings about their situation. The assessment categorizes the sibling experience into hassles (43 items) and uplifts (24 items). A sample item on the hassles subscale includes, "I get upset when my brother or sister with a disability cries or gets upset." The uplifts subscale includes the item, "When my brother or sister with a disability learns something new."

Often children need help dealing with their emotions which parents can facilitate by validating and normalizing. The objective is not to find the correct answer to their emotions or complaints. The goal is for the sibling to feel that their emotions are being heard and that the feelings are normal. See Table 6.1 for examples of common feelings and suggested parent responses.

A common emotion experienced by siblings is a sense of resentment over the disproportionate amount of responsibility they have at home. Parents can work with siblings at setting reasonable expectations by negotiating the chores they normally accomplish and assessing what would be considered an acceptable amount of family chores. This can help the sibling balance his or her own needs and the needs of the sibling with the disability.

Table 6.1   Common feelings and suggested parent responses

Common feelings by children	Suggested parent responses
Over-identification with sibling and fear of contracting the disability	Validation of fear and providing information about the disability and its causes
Embarrassment over the appearance and behaviors of sibling with the disability	Validation of feeling, providing space, offer help with answering comments from friends or bullies
Resentment, anger, and jealousy directed at sibling with the disability	Normalizing the feelings and assistance in expressing them in peaceful ways

Social needs

The attention parents place on the needs of their child with the disability may come at the expense of offering necessary social opportunities for their other children. It is important for parents to give siblings space to engage socially by going out with friends, partaking in extracurricular activities, and pursuing hobbies (Meyer & Vadasy, 2008).

Considering that parents are often busy with tending to the needs of their child with the disability, they may not have the desired amount of time to spend with their other children. In order to offer siblings an appropriate amount of social support, clinicians can work with parents at expanding the support network of their children. This can be accomplished by encouraging families to reach out to extended family or close friends or neighbors for when parents are not available.

Siblings can also be connected with agencies offering services and support groups for siblings of children with disabilities so they can join others with similar circumstances. Support groups should be run on the sibling's terms, focusing on their strengths in a non-judgmental atmosphere (Meyer & Vadasy, 2008). Siblings should not be forced into talking about "the sibling" if they are not willing to. The objective of connecting siblings with each other is to offer an opportunity for siblings to gain support and to support others, which can help foster a sense of empowerment.

Considering the mobility limitations involved in many disabilities, family outings are often confined to places or events that are limited in activity. Hence, when siblings of children with disabilities meet, they should engage in energetic activities to counter their often non-active, family activities (Meyer & Vadasy, 2008).

Parents may feel that by allowing their well children to enjoy an active social life their child with the disability is being left out. Clinicians working with parents should allow for the expression of these feelings and help parents appreciate the benefits, for their well children and for the family as a whole, of permitting and encouraging these social activities.

Academic needs

The emphasis that parents need to place on their child with the disability often comes at the expense of attending to the needs of their other children including their academic needs. As such, siblings of children with disabilities may need but not receive academic assistance. Parents should attend to all their children's academic needs and not overlook difficulties or achievements of their well children.

In some cases, siblings may feel added pressure to excel academically to prove that they do not have difficulties or to compensate for the difficulties experienced by their sibling with the disability (Meyer & Vadasy, 2008). This overachievement may trigger feelings of anxiety and stress from the sibling. Attending to these feelings and allowing for open discussions about them can help alleviate the pressure.

Provide early and ongoing information and education to siblings

Siblings of children with disabilities often feel in the dark about what is happening with their sibling (Abrams, 2009; Safer, 2002). Therefore, in addition to tending to the emotional, social, and academic needs of the sibling, clinicians and parents should provide the well sibling information about the condition of their sibling with the disability. This is particularly important in culturally diverse families considering studies that show that siblings of children with disabilities in non-Western families are especially sheltered from information about the condition of their sibling with the disability (Lobato, Kao, & Plante, 2005).

This education should be tailored to the developmental level of the children (Meyer & Vadasy, 2008). Younger children often have questions about the visible aspect of the disability such as the unusual behaviors of their sibling. They also may have their own magical explanations about their sibling that should be addressed. As children transition into elementary school, they tend to think more concretely about their sibling and have more questions about the actual disability and its causes. Adolescents may have questions about the likelihood of them, or their children, developing the disability. Uncertainty about the future and the potential of transmitting the disability to future generations often leads adolescents and emerging adults to experience difficulties in maintaining committed relationships. As such, parents may want to create opportunities for older children to seek genetic counseling to alleviate their concerns.

Similar to setting the right atmosphere for children to be comfortable expressing their emotional needs, families should work on establishing an environment that encourages questions about the sibling's condition. Creating the right atmosphere for questions is a more effective way to elicit questions than to try to confront children with a demand for questions.

Siblings can be invited to be part of meetings with medical professionals about the sibling with the disability when appropriate. They can be encouraged to provide valuable input during these meetings which can help in creating a sense of openness, cohesion, and purpose. Siblings want to know what they can do to help. Clinicians can work with parents to provide concrete ways for the sibling to contribute to caring for the sibling with the disability (Meyer & Vadasy, 2008). Siblings can be educated about techniques that calm their sibling, redirect their sibling's attention, and how to teach their sibling new skills. Offering these opportunities to the well sibling can help in conveying a sense of openness and demystifying the disability.

Allow for beginning a discussion on future planning

Siblings of children with disabilities, particularly adolescents and emerging adults, are concerned about the future (Giallo, Gavidia-Payne, Minett, & Kapoor, 2012). They may be concerned about who will take care of their sibling once the parents are unable to do so. Well siblings worry about what will be expected of them. Although they love and are committed to their sibling, they may not want to be saddled with the responsibility of taking care of their sibling full time. Parents are ambivalent about discussing these types of issues for fear of burdening their well children and for fear of talking about mortality. As such, therapists can help parents face these concerns, encourage parents to discuss these issues openly, and work with the family on creating a long-term plan for the siblings. Parents should review with their children options for the sibling with the disability regarding available services, proper activities, possible living arrangements, social issues, employment, legal issues, and advocacy.

Case study: "I hate being left in the waiting room"

Carly, a 15-year-old high-school student, was referred to treatment by her school's guidance counselor for symptoms of depression and academic difficulties. During her first session of therapy, Carly described her family life, noting that she came from a "loving and strong family," and that she was the middle of three siblings living at home with her divorced father. After reviewing other aspects of her life, including school and friends, the therapist inquired about her after-school activities, to which Carly responded that she did not have much time for those kinds of things considering all the chores she needed to do at home. When asked about these chores, she revealed that her younger brother, Jay, had Down syndrome, and therefore she needed to do lots of work at home. When pressed, Carly said that she loved her brother but would rather not talk about him. The therapist commented that it was sometimes hard talking about these things, but if she wanted, she could write a reflection about her feelings regarding being a sibling of a person with a disability.

To the therapist's surprise, Carly came to the next session with a lengthy hand-written note, including her reflections about "life as the other sibling." Carly expressed several themes common in siblings of children with disabilities, including having mixed feelings about her brother:

> I hate my brother at times but I love him even more because he suffers and goes through a lot...I take care of him a lot. Me and Jay aren't like siblings, we are like mother and son...Sometimes it is scary, because if someone would try to kidnap him, he wouldn't know what to do. He is not going to be able to scream and shout like me or somebody else would. It's kind of scary. I do have

occasional bad dreams about him dying because I cannot help him … But when I was younger, I was really jealous of all the attention my brother was getting. I would get really angry when I would come home from school and try to tell them [parents] about my day and they would ignore me to take care of my brother …

In a particularly telling part of her note reflecting on how parents often unintentionally contribute to the sibling's feelings of jealousy, neglect, and rejection, Carly wrote, "I really got angry at him once and wanted to hit him. But my mother yelled out, don't you hit my child."

Carly also noted some positive aspects of having Jay in her life:

The best part of having a sibling with a disability is not having all of the attention on me. If I get a bad grade on a test or something, sometimes I'll get away with it without getting grounded or yelled at … I like that we don't have to wait in lines for rides at parks … My family would definitely not be as close without Jay, except my mom. I probably wouldn't be planning on going to school to become a behavioral therapist. I honestly would probably be really stuck up. Things would be worse without him. Sure, sometimes I wonder what it would be like but I don't look too much into it because I wouldn't want anything other than what I have …

The therapist took some time in session to read the note and asked Carly what it was like for her writing it and bringing it into therapy. Carly said that she did not talk about these things with anyone so it felt good to express her feelings. When the therapist asked her about any other thoughts or feelings she had that she had not written about or that she had discovered since writing the note, she commented about not knowing as much as she wanted to about her brother's condition. She recalled that when she was younger, "I remember when my brother was born, my parents were always whispering … We were leaving the hospital and I remember crying and asking my mom over and over again why Jay wasn't coming home with us. I remember my mom crying, too." When asked about her experiences with these feelings currently, she said that when they went to medical appointments with her brother, "I hate being left in the waiting room ... I know him best but I have no idea what is going on with him."

When asked how she handled the difficult parts, Carly noted:

> It's very hard to handle. I never really learned how to handle the situation. My mom never really handled things well so I pretty much learned from her. When things got rough my mom walked away ... What does help is that my best friend has a little brother with a disability too, so we always are able to connect on that subject and share each other's stories on dealing with it ...

The therapist asked Carly about her thoughts about the future. Carly commented that, "I worry that when my father is gone or otherwise unable to help, who will take care of him, and whether or not he'll receive the attention he needs, and if he's happy, or that all his needs will be met financially and otherwise."

The therapist asked Carly if she would be comfortable expressing some of these feelings to her father. Initially she was resistant, but after some discussion, she said that she would be open to having her father come to a session and they could all talk about it together. After some difficulties scheduling the father, he eventually came to a session with Carly. The therapist began by thanking the father for coming and by acknowledging the difficulties he was experiencing being a single father and tending to the needs of a child with disabilities. After some rapport building, the therapist reviewed some of what Carly and he had discussed in past sessions and then allowed Carly to elaborate. Carly was careful to balance the positive and the negative but was able to express some of her mixed feelings about her brother and her feelings of being uninformed about her brother's situation.

The father was receptive to Carly's feelings and recognized that he had been neglecting some of the needs of his other children. In a subsequent session without Carly, the father described the difficulties he had experienced trying to establish a "normal" home environment for all his children. As a first step, the therapist worked with the father at developing family routines, specifically surrounding dinnertime, to help create a time of open communication and free exchange of feelings. The father was also encouraged to examine his well children's schedules to make sure that the children's family obligations were not interfering with their schoolwork and with their ability to get together with friends and do things for themselves after school. When asked about future planning, the father became emotional, commenting, "I have a difficult time thinking about what will be with Jay in the future... I know Carly needs to know. I guess that is another thing for me to start thinking about."

In a follow-up session several months later, Carly noted that things had gotten much better and that she felt that her father understood the situation much better now. She also noted that she had improved in her schoolwork and felt that she was able to do things for herself without it taking away from taking care of her brother.

Chapter summary

Siblings of children with disabilities experience hardships that can create stress for the siblings and their family. Being mindful of these challenges and having the knowledge and tools of proper intervention can help those working in disability services and therapists facing these issues in broader clinical settings offer families and siblings meaningful and efficient interventions. These siblings have a unique combination of emotional, social, academic, and informational needs. Therapists working with families can facilitate creating an atmosphere that responds to these distinct needs, producing better adjustment and enhancing the sibling bond.

Part III

Siblings in Session: Siblings in Therapy with Children, Adolescents, and Adults

7
Siblings in Child and Adolescent Individual Therapy

Part II examined ways in which clinicians work primarily with parents on creating intimacy between siblings. Part III, on the other hand, details situations where clinicians play a more active role in sibling therapy with children, adolescents, and adults. Chapter 7 identifies two primary situations where a therapist might work directly with child or adolescent siblings to help bring peace to rivaling siblings or to activate a source of compensatory support in cases of trauma (Garcia, Shaw, Winslow, & Yaggi, 2000; Gnaulati, 2002; Schibuk, 1989). Chapter 8 examines how sibling work within a family context can help in the assessment and intervention of overall marital and parental hostility.

The final two chapters examine working with adult siblings in session. Adult sibling work may include situations where the focus of treatment is helping clients build a more adaptive sibling bond. Additionally, adult sibling work may be applied using psychodynamic approaches as a means to gain insight into the way past sibling tensions permeate adulthood functioning more broadly.

Sibling relationship conflict

Beyond working with parents on appropriate sibling dispute intervention, reviewed in Chapter 4, in some situations therapists may be called upon to assist in sibling relationship conflict more directly (Lewis, 1988). In such cases, clinicians work directly with children or adolescents on their sibling conflict. This can be done independent of parent work or may be undertaken as a supplement to the parenting interventions examined in Part II. Working with both the children and the parents is especially important if the therapist observes that the parents lack appropriate basic parenting skills.

Working directly with the siblings can offer multiple advantages beyond parenting work. Engaging the siblings directly in session offers an opportunity to explore their relationship outside the parental context which allows for a more honest expression of true feelings. Furthermore, examining their relationship in session can heighten their bond which sometimes is eclipsed in the overall family context. Clinically, observing the sibling conflict in session is also necessary in order to ascertain whether the aggressive exchanges are benign or toxic (Gnaulati, 2002). Bank and Kahn (1982) distinguished between sibling *ritualistic harassments*, which include non-threatening altercations with clear engagement rules, and *humiliating attacks*, which entail uneven aggression, harassment, and manipulation. Therapeutic intervention is necessary when the aggression is humiliating and is the predominant way in which the siblings interact.

Child-focused coaching

As noted in Part II, sibling aggression is an opportunity for conflict-resolution coaching. Hence, the therapeutic goal when working on sibling conflict in session is not the complete cessation of conflict but rather using the sibling conflict as a tool to apply fundamental teachings in emotional and social understanding.

Emotional intelligence

Working with siblings directly in therapy is in essence an enhanced version of the parenting coaching approach examined in Chapter 4. However, in this case, the coaching is directed by the therapist and involves a greater emphasis on the fundamental elements of emotional and social understanding. Child-focused coaching involves enhancing the emotional intelligence and emotional regulation of the siblings.

An exhaustive review of emotional intelligence and coaching is beyond the scope of this book (see Goleman, 2006; Gottman, 1997 for a useful examination of emotional intelligence and coaching). The current discussion highlights the basic tenets of the approach as related to working with siblings.

Children with emotional intelligence possess four critical emotional and social skills along two ability dimensions. The two dimensions are the ability to identify, or be aware of, the emotions of self and others, and the ability to respond appropriately to the emotions of self and others (Goleman, 2006; Salovey & Mayer, 1990). These two dimensions produce four specific skills involved in emotional intelligence.

First, the skill to identify the emotions of self is referred to as self-awareness. Children with self-awareness are able to identify and be honest about their feelings. When situations occur that trigger an emotional reaction, these children have the ability to realize that they are experiencing an emotion and are able to identify the emotion.

The second skill associated with emotional intelligence is managing emotions by exhibiting self-control or self-management. Once the emotions are identified, children with emotional intelligence know how to control their emotions.

Knowing how to detect the emotions of others and how to respond to these emotions are the third and fourth components of emotional intelligence. Children with emotional intelligence are able to read the nonverbal cues of others and identify the emotional experiences of others based on these cues (Salovey & Mayer, 1990). Additionally, emotional intelligence involves knowing how to respond to the emotions of others.

Children with the ability to identify the emotions of others and respond to these emotions are able to engage in perspective taking more easily. Knowing what others are feeling makes it easier to understand things from the perspective of others. Furthermore, children who know how to respond based on the emotions of others are better at problem solving. For example, when a problem surfaces between two siblings, children with emotional intelligence are better at solving the problem because they constantly adjust their response to their sibling based on the sibling's emotions.

Hence, the ability to understand and manage emotions of self and sibling is a powerful tool in developing and maintaining healthy and long-lasting sibling relationships. Clinical intervention with siblings uses the sibling disputes as an opportunity to engage children in emotional-intelligence coaching.

Emotion coaching

When children lack basic emotional intelligence, they may first need to be coached in general emotional competencies, and, only once an initial level of proficiency is established, can the method be applied to sibling interactions.

Although many approaches and techniques have been suggested for emotion coaching, Gottman (1997) offers one of the most research-based and parsimonious processes for emotion coaching of children. According to his approach, emotion coaching involves five steps. First, have an awareness of the child's emotions. Next, appreciate the fact that a child's emotional moments are an opportunity for establishing closeness with the child. Third, listen compassionately to the child's expressed emotions and validate the feelings of the child. Fourth, help the child find the correct words to label the emotions they are experiencing. And finally, the fifth step in emotion coaching is to set limits on inappropriate behaviors while helping the child find a solution to the problem.

Individual therapy with children can be used as an opportunity for the facilitation of emotion coaching. For example, if a child becomes frustrated or angry during a game played with the therapist, the therapist can attend to the emotion and use the emotional expression as an opportunity for establishing closeness with the child and an opportunity to coach them through the process. After listening empathetically to the child's expressed emotion, the therapist should validate the child's feelings and help the child find the correct words to label the emotion they are experiencing. The therapist can then set limits on inappropriate behaviors while helping the child find a solution to the problem that triggered their initial emotional expression.

Setting limits on inappropriate behaviors would involve the therapist working with the child on establishing basic behavioral compliance using modeling and reinforcing of proper social conduct. Common behavior-modification techniques could be applied including ignoring negative behaviors and reinforcing positive ones using direct feedback and labeled praise (Friedberg, McClure, & Hillwig-Garcia, 2009). Hence, when the child sits peacefully and engages the therapist in the game that is being played, the therapist would respond by saying, "You are sitting so nicely. Thank you for playing with me."

Rewards can be used as a reinforcement of appropriate social behaviors. For example, the therapist can offer the child a token during play every time the child requests a toy using suitable methods. When a child requests a toy by demanding, "Give me that toy," the therapist should respond with, "That is not the nicest way of asking for things. What is a different way you can ask for the toy using nicer words?" After the child reacts with, "Can I please have that toy?" the therapist should respond with a reward or a labeled praise.

Concepts of turn-taking and sharing can be highlighted using dyadic practice and role-playing with the therapist. The therapist can set up a situation where the child is instructed to play with a specific toy and then the therapist asks the child in appropriate ways to use the toy. Once this is done, the therapist can ask the child to switch roles and be the one asking the therapist to use the toy in appropriate manners.

Although the play techniques would be less relevant for work with adolescents, a similar process can accompany general interactions between therapist and adolescent by highlighting proper turn-taking and respect during conversation.

The objective of this first phase of intervention is to use the social interactions between the therapist and child as a means to learn about and practice social and emotional understanding.

Emotion coaching applied to siblings

After several sessions of individual coaching, the siblings should be brought together to practice their new competencies. The objective of the joint sibling meetings is to apply the lessons learned during the individual meetings to sibling interactions (Chengappa, Stokes, Costello, Norman, Travers, & McNeil, 2013). When children enter therapy for sibling work, they may be anxious at first and concerned that they have done something wrong. Using classic child therapy techniques such as play and art can minimize tensions (Lewis, 1988). For sibling work, this can be accomplished by asking the children to "draw a picture of you and your sibling at your maddest and gladdest times."

With guidance from the therapist and the application of useful reinforcements and praise, the siblings can apply their skills in several manufactured situations. The therapist can instruct one of the siblings to play with a toy or game and then ask the second sibling to initiate play with the sibling in appropriate ways. Attempts at initiating play which include verbalizations such as "Can I please play with you?" should be praised. The therapist can then practice with the sibling who has received the request socially proper ways of accepting or declining the invitation to play using dyadic practice or role-playing.

Once the siblings are at play, instances of disagreement or conflict can be used to engage in conflict management including identifying and regulating emotions, perspective taking, and problem solving (Lewis, 1988). Similar to the process outlined in Chapter 4 on parenting training for sibling dispute intervention, using sibling disputes as teachable moments involves drawing the siblings' attention to their emotions during the altercation and the resulting actions brought about by their emotions. Furthermore, having both siblings share their emotional reactions during the fight fosters perspective taking. Through this process, the siblings understand that their actions can have emotional impacts on others.

After navigating emotional regulation and perspective taking, the therapist can turn to applying the lessons learned during the individual coaching to problem solving such as examining alternative ways that the siblings could have reacted during the fight and reaching a resolution. After a successful resolution, the therapist should commend the siblings on the work they have accomplished including offering them a reward for their constructive social engagement.

An extension of coaching, particularly for male siblings, may involve helping siblings acknowledge the difference between hostility and proper expressions of closeness between the siblings. Male siblings may be uncomfortable with affectionate contact and may overreact by engaging in overt rough play. Helping siblings reframe their feelings can help them find more adaptive ways of expressing a sense of brotherhood that does not involve physical altercations.

For example, Gnaulati (2002) reported on two siblings, ages 11 and 7, who were in therapy for child-centered emotional training. The siblings would often wrestle to the point where the younger one would suffer pain and hurt from the fighting. The therapist in session had the siblings wrestle using rules put in place by the therapist, including that the wrestling had to be done on top of cushions and that the wrestling had to stop at once when either of the siblings or the therapist yelled "freeze." During the wrestling, which included the boys wrapping their arms around their siblings' neck, the therapist noted the similarity between wrestling and hugging, at which time the boys began to playfully hug each other. Helping siblings reframe their feelings for each other and develop appropriate means of expressing closeness should be an additional element of sibling relationship coaching.

Parent training

As noted, direct therapeutic intervention for sibling conflict can be done in tandem with working with parents on effective sibling parenting. However, when the sibling conflict is so severe that it necessitates therapeutic intervention, parents themselves may need coaching in using emotional training and appropriate responses in their general parenting. The therapist can assess the overall parenting skills of the parents during a joint session with the parents and children (Chengappa, Stokes, Costello, Norman, Travers, & McNeil, 2013). In cases where the therapist observes that the parents are lacking basic parenting skills, intervention should include basic parent training to supplement the parent-focused sibling work reviewed in Part II.

Several useful sources are available for information on working with parents on parenting training (see Chengappa, Stokes, Costello, Norman, Travers, & McNeil, 2013; Eyberg, 1988). For the sake of sibling relationship management, parent training for sibling relationship enhancement can be supplemented by having the parents observe the therapist using the aforementioned techniques with the siblings. The therapist serves as a model for the parents in emotion training of the siblings. The modeling sessions can be followed by meeting with the parents to discuss the observed techniques. Parents can also be taught specific behavior-management skills including labeled praise, consistency, and proper reinforcement of desired behaviors (McNeil & Hembree-Kigin, 2010).

When parents attempt to use these basic parenting techniques with their children at home, they may need to master the skills with one sibling before trying it with both siblings together (Chengappa, Stokes, Costello, Norman, Travers, & McNeil, 2013). Parents should be encouraged to start applying the techniques with the "easier" sibling as training and then apply the method with the more challenging child. In addition to "testing out" the method with the easier child, using the techniques with the easier sibling can serve as a model for the other child. Furthermore, the easier child can serve as a promoter of appropriate behaviors for the other siblings

(Chengappa, Stokes, Costello, Norman, Travers, & McNeil, 2013; McNeil & Hembree-Kigin, 2010).

Parent training may also involve examining how parents react when their children fight based on their own sibling issues in childhood. Parents may be triggered by their children as a result of their own past sibling dynamics (Edward, 2013; Lewis, 1988). Past trauma relating to siblings and aggression may trigger an overreaction or under-reaction by the parents to sibling fighting which may be contributing to the sibling aggression. Openness about past sibling issues and directing parents as they apply emotion-training techniques with their children can help minimize the interference of past childhood sibling histories.

Compensatory sibling support

An additional common situation necessitating sibling integration in therapy with children and adolescents is when siblings are called upon to offer support to each other in compensation for family trauma including cases of neglect, abuse, foster care, or adoption placements (Lewis, 1988). The potential of relying on siblings therapeutically in cases of trauma emanates from a growing body of research on the buffering and compensatory effects of sibling support in cases of situational or family turmoil. As detailed in Chapter 2, studies indicate that sibling support may offer a buffer, or compensate, for children and adolescents who are experiencing ecological risk (Lockwood, Gaylord, Kitzmann, & Cohen, 2002; Vondra, Shaw, Swearingen, Cohen, & Owens, 1999), family turmoil (Hetherington, 1989; Jenkins, 1992; Linares, Li, Shrout, Brody, & Pettit, 2007), and a lack of parental support (Bank & Kahn, 1982; Bossard & Boll, 1956; Bryant & Crockenberg, 1980; Dunn & Kendrick, 1982; Kahn, 1982).

Sibling support and family turmoil

The therapeutic objective when working with siblings together in cases of family turmoil is to trigger a supportive bond that will help the children as they heal from the trauma (Lewis, 1988). Using siblings as a therapeutic milieu can be employed when children have faced parental neglect or abuse and in cases where the siblings have been placed in foster care or adoption. In many of these cases, in addition to the turmoil the children have experienced in their family of origin, child welfare agencies have made decisions for the siblings about removal and placement that may not have been sensitive to their needs (Cuornos, 2003). Children have little voice in these situations even though they are the most affected by it.

In addition to the burden of traumatic memories, children are often scared and confused about their living arrangements. Depending on sibling support during this perplexing time holds considerable therapeutic potential (McGarvey & Haen, 2005). Siblings represent the only sense of continuity the children have in what seems to them a chaotic world (Schibuk, 1989). In cases of foster placement or adoption, siblings serve as the bridge between their biological family and their new, reconstituted family. In a sense, the siblings assist each other to preserve their past and serve as an anchor to their family memories (Fishman, 1993). Ultimately, developing closeness between the siblings will enhance their well-being and assist in the establishment of attachment between the siblings and their foster or adoptive families (Maguire-Pavao, St. John, Ford-Cannole, Fischer, Maluccio, & Peining, 2007).

Therapeutic process

Bringing siblings together as the main treatment modality or as an adjunctive approach to individual treatment for family trauma can offer considerable advantages. Similar to the initiation of joint sibling work for sibling relationship conflict, children may be anxious at first and concerned that they have done something wrong. Particularly in cases of trauma, using play and art can help minimize the initial ambivalence (Bratton & Ray, 1999; Butterworth & Fulmer, 1991; Lewis, 1988; Tyndall-Lind, Landreth, & Giordano, 2001). Beyond the use of play as a means of reducing initial apprehension, play therapy can be utilized as a method of emotional expression (McGarvey & Haen, 2005) and sibling relationship enhancement (Hunter, 1993; Norris-Shortle, Donohure Colletta, Beyer Cohen, & McCombs, 1995). Play can recreate the life situation the siblings are experiencing, producing a critical turning point when the children realize that their verbal limitations in emotional expression could be "played" out in session using play. This can help the siblings move from joint sibling play about the situation to joint discussions about it (Purswell & Dillman-Taylor, 2013).

Considering the many different living conditions that children may experience, interventions need to be tailored to match the situation (Maguire-Pavao, St. John, Ford-Cannole, Fischer, Maluccio, & Peining, 2007). Some siblings may be living in different homes. In the United States foster-care system, for example, the majority of siblings are placed separately (Elstein, 1999). Arranging sibling visits when they have been separated by foster-care placement or adoption may be complicated (Maguire-Pavao, St. John, Ford-Cannole, Fischer, Maluccio, & Peining, 2007). However, when such meetings can be organized, the initial phase of therapy may involve efforts at reacquainting the siblings with each other (McGarvey & Haen, 2005). Therapists should first meet with the siblings individually to prepare them for the sibling meetings (Maguire-Pavao, St. John, Ford-Cannole, Fischer, Maluccio, & Peining, 2007). After the first joint sibling meeting, the siblings should be told when their next meeting is scheduled (Groza, Maschmeier, Jamison, & Piccola, 2003).

In cases where the siblings are living together, the therapist may be seen as an outsider and will need to begin by making efforts at gaining trust and acceptance by the siblings. Many times children within the child welfare system have a mistrust of helping professionals (McGarvey & Haen, 2005). Therapists may be viewed suspiciously and need to establish a sense of trust before intervention can be applied (Scott, McCoy, Munson, Snowden, & McMillen, 2011). Once the therapist is accepted into the sibling unit, intervention can proceed with creating a healthy and supportive bond between the siblings.

Facing difficult emotions

Sibling therapy serves as a protected space for the siblings to explore and express the myriad of emotions they may be experiencing including feelings of parental neglect, abandonment, fear, and guilt (Gnaulati, 2002; McGarvey & Haen, 2005). The process can help siblings appreciate the fact that they share similar situations, emotions, and fates. Therapy can also be used as a place for the siblings to discuss the changes in their lives and share their ideas about the future.

Siblings may also feel a sense of displaced anger at each other as a result of the past. They may act aggressively toward their siblings, particularly in cases where they experienced severe forms of abuse (Hai-Yahia & Dawud-Noursi, 1998; Tyndall-Lind, Landreth, &

Giordano, 2001). McGarvey and Haen (2005) reported on a pair of siblings who experienced past maternal neglect and abuse who blamed each other for the aggression. One of the siblings confronted the other in session by asking if the sibling wanted to hit him when their mother made him. In an additional confrontation, the sibling asked why he laughed when their mother cut him. Approaching these difficult emotions in session helped the siblings face the emotions and move from rage at each other to acceptance of each other and healing together.

Challenging unhealthy sibling dependency

Children who have experienced profound past trauma may develop an intense traumatic bond with their siblings (Creek, 2009). This bond may develop into an unhealthy dependency on siblings which may interfere with the establishment of identify and individuation (Gnaulati, 2002; Leavit, Gardner, Gallagher, & Schamess, 1998). In this case, the therapeutic process would include the formation of a healthy balance between sibling support and individuation. Siblings may need to abandon a caretaking role in exchange for a healthy balance of support and rivalry.

One way in which this overdependence on siblings can be detected is by observing compulsive mimicry behaviors. Children who have developed an unhealthy dependency on their sibling, particularly younger ones, may mimic their sibling's mannerisms, gestures, and behaviors. They may also suppress their own needs and desires in favor of the needs and desires of their siblings.

Challenging compulsive mimicry therapeutically can be accomplished by reinforcing autonomy, challenging the mimicry, and suggesting other ways siblings can love each other without the need for mimicry (Gnaulati, 2002). For example, the therapist can point out instances when the siblings disagree with each other and reinforce the sense of independence involved. When a child makes a decision in session identical to a choice made by their sibling, the therapist can challenge the decision and inquire if that is what the child really desires. The therapist can also ask if the sibling "will still love you if you made a different choice than they made."

Therapeutic goals

Ultimately, the goal of triggering compensatory sibling support is not achieving a full recovery. The therapeutic objective is to form a foundation of support which will serve the siblings now and in the future. In cases of trauma, the therapist may trigger an intense transference on behalf of the siblings (Lewis, 1988; McGarvey & Haen, 2005). Caution should be taken not to become a surrogate parent to the siblings. When transference does occur, in addition to dependency and a need for approval from the therapist, a mourning process may arise during termination leading to a regression of the sibling dynamics. This regression may be exhibited via overdependence, anger, and aggression. The therapeutic goal should be for the siblings to depend less on the therapist and support each other (Lewis, 1988).

Unique sibling issues in foster care and adoption placement

Recent increases in open adoptions have necessitated greater attention to biological sibling issues in placement deliberations (Maguire-Pavao, St. John, Ford-Cannole, Fischer, Maluccio, & Peining, 2007). Beyond the above-mentioned dynamics, sibling work with foster care and adoption placements involves several other unique and clinically relevant circumstances. Engaging in clinical practice with adoption competence is an integral part of effective intervention with foster or adoptive families (Atkinson, Gonet, Freundlich, & Riley, 2013).

When siblings are in foster care together and in the process of securing permanency, therapy can be instrumental in attending to their fears about separate placement. Joint sibling work can also be effective when joint placement is not an option or when a joint adoptive placement is discontinued. For example, therapy can be a vehicle for working on a sibling visitation plan with all parties involved. Additionally, bringing the siblings together in therapy can offer a secure place for the siblings to express their shared feelings of grief, anger, and sadness over the separation (Gnaulati, 2002; Maguire-Pavao, St. John, Ford-Cannole, Fischer, Maluccio, & Peining, 2007).

In addition to sibling support and visitation advocacy, therapists can direct case workers to programs designed to bring separately placed biological siblings together for short periods of time. Several summer and year-round programs exist, such as the Camp to Belong organization, which reunite biological siblings placed in separate foster care or other out-of-home care. Familiarity with the available options can add to a therapist's ability to support siblings during this difficult time.

In some cases, sibling work is necessary to bring the siblings together to achieve joint placement. It is important for siblings to understand how their behaviors may have real-life consequences resulting in separate placements (Lewis, 1995). For example, Gnaulati (2002) reported on two brothers, a 15-year-old and a 12-year-old, in foster placement together who were being considered for permanency by their foster mother. However, due to recent behavior difficulties of the younger brother, the foster mother was considering adopting only the older sibling. The siblings were seen in therapy together in an attempt to utilize the sibling bond as a motivator for the younger sibling's behavioral change.

In session, the older sibling was able to express his anger toward his younger brother for potentially causing them to be separated. He also reminded his brother about their past difficulties and about how fortunate they were that they had been placed in the care of a compassionate foster mother. Therapy was also used to explore the possibility that the younger sibling did not want to be placed permanently together with his older brother. This subject matter allowed the younger sibling to express some of his feelings about the older brother and his sense of inferiority to his older brother's abilities and popularity. He also expressed how sometimes he felt left out when his older brother interacted with some of the other children in the foster home. The older sibling responded that if they were separated due to adoption, he would be the one left out.

The younger sibling appreciated that expressing his anger openly may be more effective than the way he had been using his misbehaviors as an indirect way to express himself. The sense of support received from the older sibling was vital in making the younger sibling appreciate how important his brother was to him. Over time, the behavior issues subsided and the siblings were adopted jointly.

A final sibling-linked dynamic that may be encountered clinically when working with foster care and adoptions is when children are placed under kinship care, or extended family care. In such cases, children are often placed under the care of an aunt, uncle, or grandparent, triggering a realignment of preexisting extended sibling and family relationships (Crumbley & Little, 1997). For example, when a child is adopted by a grandparent, the child assumes in some senses a sibling role with his or her parent. Clinicians can play a crucial role in working with families on creating an operational definition and working model for this new combined parent/sibling role. Open communication about expectations and boundaries can serve as the foundation for finding the correct balance that accommodates the needs of the child and the family.

Additionally, when a child is adopted by a grandparent, the sibling dynamics of the parent generation may be impacted. Aunts and uncles of the adopted child may be supportive of their parent's decision to adopt or may resent their sibling, the biological mother or father, for reaching a point where they needed to give up the child for adoption. Clinicians should be cognizant of these unique subtleties in the sibling and family dynamics that may surface in cases of kinship care and work with families on facing these issues with openness and understanding.

Case study: "Guide her footsteps toward peace"

Biological siblings Dina, aged 14, and Layla, aged 16, were adopted in childhood by Bob and Karen Miller. The sisters were placed in child protective services in infancy and spent close to five years in various foster-care homes before being adopted by the Millers. The adoption was an open one, but Krissy, the sisters' biological mother, did not remain in contact. The first few years after permanency the sisters adjusted relatively well to life with their adopted parents. However, as Layla entered the adolescent years, she started to exhibit behavioral disturbances including internalizing and externalizing issues which caused considerable turmoil for the entire family. Bob and Karen found themselves getting into major arguments with Layla over her behavior, leaving them angry and exasperated.

During this time, Krissy, the sisters' biological mother, resurfaced and considering the difficulties Layla was experiencing at home, offered that Layla move back with her. Although by this point Krissy had rebuilt her life to some degree, she still lived a carefree life which was appealing to Layla. Both Krissy and Layla were pressuring the Millers to discontinue the adoption so that Layla could move in with her biological mother.

The Millers reached out to an adoption-competent therapist for help with making the decision and for guidance with how to help younger sister, Dina, cope with losing her sister. Dina was very disturbed by the fact that her parents were considering giving Layla back to her biological mother. Considering their history together, Dina had developed a very close bond with Layla and was undergoing a profound sense of grief and loss over the inevitable outcome. Dina was also fearful that Krissy was not a good influence for Layla and that something bad may happen to Layla after she moved in with Krissy.

Although reluctant to give up their child, Layla's continued belligerency and delinquency were too much to tolerate and the Millers eventually decided to transfer custody back to the biological mother. Before the transfer was finalized, the therapist suggested that both Dina and Layla come to therapy together to explore their feelings about the impending change.

Sibling therapy served to explore the displaced anger felt by both Dina and Layla. Dina expressed anger at Layla for leaving her, while Layla was angry that Dina was working behind her back at trying to keep her in that "horrible house." As the exploration continued, both Dina and Layla expressed feelings of neglect and abandonment. As the sisters reviewed their past together and explored moments of pain, anger, confusion, and tenderness with each other, they were able to identify with their shared emotions and move from anger to support.

As the time came for Layla to move out, the sisters wanted to end with a departure ceremony. Being very spiritual, they expressed comfort in some of the religious ceremonies of their Jewish tradition and wanted to incorporate some ceremony to assist in their coping. Together with the therapist, they devised a ceremony which included the recital of the traditional traveler's prayer. The prayer is a common Jewish supplication for a safe journey recited at the onset of every intercity journey.

The therapist encouraged the sisters to revise the text of the prayer to represent the journey Layla was about to embark on with her biological mother, producing the following amalgamated prayer:

> May it be Your will, God and the God of our ancestors, that You lead her toward peace, guide her footsteps toward peace, and make her reach her desired destination for life, gladness, and peace. May You rescue her from the hand of every foe, ambush along the way, and from all manner of punishments that assemble to come to earth. May You send blessing in her handiwork, and grant her grace, kindness, and mercy in Your eyes and in the eyes of all who

see her. May You hear the sound of our humble request because You are God who hears prayers and supplications. Blessed are You, Adonai, Who hears prayer.

The ceremony and prayer were conducted in session with the sisters and therapist. Dina recited the altered traveler's prayer as tears streamed down her cheeks. The experience was profoundly moving for the sisters and Dina reported, in a follow-up session, that the ceremony was a turning point in her acceptance of her sister moving away from home.

Chapter summary

There are two primary situations where a therapist might work directly with child or adolescent siblings including to bring peace to rivaling siblings or to stimulate sibling compensatory support in cases of trauma. First, in addition to working with parents on appropriate sibling dispute intervention, therapists might also be called upon to assist in sibling relationship conflict more directly. Intervention would include emotion training applied to sibling interactions. Parent training may also be included to teach parents how to apply proper emotion-based parenting at home. Parent work is especially important if the therapist observes that parents lack appropriate parenting skills. A second common situation necessitating direct sibling integration in therapy with children and adolescents is when bringing the siblings together can help trigger sibling support in compensation for family trauma including cases of neglect, abuse, foster care, or adoption placements. In such cases, intervention focuses on having the siblings appreciate their shared fate and work on depending on each other for support.

8
Siblings in Child and Adolescent Family Therapy

Attending to sibling issues in therapy with children and adolescents can offer therapeutic value beyond sibling relationship enhancement. Working with siblings within a family context can help in the assessment and intervention of overall family dysfunction. Sibling problems in some situations may be a cover for underlying marital or parenting tensions. Including siblings in therapy in these instances can help in the assessment of the marital or parental hostilities and can direct couples to focus on the real issues they are facing.

Triangulation and marital hostility

As reviewed in previous chapters, sibling tensions in families can be a result of both indirect and direct parenting processes including unhealthy modeling, parental favoritism, and counterproductive sibling dispute intervention. However, sibling problems in some families may develop in response to marital discord.

Marital hostility creates tension. In order to reduce the pressure, albeit in an unhealthy way, parents may engage in triangulation by bringing a third party into the mix (Bowen, 1993). In some cases, the triangulated party is one of the children in the family. Often, the focus on the child entails labeling the child as being "difficult," which creates a problem that the couple can bond over. Focusing on the "bad" child reduces the attention on the marital strain and the couple is able to function without confronting their own issues. It is less threatening for a couple to have a child with a problem than to acknowledge the fact that the marriage is in trouble. Having a child with problems does not shake the foundation of the entire home whereas having marital difficulties does (Namysłowska & Siewierska, 2010).

Couples experiencing marital hostility may seek treatment for their problematic child to further deflect from the true, underlying spousal tensions. In these cases, attending to the problems of the child therapeutically without an awareness of the underlying family dysfunction perpetuates the couple's secret.

Sibling integration for assessment and treatment

Based on interactions with parents or information gleaned from a child, a therapist may suspect that the child's reported problems are a cover for more systematic family difficulties. In such cases, bringing a sibling into the therapeutic mix can offer several advantages.

First, even when the therapeutic work with the parents and the child produces some understanding and the intervention results in a minimization of the parent–child tension, with the unresolved, continuous marital problems, other siblings will eventually be impacted. Ignoring other children in the family may result in the non-present siblings subsequently taking over the pathological role left behind by the original problem child.

Furthermore, focusing on the sibling relationships in the family can assist in assessing the true underlying marital problems. Talking directly to the one "problem" child may not offer the necessary insight into the overall family tension. The child may be unwilling to reveal any of the underlying family tensions out of fear or a sense of family loyalty. On the other hand, by interacting with the siblings together, the children may be more likely to open up and may offer a window into the family system (Namysłowska & Siewierska, 2010). The sibling relationships in the family often reflect the tensions that exist between the parents and the overall family relational dynamics (Bowen, 1993).

For example, Namysłowska and Siewierska (2010) reported on a case involving a family in treatment for strained relational dynamics. The family consisted of married parents with two biological children, a girl and a boy. The parents described their daughter as being rebellious whereas their son was deemed the productive and successful one. One of the main concerns of the parents was that their children engaged in constant hostility including physical fights. When the therapist inquired about the marital dynamics between the parents, both the mother and father reported that they never argued. However, after some exploration, it became evident that the parents experienced profound underlying marital tension. The couple noted that they were very hard working, spent little time together, had different interests, and slept in separate rooms.

The parents coped with their own marriage failures by keeping their distance and bonding through their children. The parents were able to express approval through their "good" son and criticism through their "bad" daughter. By doing so, the parents were able to keep a semblance of a functioning family by expressing some of their latent feelings without causing a fissure in the foundation of the marriage. The fights between the brother and sister were a reflection of the conflict between the parents who could not face confrontation as it would put the very existence of their family in danger. This case is a vivid illustration of how parents under marital strain may focus on their children to avoid their own issues. Including siblings in the therapeutic process under these circumstances can help uncover the suppressed problems.

Beyond providing a window into the family dynamics, focusing on the marital and sibling conflict concurrently can help in confronting the tensions in a systematic and holistic way. Allowing for siblings to enter the therapeutic process can help accelerate the process of change.

Setting the stage with parents

The use of siblings as part of the assessment and intervention of underlying marital hostilities may unfold in the following manner. A child or adolescent with behavioral or emotional difficulties is referred to therapy by school personnel or a parent. Ideally, as part of the evaluation process, the therapist would meet with the child and parents individually and together to hear the parents' concerns, to assess the child's behavior, and to observe the interactional dynamics between the parents and child. Based on the interaction with the parents or information gleaned from the child, the therapist may suspect that the child's difficulties reported or observed may be a function of underlying tensions between the parents.

In such cases, the therapist may request that one of the siblings of the target child should also be included in therapy. When parents respond with suspicion or outright rejection of the therapist's request, it may indicate that, in fact, wider system problems may be present. Parents may respond to the request by rejecting the idea in fear of revealing issues they don't want uncovered. The parents may be resolute that the problem is with the target child and demand the therapist work exclusively with the one child. In families with greater taboos and secrets, parents may adamantly reject the idea of bringing siblings to sessions (Namysłowska & Siewierska, 2010).

Parental rejection of bringing other children into the mix may be particularly salient when the therapist wants to meet with the children not in the presence of the parents. Private meetings with the children risks them revealing family secrets without parental supervision.

In some cases, only one of the parents may reject the idea of bringing other children to therapy. In families experiencing marital tensions, children may be drawn into the discord by aligning themselves with a particular parent (Abbey & Dallos, 2004; Wallerstein, Lewis, & Blakeslee, 2002). A parent may want the child on their side in session but not the child that has allied with the other parent. This occurrence can offer the therapist a window into the structure and loyalties of the family (Lewis, 1988).

In order to convince parents to allow their other children to come to therapy, the therapist may need to engage in some preliminary work with the parents to alleviate their anxiety about meeting with the children. The parent uneasiness may not be expressed openly. Parents may agree to bring their other children to session but may express their apprehension through missed or frequently canceled appointments (Lewis, 1988).

The therapist should talk openly with the parents about their concerns relating to bringing their other children to therapy. Parent apprehensions may include feelings of being excluded, fears about what the other children may say in session, and concerns about the children misbehaving (Lewis, 1988).

Parents may be more likely to agree to bring the other siblings into session if they feel that the process is being undertaken with their input and participation. The therapist can partner with the parents by developing specific treatment plans and goals with the parents. The therapist should also exhibit respect for the parental authority and extend an invitation to the parents to participate in some of the sibling sessions.

Setting the stage with children

Once parents agree to have their other children enter therapy, an initial meeting with the children can be arranged. Based on the arrangement agreed upon with the parents, the sibling meeting can take place with the parents or with the siblings alone. In cases where the parents agreed to bring other children into the picture with the condition that they are present during the meeting, the initial meeting will offer a preliminary picture of the family dynamics. However, in the presence of the parents, the children may act according to the family prescriptions and may not offer the therapist a window into the true overall family dysfunction (Gnaulati, 2002). Ideally, once the parents develop a sense of trust in the process, the therapist should try to meet with the siblings without the parents.

During the first meeting with the children, they may be anxious and may be concerned that they have done something wrong. As with other child meetings, using classic child therapy techniques such as play and art can minimize the tensions (Lewis, 1988). The children's feelings about the session may be indicative of parent reactions to the meetings. These reactions can help further highlight some of the underlying structure and loyalties that exist in the family. As noted, in families experiencing marital tensions, children may be drawn into the discord by aligning themselves with a particular parent (Abbey & Dallos, 2004; Wallerstein, Lewis, & Blakeslee, 2002). Attending to a specific child's reactions taking into account the initial objections of parents can help clarify the family alliances that exist.

Therapeutic process

Once in session, the children may be ambivalent about revealing the family secrets out of fear or loyalty to the family. However, having the siblings talk about "their" sibling issues can help uncover the overall family hostilities without the children feeling that they are breaking their parent's loyalty (Namysłowska & Siewierska, 2010). A sibling can also present a different perspective on the client's relationship with the parents which may offer a competing narrative about the family than the one offered by the parents.

In addition to offering a picture of what is truly transpiring in the family, sibling meetings without the parents can trigger sibling bonding and support. Considering the latent family tensions, the siblings may have had little opportunity to express closeness. Bringing siblings together in therapy may offer them an outlet for expressing closeness. When a second sibling is brought into sessions and tender moments are observed between the siblings, it may provide further indication that the narrative presented by the parents may be inaccurate and a front for deeper marital problems. A moving moment may occur when the siblings realize that the conflict that exists between them is not really theirs (Namysłowska & Siewierska, 2010).

The sibling closeness created by the joint meetings can trigger a consolidation of the sibling unit. This newly formed subsystem creates a boundary around the siblings, weakening the ability of the parents to penetrate the child unit and deflect from their own problems (Namysłowska & Siewierska, 2010). This shift in the family structure can create the setting for the therapist to discuss with the parents some of the issues presented by the siblings.

Intervention should focus on working with the parents on considering how the behaviors they engage in are contributing to the family and sibling discord. As the underlying issue in the family is the use of the children as a means to deflect from marital tensions, work with the parents should focus on open communication and family boundary formation. Strengthening intergenerational boundaries, by working individually with the parents on their relationship and with the siblings on their bond, will help in creating two, defined family subsystems. In turn, these new-formed boundaries will minimize cross-generational coalitions and the parents and siblings can fight or support each other independently in healthier ways.

Parenting message congruity

An important facet of healthy families is having parents who convey partnership and consistency in their childrearing and offer similar massages, or *message congruity*, in their parenting practices. Parents who support each other and work together on parenting decisions, known as *co-parenting*, are more likely to have adaptive and cooperative children than parents working against each other in parenting

(Groenendyk & Volling, 2007; Schoppe-Sullivan, Weldon, Cook, Davis, & Buckley, 2009). Issues of co-parenting have direct impacts on the overall family system. Working with siblings in family therapy can help highlight issues of parenting message incongruity and can offer a setting for improvements in this area.

Co-parenting and sibling relationships

Developing inter-parental cohesive and consistent parenting behaviors is a difficult task. Differences in temperament, personality, and childhood experiences between couples often produce dissimilar approaches to parenting. Developing parenting message congruity and fashioning a clear, co-parenting plan necessitates open communication between parents and a willingness to be influenced by the childrearing ideas of partners. In fact, Milevsky, Schlechter, Klem, and Kehl (2008) found that close to 45% of couples do not share similar parenting styles.

When parents disagree about parenting practices, it creates uncertainty for children in many areas of their life including family rules, procedures, and standards (Karreman, van Tuijl, van Aken, & Dekovic, 2008; Volling, 2012). Due to children's limited comprehension of the world, they view their surroundings as chaotic and disorderly. When parents impose consistent family rules and regulations, children are provided with a much-needed sense of structure (Sullivan, 1953). However, when disagreements exist between parents about family rules, system anarchy ensues. Children are uncertain about what is permitted and what is not. Subsequently, chaos is amplified when children learn to exploit these parental disagreements.

Disagreements about parenting and childrearing have been linked with several negative outcomes. First, studies indicate that couples with parenting discrepancies have higher rates of marital disharmony than couples who partner in parenting (Cummings & Davies, 2010). Parenting message incongruity has also been found to be associated with negative outcomes for children (Doherty & Beaton, 2004; Karreman, van Tuijl, van Aken, & Dekovic, 2008; Margolin, Gordis, & John, 2001; Schoppe-Sullivan, Weldon, Cook, Davis, & Buckley, 2009; Volling, 2012). Similar patterns have been found with studies on adolescents. Teens being raised in homes where there are considerable disagreements between fathers and mothers on parenting tactics have been found to experience greater levels of emotional and academic disturbances than adolescents raised in homes where parents agree on parenting approaches (McKinney, Milone, & Renk, 2011; Simons & Conger, 2007; Weiss & Schwarz, 1996).

Uncertainty about family rules goes beyond ambiguity surrounding general acceptable standards of behavior at home. Dissimilar messages children receive from their parents also produce uncertainty about the rules of engagement with siblings (Felson, 1983). Which behaviors are acceptable with siblings and which are not? What should the children do if there is a disagreement between them about personal possessions? Is fighting allowed? Is physical aggression acceptable? When parents lack cooperative co-parenting, it directly impacts the relationship between siblings.

For example, Song and Volling (2015) examined how two types of co-parenting patterns impact the way firstborn children cooperate with their second-born sibling. The authors examined *cooperative co-parenting,* which involves parents working together on parenting and supporting each other in the process, and *undermining co-parenting,* which involves parents arguing and trying to convince children to take sides in these arguments. Results showed that when couples engaged in cooperative co-parenting, their firstborn children were more likely to cooperate with the care of younger siblings.

This study suggests that when parents engage in undermining co-parenting, they create a chaotic environment conducive to sibling neglect; whereas when parents cooperate, they offer a positive model for sibling cooperation.

Co-parenting in practice

Co-parenting offers an overall sense of family cohesion and cooperation. When parents do not cooperate with each other, they showcase a damaging model for their children (Song & Volling, 2015). The children will then apply this non-cooperation in their relationships including their sibling relationships. Hence, assessing the sibling relationship in session can offer a window into the overall family functioning and parental cooperation. Meeting with siblings alone can also help uncover parent behaviors as the siblings talk about their relationship without the children feeling that they are betraying their parent's loyalty.

Therapists can help parents come to agreements about parenting practices by encouraging them to talk openly about past experiences with their parents and current goals they share for parenting their own children. This openness and agreement will then offer a direct model of cooperation for children to apply when they engage their siblings.

Assessing similarities and differences in parenting practices between the parents can be accomplished in therapy using the Authoritative Parenting Measure (Steinberg, Lamborn, Darling, Mounts, & Dornbusch, 1994) reviewed in Chapter 3. Once each parent has taken the assessment and their unique parenting style is discovered, differences can be discussed in an attempt to develop a cohesive approach to parenting shared by both parents. Furthermore, working with parents in session on co-parenting should include agreed upon rules of sibling engagement.

When therapists work with parents on agreements pertaining to parenting practices, by encouraging open communication about past experiences and current goals, they provide a direct path that will impact the family dynamics in the home. Beyond the benefits for the overall family functioning, developing a co-parenting plan with parents will assist in creating clear guidelines for children regarding sibling engagement, interactions, and fighting. This will offer children the ingredients necessary to develop a long-lasting bond with their siblings.

Case study: "What's wrong with a little fighting?"

Judy, a married 42-year-old mother of three, was seeking counseling for assistance with what she referred to as a "chaotic home." During the initial therapy session, Judy elaborated on the sense of disarray in her home and particularly emphasized the tension that existed between her three children. She described how her children, two older boys aged 15 and 12, and a younger girl of 9, would sometimes play nicely together but overall had a vitriolic relationship that often included physical fights. Judy was particularly concerned with the brutality that existed between her two older boys that would often begin as play wrestling but would rapidly descend into an aggressive fight. As Judy noted, "I think it would be better if they played other games together that do not involve any physical fighting even in play."

When the two older siblings were seen in session together, they talked about their relationship and some of the games they liked to play. They both seemed to enjoy wresting with each other. However, older brother, Derek, noted that sometimes he felt that his younger brother, Jason, took the fighting too seriously, to which Jason responded, "Well, you're just a wus." Derek seemed embarrassed by Jason's comment and apologetically told the therapist that Jason, "sometimes becomes like this." He also said that their mother hated it when Jason "goes overboard." Jason disagreed and said that "Dad has no problem with it so whatever."

The therapist asked about other things that their mother and father disagreed about, to which the boys responded with a list of other parent disagreements including video games they were allowed to play, TV shows that were acceptable, and overall family manners. Based on the conversations with the children, it became evident that Judy and her 46-year-old husband, Nick, had very different ideas about parenting including how to deal with the sibling component.

After some initial ambivalence and convincing, Nick agreed to join his wife in session. A therapist-initiated discussion about the family's leisure activities revealed that the boys and their father often watched wrestling on TV together much to the dissatisfaction of Judy. She also revealed that her husband did not find the boy's relationship problematic and would often say that "the boys have a much better relationship than I ever had with my brothers." Judy commented that she also felt that her children had a better relationship with each other than she ever had with her older siblings, but she still felt that "just because I had it bad it does not mean my kids need to suffer." When the therapist asked Judy to elaborate on how she "had it bad" growing up, she described one older brother in particular that was extremely abusive toward her in the past, including subjecting her to physical pain.

When Judy confronted Nick about the wrestling, he responded, "What's wrong with a little fighting?" This disparity in parenting approaches created a sense of confusion for the children, exemplified by them not knowing what was permitted and what was not when it came to sibling engagement and aggression.

In a series of joint sessions, Judy and Nick described their own childhood experiences with their siblings. This offered Nick an opportunity to understand how Judy's sensitivity to sibling fights was born from her past experiences with her brother. They were also able to explore their goals of parenting and were able to develop a consistent set of parenting guidelines including rules governing TV watching and sibling interactions. Sporadic ensuing sessions were used to help both Judy and Nick follow the established guidelines consistently. Both Judy and Nick reported that the congruity in parenting messages created a more peaceful home environment and better sibling interactions.

Chapter summary

In addition to working with siblings in therapy on sibling relationship enhancement or on creating a compensatory bond in cases of trauma, working with siblings within a family context can help in the assessment and intervention of overall family dysfunction. Sibling issues in some cases may be indicative of systematic, underlying marital or parenting tensions. Including siblings in therapy in these situations can assist in the assessment and intervention for the marital or parental hostilities. In cases where the sibling tensions may be a cover for martial issues, work with the parents should focus on open communication and family boundary formation. Sibling strain as a result of parental message incongruity necessitates working with parents on coming to agreements about parenting practices by encouraging them to talk openly about past experiences and current goals.

9
Cognitive-Behavior Interventions for Adult Sibling Issues

Cognitive-behavior intervention with adult sibling issues is used when the focus of treatment is repairing the contentious sibling relationships of clients. As examined in the next chapter, the integration of sibling issues in treatment can also be used when the presenting problem of a client is not sibling-linked as a means to gain insight into the way past sibling tensions may be permeating psychological well-being more broadly. In these situations, the sibling tensions and their consequences are obscured and need to be assessed and examined using psychodynamic approaches.

The current chapter, on the other hand, examines situations where the focus of treatment is helping clients build a more adaptive sibling bond. This focus is often the expressed goal of the client at intake. Sibling difficulties necessitating treatment may develop as a result of an external life event, such as a death of a parent, or as a result of fermenting tensions that have been overlooked over time. Sibling issues encountered in therapy may also include situations of step-siblings and blended families that have been created as a result of the remarriage of older adults (Schulman, 1999).

When the goal of therapy is helping clients build a more adaptive sibling bond, the therapeutic integration of sibling issues is undertaken at the start of treatment. In other cases, the need to focus on siblings in therapy may be initiated by the therapist when, in the course of treatment, it becomes evident that sibling tensions are actively creating turmoil in a client's life. In this latter case, a therapist may need to convey to a client how the sibling tensions are impacting his or her life and how working on mending the sibling bond holds considerable therapeutic value.

Therapeutic value

In addition to the importance of merely minimizing sibling tensions, therapists can express to clients that enhancing the sibling bond can provide an important source of support as they transition into their older adult years. Numerous societal shifts are creating a situation where a growing number of older adults are living lonely lives. Considering the increasing life expectancy, high divorce rate, and low birthrate, many adults are reaching older adulthood alone. In Western populations by age 55, over 10% of people live alone, and by age 75, close to 40% live alone. Hence, enhancing the sibling bond in therapy can serve as a relational anchor and reciprocal source of support in preparation for older adulthood (Weisner, 1982).

Clients may further be persuaded that attending to sibling issues in therapy is beneficial by examining how unresolved sibling problems often surface in very destructive ways after parental death. Parental death is a naturally painful experience. Unfortunately, when underlying sibling tensions exist, the emotional experience of the death coupled with the increased amount of time families spend together before and after the loss often creates a contentious environment that makes dealing with the entire death process exponentially more difficult.

For example, in response to reading a column about sibling dynamics after parental death, a woman sent the following note to the author.

> Dear Dr. Milevsky, I have just read your article "Til Death (of our parents) Do Us Part" but how do you begin to repair sibling relationships now? We buried our father today and throughout the week long mourning process, our nieces and nephews behaved remarkably, working together and consoling one another while we, the adults aged 48 through 57, did not fare as well. Is there any reading material you can recommend? Thank you, Margie.

Working with clients at repairing the antagonistic interactions with their siblings can help avoid the painful dynamics that may surface after the death of their parents. More importantly, the close sibling bond that may develop as a result of tending to sibling issues in therapy can serve as a vital source of much-needed support in the event of parental death.

A final point that can be raised with clients is that focusing on repairing their sibling bond is important considering the intergenerational transmission of sibling conflict (Donley & Likins, 2010). Children replicate the sibling dynamics that exist between their parents and the parents' siblings (Schulman, 1999). Hence, working on enhancing the sibling dynamics of the family can produce benefits for the current and future generations.

Setting the stage

Once the goal of repairing the sibling relationship has been established in therapy, the initial focus of cognitive-behavior intervention entails an assessment of the client's current sibling relationships. The investigation of the client's sibling dynamics can be done using both a clinical interview and quantitative tools. The clinical interview should begin with the client providing a general picture of the ages and genders of all their siblings and then continue with asking the client to describe the relationship with each of their siblings. Questions should include cognitive, emotional, and behavioral aspects of the relationship (Goldenthal, 2002). Queries to assist in directing the review can include:

> Tell me about the relationship you currently have with each of your siblings starting with the oldest. Do you know what is happening in their lives? Do you know what stress they are currently experiencing in their life? Do you know what personal improvements they are engaged in currently? Do you know what gift they would appreciate receiving? When was the last time you got together with them? How often do you have contact with them? How do you reach out to them; is it by phone, email etc.? Who usually initiates contact? When you know that you are about to talk to them or see them do you experience any anticipatory stress? During your interactions with them do you enjoy yourself? What do you usually talk about when you are connecting? How open are your conversations? Do you talk to each other about private things happening in your lives? Are there any conversation taboo items? After your interactions with them, do you

require any contact recovery time? How do your sibling relationships currently compare to the relationship you had with them growing up?

The clinical interview questions can be supplemented with the use of the Adult Sibling Relationship Questionnaire (ASRQ) (Lanthier, Stocker, & Furman, 2001). This instrument, originally established as a research tool, can be easily adapted for clinical use. The measure can be used to assess multiple aspects of a client's current sibling relationships. Clients are asked to respond to the items on the scale based on their relationship with their closest or most important sibling. The measure can be repeated to gain information about the relationship the client has with each of his or her siblings. The ASRQ includes 81 questions representing 14 relationship dimensions including similarity, intimacy, quarreling, affection, antagonism, admiration, maternal rivalry, emotional support, competition, instrumental support, dominance, acceptance, paternal rivalry, and knowledge. These relationship dimensions are combined to create a profile of the sibling relationship along three broad categories including sibling warmth, conflict, and rivalry. A sample item on the warmth category includes, "How much do you know about this sibling?" A sample item on the conflict category includes, "How much do you put this sibling down?" And a sample item on the rivalry category includes, "Does this sibling think your father supports him/her or you more?" Although the scoring of this instrument is meant to be applied in group administrations for norm-referenced comparisons, individual scores can be used to gain a general picture of the sibling dynamics along the relationship dimensions.

Cognitive-behavior interventions

Once a clear picture of the client's sibling relationship is established, cognitive-behavior techniques can be applied to challenge the contentious aspects of the relationship. When applying cognitive-behavior interventions in sibling therapy, the process involves the application of classic cognitive-behavior techniques as it relates to the cognitions and behaviors involved in the antagonistic sibling relational dynamics (Dattilio, 2013). An exhaustive review of cognitive-behavior therapy is beyond the scope of this book. For a comprehensive review of cognitive-behavior therapy and its use in practice, see Beck (2011) and Leahy (2003). However, the basic premise of this therapeutic orientation entails challenging the cognitive distortions that produce maladaptive emotions and behaviors coupled with encouraging positive behavioral change.

Cognitive tools

In line with classic cognitive-behavior therapy, the cognitive aspects of intervention involve working with clients to challenge some of the unhealthy ways they think about themselves and their siblings (Beck, 1995). Faulty thinking about siblings and the sibling relationship often leads to incessant mental turmoil which perpetuates negative engagements with siblings. For example, if a client believes that their sibling is out to get them or that their sibling thinks they are better than them, the client will assume that every benign gesture by this sibling is nefarious. In turn, during sibling interactions, the client will be on guard and respond to his or her sibling in antagonistic ways. The cognitive restructuring that is undertaken in therapy focuses on redefining the relationship, challenging core sibling beliefs and distortions, and confronting obsessive jealousy.

Redefining the relationship

The first step in redefining the relationship includes challenging unhealthy, underlying beliefs that the client has about a specific sibling. This is accomplished by examining the thoughts behind the emotions triggered during interactions with the sibling. Clients should recall a recent interaction with the target sibling and the resulting feelings. Once the feelings are identified, the objective is to isolate the thoughts about the situation that trigger the negative emotions. The client can be asked, "You felt _____ because you thought what?" Once a set of thoughts are generated, the thoughts or core beliefs need to be identified and challenged. This identification and challenge of core beliefs about the sibling may necessitate an exploration of early sibling memories.

Examining the relationship the client had with his or her sibling growing up can help in identifying the core beliefs about the client in relation to the sibling that have been imprinted over time. The exploration attempts to assess how past themes of rivalry, competition, and jealousy have defined and labeled the siblings and their current relationship (Schulman, 1999). Challenging these themes requires an honest contrast between how these dynamics are understood in childhood as opposed to how they should be perceived in a more mature, adult way.

Therapists can explore how rivalry is a common part of childhood interactions driven by competition over parental love and attention. However, maturity requires moving beyond these childhood characterizations and redefining the rivalry in more adaptive ways. For example, in childhood, the rivalry may have entailed contentious competition triggering avoidance, resentment, hostility, and constant comparisons. On the other hand, in adulthood, this rivalry can be redefined as a fun, playful, and open competition. In childhood, the rivalry was a source of latent resentment and was unspoken about in honest ways. On the other hand, in adulthood, the rivalry can be viewed as an appreciation and acceptance of differences in abilities, intellect, and values.

These childhood expectations may have created a script that clients follow during their interactions with their family (Beck, 2011). Some children may have taken on the passive role within the sibling group while others may have acquired the label of being the argumentative one. Each of these childhood definitions play out in adulthood in the way siblings relate to one another. Often, these scripts create resentment within the sibling group. For example, the passive siblings may be resentful that others disregard their opinions. The argumentative offspring may feel that the other siblings in the family respond aggressively to him or her even when no hostility was intended. In order to undo these childhood definitions, clients need to challenge the past definitions and act in ways that are contrary to the expectations when they interact with their siblings.

Challenging core sibling beliefs

Beyond challenging past sibling definitions, clients need to be directed in appreciating how their underlying core beliefs about their siblings impact their interactions with them. When clients hold specific underlying beliefs about themselves and about the way they are viewed by their siblings, interactions between the clients and their siblings are filtered through these underlying beliefs. For example, clients who believe, due to early childhood sibling experiences, that their sibling is more successful than they are will misinterpret nonthreatening comments from their siblings as being malicious. Challenging these core beliefs can help clients respond to their siblings in more mature ways.

Beck (2011) offers a useful visual illustration of how core beliefs impact the perceptions of both verbal and nonverbal cues from others. This model can be easily applied to sibling work and can be presented to clients in helping them comprehend the way core beliefs impact their engagement with their siblings. Once a sibling-related core belief is established, such as "My sibling thinks he is better than me" or "I am no good," the statement is written on a sheet of paper and a big circle, with a small opening, is placed around the statement. The therapist and client then generate two categories of declarations that the client may hear from their sibling. The first category includes clear negative statements such as "You really are hopeless" or "When will you ever do something with your life?" These objectively offensive comments are written down on the same sheet of paper and placed within small squares, small enough that the squares can fit into the opening in the big circle.

The second set of sibling comments are statements that are innocuous but can be perceived as offensive by someone with a negative core belief, such as "How is that new job going?" or "Let me pay for that coffee." Although these statements seem quite innocent, they can be viewed as offensive by a client with a negative core belief about being less than a sibling. The job comment may be perceived as a brother saying "So you have a new job again? You slacker" or the offer to pay for the coffee may be perceived as a sister hinting that she is more financially secure than the client. This second category of comments is also written down and placed within triangles. The therapist then explains that these "triangles" don't fit into the opening in the big circle. Hence, in order to be able to fit these seemingly innocent comments into the opening in the big circle, these "triangles" must be changed into squares that can now fit into the big circle. This is a visual illustration of how the client changes the innocent comments about the job and the coffee into offensive comments in order for them to fit into the negative core belief. Using this visual illustration is a powerful tool to elucidate to clients how their core beliefs are impacting the way they interact with their siblings (Beck, 2011).

In order to help the client differentiate between truly offensive comments and the more common, innocent comments perceived as threatening, the therapist can ask the client to think how the therapist would perceive the various comments they hear from their siblings. Stepping back and trying to view sibling interactions as an outside observer can help clients perceive comments by their siblings in more accurate and healthy manners. Once the client understands this cognitive model, therapy can proceed with challenging the core beliefs. This can be undertaken by allowing the client to entertain the notion that the core belief is false and that it was established based on inaccurate childhood definitions.

In some cases, clients may comment that they understand the cognitive process but still don't "feel it." For clients with these concerns, the cognitive-behavioral model offers an emotion-based task for general treatment that can easily be applied in sibling work as well (Beck, 2005). The technique seeks to create a link between the cognitive and emotional via a guided imagery task. The client is encouraged to recall a past archetype memory linked with the negative core belief and is then asked to visualize their current self entering the memory and offering support to their past self. This method has been found to help clients confront their core beliefs on an emotional level. The forthcoming case study will offer an illustration of the use of this technique in sibling work.

Challenging distortions

Clients experiencing negativity in their sibling interactions may have several cognitive distortions that need to be challenged. In cognitive-behavior literature, a number of cognitive distortions that clients hold have been identified as creating mental blocks that impact emotions and impede positive behavior (Beck, 1995). Applied to sibling work, several cognitive distortions by clients about their sibling relationships may be generating negative feelings about their siblings which, in turn, produce acrimonious behaviors exhibited by clients with their siblings. For example, if clients believe that their sibling "must" call them on their birthday or that their sibling "must" respect the work they do, then when these demands are not met, clients feel dejected, which results in unfriendly interactions with siblings.

Similarly, if clients believe that their sibling "should" make efforts to get together more often or that their sibling "should" respond more quickly when they leave them a message, then, when these requirements are not met, clients are infuriated and respond to their sibling in anger. In order to avoid these unhealthy patterns, therapists can assist clients in challenging the distortions by reframing the "musts" and "shoulds" of sibling relationships and redefining them as preferences. For example, instead of "My sibling must call me on my birthday," the client can be encouraged to reframe the thought as "It would be nice if my sibling would call me on my birthday." Similarly, instead of "My sibling should make efforts to get together more often," the client can be coached to reframe the thought as "It would be nice if my sibling would make an effort to reach out to me more often." Reframing the "musts" and the "shoulds" as preferences minimizes the tension when the demands are not met, resulting in less negativity during sibling interactions.

An additional common cognitive distortion is to tag a sibling as "bad" when the sibling does something hurtful to the client. When a sibling is labeled as bad, then even when they exhibit harmless behaviors, they are viewed as bad, which leads to an endless cycle of contentious interactions. In such cases, clients can be encouraged to challenge the label of "My bad sibling" and redefine it as "They did something upsetting." Likewise, clients may have defined their sibling relationship as a "bad relationship," which, in turn, leads to an expectation of negativity every time they get together with their sibling. Reclassifying the relationship from "bad" to "not where it should be" can help clients interact with their sibling in more accepting ways.

An additional way cognitive distortions impact the sibling bond is when a client's brother or sister is emotionally or psychologically unhealthy. In such cases, clients may have taken on more responsibility over the relationship than is appropriate. They may need to redefine their role and understand how their sibling's behaviors are driven by entrenched personality or psychopathology and are not a function of the client's efforts. This may help clients minimize their expectations and create less tension during sibling interactions.

Confronting obsessive jealousy

As noted, adult sibling dynamics often contain similar feelings that afflict childhood sibling relationships. These feelings lead to childhood definitions that impact the way clients interact with their siblings. Adult sibling disputes are frequently a manifestation of definitions born from childhood themes of parental favoritism and rivalry. In adulthood, these definitions often lead to jealousy. The cognitive-behavior model has greatly impacted the conceptualization of jealousy and has published a considerable body of clinical work on overcoming jealousy in general. This work can be applied to sibling jealously in effective ways.

Cognitive-behavior approaches define jealousy as "angry, agitated worry." Thus, jealousy is conceptualized within the framework of the cognitive approach to anxiety (Leahy, 2003). This definition and conceptualization of jealous thoughts and feelings can clarify some of the features of sibling jealousy.

First, sibling jealousy may entail a fear that the success of the sibling in some way may detract from the client's achievements. The client may fear that their sibling is engaging in behaviors meant to harm him or her. This produces a hyperawareness or a constant worry about threats from the sibling. A simple neutral gesture from the sibling is rapidly misinterpreted and is assumed to be a personal attack. For example, when the sibling simply asks, "So, how is that new job going?" the client may perceive the question as, "So, how long will it take until you get fired from this job as well? I have been working in the same place for years and am up for promotion."

Second, this hypersensitivity is often a result of anxiety about self or one's own success. A client is more likely to misinterpret neutral gestures from siblings as malicious if they have anxieties about themselves such as, "I am no good; I am flawed."

There are many tested, classic cognitive-behavioral techniques to use in an effort to minimize this type of worry. Two of the approaches can easily be applied to helping clients deal with the obsessive worry of sibling jealousy.

First, therapists can discuss with their clients the distinction between productive worry and unproductive worry. Productive worry is when the worry, or jealousy, produces some positive outcome. The client can be presented with the following questions: "Does your jealousy motivate you to change things about your life? Does it motivate you to develop better relationships with your family? Does it motivate you to work harder at securing a better job?" In cases where the client determines that their thoughts about their sibling actually motivates them to do better, the jealousy can be redefined as a healthy motivator.

On the other hand, unproductive worry is when the jealousy does not result in any type of productive behavior. It is when the jealousy only makes clients anxious as they continually ruminate about their sibling, about how good their sibling has it, and about how bad things are for them. These thoughts and feelings only serve to increase the jealousy and distress.

Second, jealous feelings are often coupled with negative behaviors toward the siblings. Clients think that being offensive toward siblings may help them in expressing the negativity which will minimize the jealousy. However, due to the interactive nature of behaviors, thoughts, and emotions, acting in belligerent ways toward siblings actually increases the negative feelings toward the sibling which, in turn, increases the jealousy. Keeping this in mind, clients can be encouraged to engage in positive behaviors toward their siblings, as reviewed in the next section. Clients can make an effort to reach out to siblings, spend some time together, and express genuine interest in their lives. This positive engagement can help clients realize that their siblings are no threat to them at all. On the contrary, the relationship they build with siblings may turn out to be very enjoyable.

Sibling jealousy is a common aspect of adult sibling dynamics. However, an awareness of its existence and active steps to challenge the thoughts and behaviors that accompany the jealousy can help minimize the feelings. This process can help move the siblings toward developing a healthy, supportive, and meaningful sibling relationship.

Behavioral interventions

The effectiveness of the cognitive tools reviewed can be enhanced by combining specific behavioral techniques to the therapeutic intervention (Beck, 1995). The process of the behavioral intervention involves the client engaging their siblings using specific, practical, and measurable actions toward rebuilding the relationship. The goal is for clients to take responsibility for the relationship and acknowledge their part in keeping the detachment from their sibling active. Furthermore, engaging in actual behavioral tasks serves as experiments to test and dispute some of the faulty cognitions (Beck, 2011). These objectives are accomplished using specific homework assignments to build positive engagement and communicate openly and more effectively with siblings.

Positive engagement

When clients are seeking to build better relationships with multiple siblings, the behavioral interventions can begin by focusing on repairing the relationship with the sibling that the client has the least problematic relationship with and then can proceed with other siblings. By starting with the easier sibling, clients can master the behavioral techniques in a calmer relational context and then apply their newly-found success with the more challenging siblings.

Therapists can begin by asking clients to describe what a better relationship with their sibling would look like. Using the classic, therapeutic, miracle question, the client can be asked, "Visualize a new future with your sibling, what does it look like?" Once a relationship goal is established, therapists can assess the strengths and weaknesses of the relationship. This can be accomplished by revisiting the relationship assessments from earlier in the chapter and examining what would make the relationship better, what would bring the siblings closer, and what can be done to enhance the relationship.

Once specific steps have been identified that would enhance the connection, the client can begin working on the new relationship by creating a new paradigm for the relationship. However, often this ostentatious objective of creating a new relationship can seem daunting to clients. Hence, it is important to clarify to clients that the goal is not changing the relationship overnight. The initial objective is a realization that a relationship is possible and that small steps can restore the connection. Clients may also think that having a close relationship with a sibling requires living close to them or necessitates a considerable time investment. However, studies have shown that sibling closeness is not linked with proximity or frequency of contact (McGhee, 1985; Van Volkom, 2006). Hence, small steps not requiring a significant time commitment can make a difference.

The client can be encouraged to begin the process by reaching out to the sibling via the phone or email and inviting them out for coffee or lunch (Rosenberg, 1980). The client can bring a small gift to the meeting for their sibling as a token of their commitment to a new future. When the client reaches out to their sibling, they should set a specific time and date for the get-together as opposed to just offering that "we should get together sometime." These specific tasks should be prescribed in session as homework and the client should be instructed to report on their progress in a future session (Beck, 2011).

The therapist can use client rewards and clear weekly assignments to achieve these goals.

Open communication

In order for the overtures toward the sibling to be successful, it is important to work with clients on having open communication with their sibling. When siblings do not communicate openly about their current relationship, their childhood definitions fill the void and become the present reality. These past, unhealthy definitions perpetuate the hostility between the siblings. A childhood definition of rivalry, for example, may be based on projection and not based on reality. Communication about these issues is important considering that each sibling may have his or her version of the past which does not represent the current state of the relationship.

For example, if a past childhood definition entailed jealousy, the sibling may hold back sharing details about their life for fear of making their brother or sister jealous. The sibling, who has moved past being jealous, may perceive their sibling's lack of sharing as detachment. Openly communicating with each other can help the siblings move beyond this impasse. Goldenthal (2002) reported on a dying individual who commented to his siblings on his deathbed that "No one is there for me" when in fact his siblings had been by his side for over a decade. Holding on to the detachment he felt as a child coupled with a lack of communication with his siblings about their current relationship contributed to the individual retaining his childhood narrative throughout life.

Open communication is further essential when repairing sibling relationships considering that, even when siblings are close to one another, misunderstandings can occur. Delaying talking about misunderstandings can build resentment and can retrigger past sibling hostility. Hence, integrating communication techniques in therapy with specific in-session and homework tasks is an essential component of repairing adult sibling relationships.

Effective communication techniques

Successful integration of communication techniques in sibling work entails the application of the extensive, empirical and clinical literature on effective communication combined with sensitivity to the sibling context (Caughlin, Koerner, Schrodt, & Fitzpatrick, 2011;

Knapp, Vangelisti, & Caughlin, 2013). This pairing can be applied as a means to work with clients on improving their communication with a specific focus on effective talking, careful listening, and attending to nonverbal signals. As with other behavioral interventions, competencies in these three areas are achieved using specific, practical, and measurable actions, using in-session practice, and specific homework assignments to be applied when interacting with siblings.

Therapists can encourage their clients to think before talking and to consider if what they plan on saying to their sibling will help or hinder the relationship. Clients can be asked to monitor when they hold back saying hurtful things when they are with their siblings and report on their progress in subsequent sessions. Attention can also be placed on helping clients focus on what is heard by their siblings when they communicate and appreciate that often the intent behind words is not necessarily what is received by the listener. This awareness can also be prescribed as homework by having clients note the number of times they intentionally reconsidered the words they were about to utter to their sibling due to the potential of misunderstandings.

Furthermore, the importance of focusing on facts and being honest in conversations should also be highlighted. When presenting a sibling with a grievance, therapists should encourage clients to stick to a specific issue as opposed to globalizing the problem. A conversation beginning with "When you said I was lazy last night I was hurt" will be more effective in trying to rectify the problem as opposed to a conversation that begins with "You always offend me."

When a conversation with a sibling is derailed, clients should be encouraged to highlight the process of the conversation by saying to the sibling something similar to "Look what just happened." Focusing on the process of the conversation can help bring the discussion back to a productive track. It is also important for clients to learn to admit when they are wrong and acknowledge positivity in their siblings. All these elements of effective communication can be discussed in session, practiced, and then assigned as specific homework tasks to be tested when engaging siblings.

In terms of careful listening, the therapist and client can practice active listening by paraphrasing and asking questions during conversations. Listeners should not assume intent. Inquiring about the meaning of vague statements by siblings can help minimize confusion. Careful listening also entails reacting to what is being said by the sibling and not reacting based on past exchanges or insecurities. Similarly, it is vital for clients to understand that what is said by their sibling may be driven by the sibling's own insecurities and past definitions. Having this awareness can help clients consider the underlying meaning behind their sibling's position. By being aware of the underlying tensions behind what is being said by a sibling, clients can avoid responding with defensiveness.

For example, when a sibling complains to a sister that "You are so self-centered, you never listen," they may be responding to deeper feelings of loneliness growing up and not based on any current behaviors. An awareness of this can help the sister respond with empathy as opposed to defensiveness. Levitt, Levitt, and Levitt (2001) reported on an altercation pertaining to inheritance between a sister and brother following the death of their parents. Once the sister attended to the deeper meaning of the messages conveyed by her brother, she appreciated that the fight was not about the money but rather about hidden emotions based on past feelings of parental favoritism. This realization helped her avoid defensiveness, thus preventing an escalation.

Attention also needs to be placed on helping clients notice nonverbal communication on both ends. They need to be cognizant of the way they express nonverbal messages and they need to attend to the nonverbal messages conveyed by their sibling when communicating. For example, what messages are conveyed or received while the conveyer is folding their hands? What is the context of the message if the talker is standing while the receiver is sitting? What is the message being conveyed when the sibling is finger pointing? Based on past histories, these nonverbal elements of communication may contain specific meanings. For example, a younger sibling with a childhood definition of always being bossed around by an older sibling may respond particularly harshly when an older sibling points a finger during conversations. Hence, being cognizant of these elements of communication is an integral part of enhancing proper communication.

An additional, nonverbal element of conversation that can be effective in enhancing the sibling bond is touch. An extensive literature exists on the interpersonal and therapeutic value of touch (Barnett, 2005; Duhn, 2010). Drawing from evolutionary and ecological theory, Montague (1995) highlights the importance of touch across species as a form of communication and enumerates the devastating physical, familial, and societal consequences of lacking touch. Encouraging clients to reach out and touch a sibling in the form of a hug or a pat on the back can be an effective nonverbal way of expressing warmth.

Although the cognitive and behavioral dimensions have been presented as separate procedures, the therapeutic process necessitates a constant interplay between attending to the cognitive elements of the relational detachment and integrating behavioral interventions. For example, as noted, challenging the cognitive distortions of jealousy is made easier once the client reaches out to a sibling and realizes that their sibling is not a threat. Similarly, cognitive dimensions may be required throughout the behavioral interventions in reaction to how siblings respond to the client's overtures. Clients may perceive the lack of enthusiasm of the sibling to their reconciliation attempts as a personal rejection. In such cases, cognitive tools may be needed to help the client understand that "after all was said and done you did what you could." Clients may also need encouragement in appreciating that they did their part and created a context for potential future resolution.

Case study: "The little pipsqueak"

Adam, a married 36-year-old with two young children, came to therapy to deal with a general sense of unhappiness in his life. Adam reported that he adored his wife and children but had found recently that he was "a bit down" and not very enthusiastic about life. When discussing his family of origin, Adam reported that he was the youngest of three siblings, having an older brother and a middle sister, and that he, his parents, and his sister, all lived in the city where they grew up. Recently, his 40-year-old brother, Chris, relocated back home and now also lived nearby. Adam noted that he felt a bit uneasy at a recent family gathering when his brother was talking about his new job.

When the therapist suggested that his recent mood shift may be linked to his brother's relocation, Adam was hesitant but willing to explore. After assessing his current and past relationship with his brother, Adam revealed that he felt that Chris was arrogant and was always talking about his career success. Growing up, Adam felt that

Chris looked down at him and often referred to him as "the little pip-squeak." Even with the mistreatment, Adam looked up to his brother and was jealous of "how cool he seemed."

When examining how the childhood jealousy was manifested in their present relationship, Adam thought that Chris was in competition with him and talked about his career to point out how much more successful he was than Adam. This thought compelled Adam to try to avoid his brother by not visiting his parent's house when he knew Chris was there.

The cognitive therapeutic intervention entailed revealing how the core belief that "Chris is better than me" impacted the way Adam reacted to Chris and behaved around him. The therapist worked with Adam at generating two categories of statements or behaviors that Adam may hear or experience from Chris. The first were blatantly negative statements or behaviors and the second were harmless statements or behaviors that were perceived as offensive by Adam because of his negative core belief. Hence, when Chris would talk about his job, a harmless behavior to most, Adam would perceive that as offensive, as it confirmed his negative core belief about being less than his brother. Using this tool, Adam was able to appreciate how he may be misinterpreting his brother's words and actions.

In order to create a link between the cognitive and emotional, Adam was asked to recall a past memory that most represented his brother being better than him. With his eyes closed, Adam recalled a childhood memory of him during an extended family vacation losing a swim race to Chris. The memory of the cousins applauding his brother as he struggled to swim to the other end of the pool was particularly painful for Adam. The therapist instructed Adam to imagine his adult self entering the memory and offering words of encouragement to his childhood self. Adam responded by supporting his childhood self, commenting loudly, "Don't be sad, Adam. You will one day be very good at school and graduate with an MBA. You will marry a great girl and you will have such great kids. Chris is good at sports but you are good at so many other things." Once the recollection was over, Adam was very emotional and, that evening, sent an email to the therapist expressing how the session was "transformative."

Using these cognitive tools provided Adam the necessary courage to reach out to Chris and offer to meet for lunch. Chris readily agreed and Adam reported in a future session that the meeting was surprisingly pleasant. Adam was able to talk with Chris about some of his feelings of jealousy. Although Chris was initially defensive about the topic, in a subsequent discussion, Chris was able to admit that in the past he felt similarly but now was actually very proud of Adam. Adam found the rekindling of the sibling bond very supportive and his initial sense of discontent was eased.

Working jointly with siblings

The cognitive tools and behavioral interventions examined are geared toward working individually with one sibling in a family. However, the above techniques can be applied when working jointly with siblings as well with a particular awareness about common sibling interactional difficulties. An advantage of having the siblings in session together is that a joint meeting can trigger siblings to reveal in their affect and behavior aspects of the relationship that may not have been expressed explicitly in the past.

Several family dysfunction themes common in systems therapy can have a considerable impact on sibling relationships. Attending to these issues in an honest way in joint therapy with siblings can be an important supplement to individual cognitive-behavior interventions.

Family boundaries

Siblings can examine if the overall family system has appropriate boundaries. Boundary violations can occur when members of a family cross personal or relational boundaries (Goldenberg & Goldenberg, 2012; Minuchin, 1981). Personal boundary violations entail invading a family member's privacy by being intrusive. Personal boundary violations can also occur by being overly involved or controlling of a family member. Relational boundary violations transpire when a family member inserts themselves in a relationship between other family members in inappropriate ways.

For example, the parental unit in a family has a unique relationship that should be distinct from other family relationships. Similarly, the siblings in a family have a distinct relationship that should be respected by parents. When children invade the parental unit or when parents invade the sibling system, dysfunction ensues. Siblings in therapy can assess if these types of violations have occurred in the family and practical steps can be implemented to minimize such invasions.

Joint communication

When siblings are in session together, the significance of open communication can be emphasized further by identifying times in the past when both siblings begrudgingly engaged in some activity together because they each thought that the other one wanted to. This common breakdown in communication emanates from a similar concept identified by the fields of social psychology and management theory referred to as the "Abilene paradox" (Harvey, 1974).

For example, a brother is planning on making a small birthday party for one of his children. He would rather not invite his siblings considering that he wants the party to be a small event for children that ends early. However, fearing that his siblings may get offended, he invites them anyway. His siblings would rather not go to the party as they each have other obligations that day. Fearing that the brother may get offended if they decline the invitation, they accept, much to the chagrin of the brother. As a result, during the party, both the brother and his siblings are annoyed. Having open communication among siblings about their likes and dislikes can help minimize misunderstandings that lead to siblings engaging each other insincerely.

Triangulation

Finally, a common dynamic found in family dysfunction is triangulation (Bowen, 1974, 1993; Goldenberg & Goldenberg, 2012). As reviewed in past chapters, triangulation occurs when family members with a strained relationship use their relationship with another family member as a way to gain access to or influence each other. This pulls the third party into the conflict between the rivaling family members, creating an unhealthy triangle. Siblings can often be pulled into battles between parents or between other siblings in the family. By serving as the triangulated family member, the lack of family communication spreads and the family dispute is prolonged.

For example, a mother not on speaking terms with her daughter due to some grievance may reach out to another of her children to have them provide information about her daughter or have them influence the daughter in some way. This can cause resentment by the triangulated sibling toward the mother, the sister, or toward both, furthering the detachment and family aggression.

Siblings in joint therapy can discuss the occurrence of this phenomenon in their family and develop concrete ways to limit its manifestation. Openly communicating about the destructive nature of triangulation and applying specific behavioral interventions to be monitored and reviewed in session can help siblings confront this destructive family dynamic and enhance their bond.

Chapter summary

Helping adults develop a closer sibling bond can have multiple benefits. First, it can minimize sibling hostility that often creates tension in people's lives. Furthermore, enhancing the sibling bond can provide an important source of support as people transition into their older adult years. Attending to sibling issues in therapy is also crucial considering how unresolved sibling problems can often surface after parental death in damaging ways. After a clear picture of the client's sibling dynamics is reviewed in therapy, cognitive-behavior techniques can be applied to challenging the cognitive distortions that keep siblings apart. The cognitive tools can be enhanced by combining specific behavioral techniques to the therapeutic intervention. The behavioral objectives are accomplished using specific homework assignments to build positive engagement and communicate openly and more effectively with siblings.

10
Brief Psychodynamic Interventions for Adult Sibling Issues

The use of brief psychodynamic interventions when integrating sibling issues in therapy with adults can be applied in two primary situations. First is when the sibling issues are presented by the client during the intake process. In this situation, referred to as overt sibling issues, a client enters therapy with the explicit goal of repairing their sibling relationship. The focus of therapy in this situation is the exploration of underlying sibling tensions with the goal of repairing the negative sibling bond. An examination of this process is presented later in this chapter.

However, the powerful role played by past sibling dynamics in adult well-being calls for a broader use of sibling issues in therapy (Coles, 2003; Lewin & Sharp, 2009; Schulman, 1999). Even in situations where a client enters therapy for other difficulties which are seemingly unrelated to siblings, such as anxiety or depression, a sibling-sensitive therapist should allow for an exploration of sibling issues. This exploration can help uncover the core sibling issues underlying the broader tensions which in turn can help relieve the client of these other difficulties (Kivowitz, 1995; Schulman, 1999). In this situation, referred to as covert sibling issues, therapy begins with an examination of the presenting problem but soon evolves into an exploration of underlying sibling tensions and past family dynamics in order to shed light on the accurate nature of what is truly bothering the client.

This chapter begins with a review of the integration of psychodynamic interventions in covert sibling issues considering that in due course, even in this situation, therapy will ultimately transition to exploring the sibling issues more overtly, a topic forth-coming in this chapter.

Covert sibling issues

Covert sibling issues entail sibling-related childhood introjections penetrating current functioning and well-being. As reviewed in Part I, childhood sibling interactions within the family context create pow-erful dynamics, models, and definitions which impact future adult relationships, personalities, and well-being (Bank, 1992; Bank & Kahn, 1982; Mitchell, 2003). Considering the importance of past sib-ling associations for current adult functioning, several early theoreti-cal perspectives have highlighted the therapeutic value of integrating sibling histories in therapy.

For example, although much has been written about the psychoanalytic emphasis on early parent–child relationships, a care-ful examination of the writings of Freud reveals a vast literature on many aspects of sibling psychology. These writings emphasize the prominence of siblings in the development of the psyche and its impact on adolescence and adulthood. Beyond the many mentions in his papers, his *The Interpretation of Dreams* (Freud, 1900) has over 40 references to brothers and sisters. As Sherwin-White (2007) noted, "Freud had a wide and judicious grasp of the potential importance of sibling dynamics for therapeutic work, still relevant today" (p. 5).

As introduced in Part I, several sibling-related themes can be seen in Freud's writing, all of which contain lifelong and therapeutic implica-tions. Sexual development and the ability to form true love partners later in life has been suggested as linked with early childhood inces-tuous feelings toward brothers and sisters. Broader social dynamics have also been suggested by Freud as driven by childhood reactions to the birth of a sibling which may entail feelings of jealousy, rivalry, and competition over maternal affection (Freud, 1955).

Siblings continue to play a role in future socialization by serving as original "objects" which are later substituted by other social relation-ships. Even intellectual inquisitiveness has been linked theoretically to the arrival of a new sibling through the natural curiosity regard-ing conception, pregnancy, and the birth process triggered by the arrival of the new sibling (Colonna & Newman, 1983; Kivowitz, 1995; Sherwin-White, 2007).

The neo-analytic theory of self-psychology is an additional model to assist in framing the theoretical significance of clinically tending to covert sibling dynamics. According to self-psychology, the availability of reliable and stable others in childhood who provide specific "selfobject" experiences is a key feature in the development of a healthy and secure adult personality (Kohut, 1971; Schermer, 2000). When these experiences, or needs, are consistently provided, they become engrained in a child's inner self producing a sense of personal unity. The three primary selfobject needs are referred to as *mirroring needs,* which is the need to feel recognized and valued, *idealizing needs,* the need to have a sense of oneness with a dominant selfobject, and *twinship needs,* the need to feel a sense of being together with others (Banai, Mikulincer, & Shaver, 2005). When these three needs are offered regularly by significant people in the lives of children, they transition into the adolescent and adult years feeling a sense of motivation, self-importance, security, and belongingness (Wolf, 1988).

When parents do not offer these needs to children, they often rely on their siblings for the provision of these selfobject needs (Kahn, 1988; Wittenberg, 2009). Hence, a sibling may offer recognition and value to a child. Furthermore, they may also serve as a dominant selfobject and may provide a sense of belongingness for a child. However, due to the immaturity of children, and their own developmental process, their ability to truly provide for the selfobject needs of their siblings may lead to difficulties.

For example, when providing a child's idealizing needs, a sibling serving as the dominant selfobject may continue serving this role over time by taking on a burdensome amount of responsibilities and denying their own needs which can lead to an internalization of resentment in adulthood. Furthermore, the receiving sibling may not feel adequately satisfied by the provision of the selfobject, leading to bitterness. Although these feelings of resentment or bitterness are directed at siblings, the sentiment is veiled and may be displayed in other areas of functioning.

Hence, clients entering therapy for a myriad of issues can gain insight into their difficulties through an exploration of early childhood sibling interactions (Agger, 1988; Rosner, 1985; Schulman, 1999). As Wittenberg (2009) noted, children who seek out their siblings to fulfill selfobject functions face lasting consequences to their adult psychology because their siblings almost inevitably fail to fully meet their needs, so for clients who appear to have had idealizing or mirroring selfobject needs met by a sibling in childhood it is likely that therapy will uncover hidden disappointment and rage at the sibling. (p. 53)

Past sibling issues in relationships

In the empirical literature, early sibling dynamics have been shown to impact adult functioning in several ways. Considering that the sibling relationship early in life served as the original reciprocal relationship, unfinished business with a sibling may permeate other adult relationships. Shalash, Wood, and Parker (2013) found that conflict styles in adult romantic relationships follow similar patterns as conflict styles employed during adolescence with siblings. Hence, a client in therapy for difficulties in romantic or other relationships can be served by exploring the primal mutual relationship they developed with their sibling. By studying past and present sibling relationship dynamics, and how these patterns may be playing themselves out in the client's present relationships, clients can gain important insight into their underlying relational devices and approach their difficulties in a more meaningful and systematic way (Coles, 2003).

Furthermore, parent–child relationships may be driven by past underlying sibling tensions. Edward (2013) reported on a mother who was seeking treatment for anxious feelings in the lead-up to the birth of a second child. After the birth, the mother felt extremely detached from the newborn baby boy and attempted to protect the interests of her firstborn daughter. Sibling-focused therapy uncovered intense feelings of resentment this mother harbored against her younger brother from childhood which began soon after his birth. The mother reported that she felt that the attention her younger brother received after being born took away her unique status in the family as being the only child. Her feelings of bitterness toward her brother continued to propagate throughout her childhood and adolescent years. This exploration helped the mother appreciate how her reaction to her second child was an expression of her past, concealed feelings toward her younger brother.

Broader social/relational dynamics may also be driven by past sibling interactions (Bank & Kahn, 1982; Caffaro & Conn-Caffaro, 2003; Cicirelli, 1989; Lam, Solmeyer, & McHale, 2012; Sulloway, 1996). A person's comfort level in social situations may be motivated by past engrained memories of public ridicule by an older sibling. For example, a client recalling how her older sister would "make fun of me in front of everyone" and how the embarrassment from these episodes impacted her social engagement for many years would benefit from an examination of those early sibling ridicules to help overcome her current social anxieties.

Sibling dynamics and identity

Early sibling interactions may impact a person's identity (Caffaro & Conn-Caffaro, 2003; Sherwin-White, 2007). Sibling modeling and de-identification are powerful processes which influence adulthood in many mays. For example, an adult's occupational choices may be driven by an older sibling's choice or by early family sibling labeling. An adult may have chosen a specific career path to mimic an older brother or may have avoided some occupations, even desired occupations, simply to try to distance himself or herself from an older sibling who chose that specific occupation. In some cases, a client may have chosen a specific career to gain approval from a sibling. In other circumstances, occupational choices may have been driven by early labels arbitrarily placed on each sibling within the family. A child known as the intellectually inferior child, in comparison to a more gifted older sibling, may have chosen an occupation necessitating little talent or training simply in response to this childhood label.

Hence, a client presenting with job dissatisfaction, for example, may gain substantial insight into their underlying difficulties if the therapeutic intervention includes an exploration of these early childhood sibling relational dynamics and family sibling labels. For example, while exploring these dynamics in session with a client encountering occupational dissatisfaction, a middle-aged client commented that "I never wanted to be a physician but my older brother was one and I wanted to please him." This type of sentiment is a prime example of how something as powerful as an individual's occupational identity can be driven by sibling dynamics. Allowing for an exploration of these sibling features in therapy can uncover important elements integral to a client's difficulties.

Siblings and well-being

Beyond occupational identity, other aspects of adulthood identity and personality impacting psychological well-being may be driven by early sibling dynamics (Cicirelli, 1995; Vaillant & Vaillant, 1990). For example, issues of self-worth may be a function of past sibling approval and rivalry. Barnes and Austin (1995) found that self-esteem was linked to early sibling dynamics to a greater degree than was maternal affection. Clients suffering from low self-esteem may be responding to feelings of inadequacy born during early childhood sibling interactions. A client may present with depressive symptomology which, after an initial phase of assessment, is determined to be driven by feelings of worthlessness. Engaging a client, in such a case, in an elaboration on his or her early sibling relationship dynamics may reveal that these feelings of low self-worth or depression have been engrained early in life via a sense of inferiority toward an older sibling. An assessment of these early sibling relational feelings can then be used as the foundation for a broader examination of the low self-esteem or depressive symptomology.

In all of these examples, the presenting problem is not initially seen as connected to siblings in any way. It is only after an initial phase of intake and assessment that a sibling-sensitive therapist would breach the topic of sibling relationships to examine how the presenting problem may be a symptom of deep-seeded past sibling dynamics.

The clinical process

Clients may respond initially with skepticism to questions about past siblings relationships. Many clients reply with some variation of "this is not what I came here to talk about." However, like any other therapeutic plan of the therapist, a client is more likely to agree to enter an exploration of past sibling dynamics after a sense of trust has been established between therapist and client (Wallin, 2007). Once trust has been developed and an initial examination of past sibling relationships has been undertaken, the clinical objective would be for the client to realize how these past sibling issues may be linked with his or her current functioning. Once this realization is achieved, a more direct, elaborate examination of the sibling bond commences.

The therapeutic focus on the sibling relationship can serve multiple functions. In addition to using this exploration to help shed light on the client's seemingly unrelated presenting problem, embarking upon an open discussion about the client's sibling relationships has the additional benefit of potentially helping to create a closer bond between the client and his or her siblings. This renewed sibling bond can serve as an additional source of positive support for the client (Avioli, 1989). Schulman (1999) noted that siblings can be called upon to offer "protectiveness, sharing, and companionship" (p. 518) with an examination of sibling issues in therapy. Hence, the sibling focus may influence both the covert and overt aspects of the sibling dynamic.

Overt sibling issues

In many cases, sibling issues are the focus of therapy from the beginning. In these cases, a client seeks therapy for the explicit goal of repairing his or her tumultuous sibling relationship. The turmoil in the relationship may be present due to a number of possibilities. First, the conflict may have been present for many years as an undercurrent and is now being attended to by one or both siblings. Additionally, sibling conflict may have been triggered by a negative life event such as the death or illness of a parent (Schulman, 1999).

Psychodynamic and neo-analytic theories can help provide a framework by which to conceptualize the importance of clinically attending to past sibling dynamics in overt sibling issues. The focus of therapy in overt situations is the examination of underlying sibling tensions, by exploring past family dynamics, with the goal of repairing the destructive sibling dynamics and creating a supportive bond. Wittenberg (2009) reported on interviews conducted with six licensed psychotherapists about their use of siblings in psychotherapy. In multiple accounts provided by the clinicians, the integration of past sibling issues in therapy was a catalyst for clients to reconnect with siblings, activating a reflective and meaningful relationship.

The therapeutic process entails an exploration of present and past sibling relationships, an examination of past personal identities, illuminating the parental context in the sibling relationship, and an awareness of transference issues. The procedure described here for overt sibling issues would progress similarly in cases of covert sibling issues once the link between the presenting problem and the past sibling narrative is established in session.

Exploring the sibling relationship

Facing overt sibling issues in therapy begins with an exploration of current and past sibling relationships. The assessment of both past and current sibling dynamics assists in providing a clear picture of the way past sibling interactions may be impacting current sibling engagement (Sanders, 2004). The assessment of the current sibling relationships can be conducted similarly to the process described in Chapter 9 with both qualitative and quantitative tools. Questions should include cognitive, emotional, and behavioral aspects describing the relationship with each sibling, their level of knowledge about their sibling's lives, when was the last get-together with their siblings, frequency of contact, means of contact, who initiates the contact, anticipatory stress, pleasantness of the interactions, topics of conversation during get-togethers, how open are the discussions, taboo items of conversations, and is there a need for contact recovery time after sibling get-togethers (Goldenthal, 2002). The questions can be supplemented with the use of the ASRQ (Lanthier, Stocker, & Furman, 2001), as reviewed in Chapter 9.

Once a clear portrait of the current state of the relationship has been established, a review of past sibling relationship quality can be initiated. The objective here is to assist the client in recollecting early sibling memories. The initiation of the reminiscence can begin with some form of a relaxation technique. Once the client has reached a point of relaxation, the therapist can begin by asking the client to recall some early sibling memories. Recollection can be aided by having the client draw their childhood home and talk about the drawing and events that occurred with siblings in the home (Goldenthal, 2002). The recollection should include the context of the first memory, including a description of the location, surrounding, and any other sensory recollection associated with the memory. The client should talk about what occurred in the memory, the thoughts and feelings of the memory, and any childhood reactions and conclusions linked with the memory. After the memory recollection, the client should be asked if they noticed any new dimensions to the memories recalled. Clients should also discuss any current thoughts, feelings, or body experiences occurring as a result of the memory recollection.

The therapeutic process continues with a dialogue about how these childhood memories have created certain conclusions about the client, the siblings, the relationship between the client and their siblings, and how these conclusions may relate to the client's current sibling issues. For example, the therapist may ask, "How have these childhood interactions defined and labeled you, your siblings, and your relationship with them?" to encourage a discussion about how the client's current interactions with their siblings are driven by childhood dynamics. By appreciating how adult sibling relationships and interactions are fueled by "frozen misunderstandings" of the past, clients can gain awareness of their tendency to resort to familiar, and unhealthy, childhood "auto-pilot" when they engage their siblings (Kahn & Lewis, 1988).

For example, Edward (2013) reported on a client, Helen, who was upset by her sister's offer to help during the upcoming wedding of Helen's daughter. After exploration, it became evident that her aversive reaction to her sister's benign gesture was driven by childhood feelings of being excluded as a result of the close relationship that existed between Helen's sister and mother. This frozen past sibling framework triggered a fear that if her sister helped with the wedding, she would be excluded once again.

Additionally, adults may return to their childhood roles when interacting with their siblings when they permit a sibling to serve as their parent, a common sibling engagement role during childhood (Schulman, 1999). Alternatively, siblings may revert back to childhood roles in the way they label the competency level of each of their siblings. During childhood, specific definitions about which sibling was the smart one and which the thoughtless one may have been established. Now, as adults, siblings may revert back to these definitions. When adults permit these past roles to permeate their current sibling relationships it may trigger past negative feelings about these roles, obscuring the present situation. Clients should be encouraged to examine how past childhood roles infiltrate their current life, creating negativity in their existing sibling relationships (Schulman, 1999).

The regression to childhood sibling labels may occur more blatantly in the presence of parents. The development of childhood sibling definitions is often initiated by parent and family dynamics (Wittenberg, 2009). Hence, the presence of parents may heighten the intrusion of past labels into current interactions. For example, past sibling definitions may be activated when parents ask adult children about their careers in the presence of siblings, triggering regression to childhood feelings about competition.

Once clients are aware of the way past childhood definitions serve as the template for the way they perceive their siblings currently, and act toward them in return, they can apply this understanding in practice. For example, clients may be encouraged to monitor their emotions during interactions with their siblings to refrain from regressing to childhood reactions. Clients could be directed to pay attention to their automatic reactions during sibling interactions and try to respond to sibling comments or requests more honestly and based on the present circumstances.

Examining past personal identities

An additional, more systematic, and pervasive way that past childhood sibling definitions constrain current sibling dynamics is how the family of origin confronted sibling de-identification processes. As reviewed at length in Chapter 4, siblings may choose divergent life paths in many areas of functioning, such as personality and academics, in order to create separate identities between themselves. This de-identification may help in minimizing sibling comparisons and rivalry. Often, de-identification processes are initiated early and are directed intentionally by parents (Saudino, McGuire, Hetherington, Reiss, & Plomin, 1995; Schachter, Gilutz, Shore, & Adler, 1978; Whiteman, McHale, & Crouter, 2007). Although this process can be an adaptive way to minimize sibling rivalry, if the identities accepted by each individual sibling were determined arbitrarily, the process may result in counterproductive outcomes (Caffaro & Conn-Caffaro, 2003). In some cases, childhood rivalry may have been minimized by choosing, or being forced into, dissimilar identities, even when the natural personality and desires of the siblings were, in fact, similar. Under these circumstances, the personal identity developed by some children in the family was purely for the sake of minimizing rivalry and not based on their true disposition and talent. Hence, over time, adults may be living a life that is not truly driven by their personal character, creating overt resentment and covert personal identity issues.

In such circumstances, clients may need to recreate a more authentic sense of self. They may need to re-identify and reclaim their true self even if this new persona is similar to that of a sibling.

Through the process of examining childhood definitions of rivalry and identity, clients can consider new, and more accurate, ways of thinking about self and sibling free from childhood defaults and automatic reactions.

Beyond the significance of engaging in re-identification for overt sibling tensions, this process can also be valuable in cases of covert sibling issues reviewed in the previous section. For example, self-esteem problems may be driven by sibling de-identification processes and an examination of how a client's personal identity was born from early sibling dynamics can assist in approaching the self-esteem difficulties more comprehensively.

In order to initiate this reexamination of personal identities in the context of past sibling definitions, clients can begin with creating a list of childhood family roles (Goldenthal, 2002). Questions to prompt this discovery can include:

> What was your father, mother, and each of your siblings known for/as? What labels were given to each of your family members? Were there any labels given to individual relationships that existed between dyads in your family? How did these individual and dyadic labels develop? Were these labels accurate? Did these labels truly represent the reality of the circumstance at the time? What was your reaction to your individual label? In what way did you try and live up to those labels? Can you think of times when you behaved in ways that did not match with your given label? How was that experience for you? How did others react to it? How do current family and sibling realities match up to those past labels? Do these labels match up to how you are nowadays?

Clients can use this discovery to examine the authenticity of their current identities. This process can impact both overt and covert sibling issues. Adult sibling interactions are often driven by these past, arbitrary childhood identities (Moorman, 1994). Challenging these forged identities can induce clients to develop an awareness of how childhood labels feed current negative reactions when they are with their siblings. This awareness can encourage them to engage their siblings in more authentic ways.

On the covert level, an exploration of how past sibling-based labels about self and others impact current functioning can assist clients in developing honesty about their personal identity. This newfound genuine individuality may impact clients on many levels including self-esteem enhancements, general well-being improvements, and occupational satisfaction.

For example, after an examination of how past family dynamics prescribed specific roles for each sibling in the family, a client commented that his current job dissatisfaction may be a function of failed sibling expectations. The client described how his older brother pursued a professional career and due to modeling and sibling pressures, it was expected of him to continue the tradition initiated by his sibling. Through this discovery in session of past and present sibling-based identities, the client was able to acknowledge that his entire career choice was driven not by his desires or talents but rather was based on faulty past identities. The integration of sibling issues in therapy, in this case, was the catalyst for this client to abandon his chosen occupation and pursue a different occupational path producing a more authentic and satisfying existence.

The parental context

An additional crucial aspect of confronting adult sibling tensions is highlighting the parental role, or parental context, in the development of the hostile sibling dynamics (Kahn & Lewis, 1988). Current hostilities in the sibling relationship were born from past sibling struggles. These intense childhood sibling conflicts could not have been the child's "fault." The development of positive or negative sibling relationships in childhood is primarily driven by parenting behaviors. For example, using the self-psychology theoretical model, Wittenberg (2009) documented several clinical accounts of parents encouraging siblings to provide for the selfobject needs of each other, resulting in negativity between the siblings. This interconnection between parent and sibling relationships may continue into adulthood as well (Voorpostel & Blieszner, 2008).

Hence, when facing overt sibling tensions in session, it is important to discuss how these dynamics developed, as reviewed in the previous section, together with examining the role played by parents in creating these sibling hostilities. Ultimately it was the parents, not the siblings, who were involved in what went wrong. Parents were unavailable, unwilling, incapable, or even inflamed the situation over the years by making comparisons between the siblings or even encouraging competition for approval. The objective is to demonstrate to the client in a non-accusatory way that, despite good intentions, parents failed (Bank, 1988).

For example, a client with resentment toward a sibling for past physical aggression can be encouraged to examine the childhood family dynamics that allowed for such aggression and how it may have been parental modeling of aggression that caused the sibling violence. A client angry over a detached and unsympathetic relationship with a sibling can explore how such a cold relationship developed during childhood and the role that his or her parents played in creating an emotionless early home environment. Anger toward a sibling for being "a brat" and for "ruining my life by getting all the attention and taking everything from me" can be reframed as parental abdication of healthy parenting practices early in life. In this case, the client can also benefit from examining how the parental permissiveness resulted in negative life outcomes for the "privileged" sibling as well.

Removing the blame from the sibling can help clients reclaim their birthright of sibling closeness and realize that due to parental behaviors, the natural, heartfelt, and treasurable relationship that they should have had with their brother or sister failed to launch (Kahn & Lewis, 1988). By highlighting how years of negative feelings toward a sibling may have been misplaced and that the true culprits in what went wrong were parents, clients can gain permission to reach out to the sibling and engage them with a new perspective.

In many cases, loyalty to parents may hinder the ability of a client to accept the parental involvement (Bank, 1988). Clients may need to discuss how to exonerate parents before moving forward. Clients should be encouraged to consider what their parents did in the context of the parents' childhood or in the context of parents' hardships during the client's childhood. However, the ultimate objective is to help clients realize that the negative feelings they harbored toward their siblings have been misdirected all along.

Case study: "What would make mom happy?"

Julie, a married 36-year-old, entered therapy with the explicit objective of mending her destructive sibling relationships. Julie was the second of four children, the older being 38-year-old Mark, followed by Julie, then 34-year-old Laura, and 30-year-old Steve. Her parents had been married for over 40 years and the entire family lived in close proximity to one another. Julie reported that she suspected that her parents were not very satisfied in their marriage and that the family rarely talked about family problems openly. She noted that her father, Tom, was very successful at business but was a workaholic, and that her mother, Barbra, was primarily a stay-at-home mom. Julie reported that all her siblings had unhealthy interactions between each other to various degrees. Her relationship with younger brother, Steve, was somewhat detached. However, the real concern she had was with the antagonistic relationship she had with her older brother, Mark, and younger sister, Laura.

While reviewing childhood sibling relationships and family dynamics, it became clear that the family system suffered from intense boundary violations orchestrated by Julie's mother, Barbra. First, Barbra would violate the sibling's privacy by invading their personal lives and by openly discussing personal aspects of one sibling's life with the other siblings. Second, she would treat her adult children with disrespect by disregarding their opinion and making decisions for them. Finally, due to the fact that Julie's father, Tom, was a workaholic and was rarely home, Julie reported that her mother would depend on her oldest brother, Mark, for closeness and conversation. Julie noted that growing up she felt that her brother and mother were "too close." When the therapist introduced the concept of spousification to Julie, she was convinced that this process was exactly what occurred with her mother and brother. Julie also noted that when Mark left for college, her mother then elevated her younger sister, Laura, to spouse status, sharing with her confidences and engaging her "like more of a friend than a mother."

Julie was able to appreciate how her past and current sibling relationships were driven by her mother's behaviors. First, the overall lack of personal privacy compelled her to hide much of her life from her siblings in reaction to feeling invaded. Second, her mother's lack of open communication about family problems served as a model for her siblings in their inability to express themselves openly.

Most importantly was the reaction of the siblings to the spousification. Julie and her younger brother, Steve, felt resentment and jealousy toward the two spousified siblings. On the other hand, the two spousified siblings, Mark and Laura, were in constant competition over the affection of their mother. These dynamics created a constant state of jealousy and competition throughout the family system.

The awareness of the parental context in her situation helped Julie in her decision to try to reach out to her siblings. She started by reaching out to her youngest brother, Steve, considering that she felt he would be the easiest one to begin repairing the relationship with. Her overtures toward Steve were successful and she was able to have an honest conversation with him, over coffee, about how some of the things their mother did in the past may have interfered with their relationship. They decided to try to reconnect without allowing their mother to interfere.

However, when she tried to reach out to her other two siblings, the spousified ones, her efforts were met with resistance. Julie's attempt at initiating an open exchange with them about how their sibling dynamics may have been driven by their mother's behaviors was met with antagonism. Considering that they served as the mother's surrogate spouse, any effort by Julie to paint their mother in a negative light, in any way, was responded to with hostility, full support of their mother, and harsh attacks blaming Julie for their family problems. At one point, her older brother shouted at her that she "needs to respect our mother and stop trying to tear this family apart." Julie was disheartened by this considering that all she was trying to do was begin some open communication in her family.

In order to demonstrate her family dynamics and the difficulties she was experiencing in removing her mother's influence on her relationship with her older siblings, Julie shared with her therapist the following email exchange between her mother and siblings. The first email from her mother was prompted by her siblings forgetting to celebrate a recent Mother's Day. In response, Barbra emailed her four adult children the following note:

From: Mother

To: Siblings

Subject: Mother's Day

I want to comment on your Mother's Day opinions: too commercialized, superficial, or need to spend the day with friends etc. May I suggest another option for next year? What would make Mom happy????? Flowers, a card, a BBQ. I am not interested in explanations. The only response that I would hear is next year we will do better.

Mom

Considering that by the time of this email exchange Julie was in therapy for an extended period of time and developed insight into her maladaptive family dynamics, she was able to appreciate how this email was indicative of several unhealthy family boundary violations. First, she noted "Why is it our job to make our mother happy?" Julie was also taken by the fact that her mother was once again treating her adult children like little kids and was shutting down any attempt of having an open exchange between the family members.

Feeling encouraged by her successful efforts at reigniting the relationship with her younger brother, Steve, Julie decided to respond to this email with a subtle attempt at opening an honest conversation about the family's situation. In response to the mother's email Julie wrote:

From: Julie

To: Family

Subject: Mother's Day

Is this a general comment/request/demand or a response to an ongoing discussion that I missed the beginning of? I'm not sure I understand where this is coming from.

Julie

As expected, her attempt at communicating openly about her family dynamics in an effort to create harmony between her siblings was met with resistance by her spousified older brother Mark:

From: Mark

To: Family

Subject: Mother's Day

I agree with Mom on all her points. Most importantly I agree that we should not discuss this (as Mom asked). We did wrong, and we have done wrong for the past few years. It is egregious as we were lazy, busy, inconsiderate, etc. It is even more egregious (and stupid), if someone neglected Mother's Day because of some opinion. As Mom asked, the response should be, we are sorry, and we will do better in the future. I think this discussion should end. I respectfully request to be removed from this discussion. Not sure why everyone else besides one person recognized that the only appropriate response was "mea culpa". Regardless, please remove me from further discussions on this topic. As Mom said, she is not interested in excuses. A little respect is in order.

Mark

Julie was not surprised that her older brother was backing their mother without any insight into the unhealthy mentality conveyed by their mother in the initial email. She appreciated the fact that an awareness of the parental context in her sibling dynamics was the catalyst for her to strengthen her relationship with her younger brother. However, Julie feared that, being spousified, her two older siblings were too entrenched with their mother and that her attempts at repairing the relationship with them were not going to be successful. As a last effort she responded to Mark's email:

From: Julie

To: Family

Subject: Mother's Day

You are so right. Mother's Day is meaningful for mom regardless of what it means for us. However, we all would have benefited from an email or phone call from Mom a week ago or even yesterday saying that Mother's Day is very important to her especially since grandma died and a request to acknowledge Mother's Day now and in the future in some way. Instead, Mom responded with an email to her "naughty children" requiring us to reform our ways without talking or communicating. It sounded like a mother scolding her toddlers for misbehaving. We are all adult children now and our relationships with our parents need to reflect that. I think we can show our love and support and appreciation for Mom better if we can have some open communication. I would love to talk about plans for next year or sooner that we can acknowledge

Mom, but it should be done out of love and not fear that we are pissing Mom off or that she is unhappy because of us.

Julie

Julie received the following response from Mark, putting to a close her attempts:

From: Mark

To: Siblings

Subject: Mother's Day

Do you not know how to remove people from an email chain? I've removed Mom & Dad. Did you not realize that your previous email included them? Please remove me as well, from any further emails on this topic.

Mark

Although the focus on the parental context in sibling dynamics can help siblings remove the blame from one another and reconnect, as Julie was able to do with Steve, this situation also demonstrated that in some cases, emphasizing the parental context does not produce results. Where the parental context is profoundly entrenched in the past and in the present, like in cases of continuous spousification, trying to introduce openness to the family system about parental involvement may be met with defensiveness and denial.

Transference issues

The final element of the therapeutic process when using brief psychodynamic interventions with sibling issues is an awareness of sibling transference in therapy. In traditional psychodynamic theory, transference may occur in session when past unresolved parent feelings are reenacted in the here and now of therapy by placing those feelings onto the therapist (Freud, 1938). However, an exclusive focus on parental transference comes at the expense of tending to an additional important transference process that may occur in therapy: that of sibling transference. In sibling transference, which is noted in traditional theoretical psychodynamic literature as well, a client's past, unresolved feelings about a sibling are reenacted in therapy and directed toward the therapist (Edward, 2013; Kivowitz, 1995; Rabin, 1989; Shapiro & Ginzberg, 2001; Sherwin-White, 2007).

Hence, a client shouting at a therapist after a contentious moment, "You are just like my brother," is recreating a sibling-linked dynamic with the therapist. Working with sibling transference requires moving beyond a vertical therapeutic orientation, where transference occurs when unresolved parental issues are placed onto the therapist, to a horizontal orientation, which is the transference onto therapists of a client's unresolved sibling issues (Blessing, 2007; van Beekum, 2013).

When stressing sibling transference instead of parental transference, a therapist can no longer therapeutically use the transferred parental authority dynamic and must contend with being transferred as a peer. In such cases, attending to sibling transference reactions can create an opportunity for exploring sibling-related, unresolved issues such as competency, envy, and rivalry. For example, a client with a competitive sibling relationship commenting to a therapist about his uneasiness with the therapist's career success may be transferring sibling feeling onto the therapist. Exploring those negative feelings toward the therapist in the context of the client's sibling relationship can produce an important and therapeutic dialogue.

Sibling transference can occur in various forms (Agger, 1988). The transference may symbolize the client's past or current sibling relationship, such as when a client comments to a therapist, "You are just like my brother." It may also represent a desired sibling relationship. For example, a client may express warm feelings to a therapist and note that the relationship with the therapist is the opposite of the relationship they have with a sibling. Attending to these transference forces at work can enlighten both the therapeutic relationship and provide a deeper portrait of the underlying sibling tensions (Cabaniss, Cherry, Douglas, & Schwartz, 2011).

Lastly, it is important to attend to sibling countertransference dynamics as well (Edward, 2013; Lesser, 1978). Therapists may have their own unresolved, sibling issues and their reactions to specific actions or comments by their clients may be driven by their own sibling-related complications (Kivowitz, 1995). A therapist taking offense to a client's insult may be responding based on their own feelings of sibling inferiority. Alternatively, desiring affirmation from a client may be a reenactment of an unresolved desire that the therapist has for acknowledgment from a sibling. An awareness of sibling countertransference dynamics in therapy can assist therapists in offering their clients a supportive therapeutic environment free from interferences.

Chapter summary

Brief psychodynamic interventions when integrating sibling issues in therapy can be applied in cases where the sibling issue is the presenting problem, or overt sibling issues. Additionally, it can be applied in cases of covert sibling tensions in which the client enters therapy for other difficulties and an exploration of underlying sibling issues can assist in uncovering core sibling issues that lie beneath the broader tensions. In covert sibling issues, clients entering therapy for numerous psychological problems can gain insight into their difficulties by exploring their early childhood sibling interactions. The therapeutic process for both overt and covert sibling issues entails an exploration of present and past sibling relationships, an examination of past personal identities, revealing the parental context in the sibling relationship, and an awareness of transference and countertransference issues.

References

Abbey, C., & Dallos, R. (2004). The experience of the impact of divorce on sibling relationships: A qualitative study. *Clinical Child Psychology and Psychiatry, 9,* 1359–1045.

Abrams, M. S. (2009). The well sibling: Challenges and possibilities. *American Journal of Psychotherapy, 63,* 305–317.

Achenbach, T. M., & Edelbrock, C. (1983). *Manual for the child behavior checklist and revised child behavior profile.* Burlington, VT: Queen City Printers.

Adler-Baeder, F., & Higginbotham, B. (2004). Implications of remarriage and stepfamily formation for marriage education. *Family Relations, 53,* 448–458.

Agger, E. M. (1988). Psychoanalytic perspectives on sibling relationships. *Psychoanalytic Inquiry, 8,* 3–30.

Ainsworth, M. D. S., & Wittig, B. A. (1969). Attachment and exploratory behavior of one-year-olds in a strange situation. In B. M. Foss (Ed.), *Determinants of infant behavior, 4* (pp. 111–136). London: Methuen.

Ainsworth, M. D. S., Blehar, M. C., Waters, E., & Wall, S. (1978). *Patterns of attachment: A psychological study of the strange situation.* Hillsdale, NJ: Laurence Erlbaum Associates.

Amato, P. R. (1996). Explaining the intergenerational transmission of divorce. *Journal of Marriage and the Family, 58,* 628–640.

Amato, P. R., & Keith, B. (1991). Consequences of parental divorce on children's well-being: A meta-analysis. *Psychological Bulletin, 110,* 26–46.

Ansbacher, H. L., & Ansbacher, R. R. (1956). *The individual psychology of Alfred Adler.* New York: Basic Books.

Arnold, J. E., Levine, A. G., & Patterson, G. R. (1975). Changes in sibling behavior following family intervention. *Journal of Consulting and Clinical Psychology, 43,* 683–688.

Atkinson, A. J., Gonet, P. A., Freundlich, M., & Riley, D. B. (2013). Adoption competent clinical practice: Defining its meaning and development. *Adoption Quarterly, 16,* 156–174.

Avioli, P. S. (1989). The social support functions of siblings in later life. *American Behavioral Scientist, 33,* 45–57.

Banai, E., Mikulincer, M., & Shaver, P. R. (2005). "Selfobject" needs in Kohut's self psychology: Links with attachment, self-cohesion, affect regulation, and adjustment. *Psychoanalytic Psychology, 22,* 224–260.

Bandura, A. (1962). Social learning through imitation. In M. R. Jones (Ed.), *Nebraska symposium on motivation, Vol. 10* (pp. 211–274). Lincoln, NE: University of Nebraska Press.

Bandura, A., & Huston, A. C. (1961). Identification as a process of incidental learning. *Journal of Abnormal and Social Psychology, 65,* 311–318.

Bandura, A., Ross, D., & Ross, A. A. (1963). Comparative test of the status envy, social power, and secondary reinforcement theories of identificatory learning. *Journal of Abnormal and Social Psychology, 67*, 527–534.

Bank, L., Burraston, B., & Snyder, J. (2004). Sibling conflict and ineffective parenting as predictors of adolescent boys' antisocial behavior and peer difficulties: Additive and interactional effects. *Journal of Research on Adolescence, 14*, 99–125.

Bank, L., Patterson, G. R., & Reid, J. B. (1996). Negative sibling interaction patterns as predictors of later adjustment problems in adolescent youth and adult males. In G. H. Brody (Ed.), *Sibling relationships: Their causes and consequences* (pp. 197–229). Westport, CT: Ablex Publishing.

Bank, S. P. (1988). The stolen birthright: The adult sibling in individual therapy. In M. D. Kahn & K. G. Lewis (Eds.), *Siblings in therapy: Life span and clinical issues* (pp. 341–355). New York: Norton.

Bank, S. P. (1992). Remembering and reinterpreting the sibling bond. In F. Boer & J. Dunn (Eds.), *Children's sibling relationships: Developmental and clinical issues* (pp. 139–151). Hillsdale, NJ: Lawrence Erlbaum Associates.

Bank, S. P., & Kahn, M. D. (1982). *The sibling bond.* New York: Basic Books.

Barnes, T. P., & Austin, A. M. B. (1995). The influence of parents and siblings on the development of a personal premise system in middle childhood. *Journal of Genetic Psychology, 156*, 73–85.

Barnett, L. (2005). Keep in touch: The importance of touch in infant development. *Infant Observation, 8*, 115–123.

Bat-Chava, Y., & Martin, D. (2002). Sibling relationships of deaf children: The impact of child and family characteristics. *Rehabilitation Psychology, 47*, 73–91.

Baumrind, D. (1971). Current patterns of parental authority. *Developmental Psychology Monographs, 4*, Part 1.

Beck, J. S. (1995). *Cognitive therapy: Basics and beyond.* New York: Guilford Press.

Beck, J. S. (2005). *Cognitive therapy for challenging problems: What to do when the basics don't work.* New York: Guilford Press.

Beck, J. S. (2011). *Cognitive therapy: Basics and beyond* (2nd ed.). New York: Guilford Press.

Bhavnagri, N., & Parke, R. D. (1991). Parents as direct facilitators of children's peer relationships: Effects of age of child and sex of parent. *Journal of Personal and Social Relationships, 8*, 423–440.

Blasinsky, M. (1998). Family dynamics: Influencing the care of the older adult. *Adaptation and Aging Activities, 22*, 65–72.

Blessing, D. (2007). Hiding in plain sight: The sibling connection in eating disorders. *Journal of Child Psychotherapy, 33*, 36–50.

Boer, F. (1990). *Sibling relationships in middle childhood.* Leiden, Netherlands: University of Leiden Press.

Bossard, J. H. S., & Boll, E. S. (1956). *The large family system.* Philadelphia, PA: University of Pennsylvania Press.

Boszormenyi-Nagy, I., & Spark, G. (1973). *Invisible loyalties: Reciprocity in intergenerational family therapy.* Hagerstown, MD: Harper & Row.

Bowen, M. (1974). Theory in the practice of psychotherapy. In P. J. Guerin (Ed.), *Family therapy: Theory and practice* (pp. 314–342). New York: Gardner Press.

Bowen, M. (1993). *Family therapy in clinical practice.* New York: Jason Aronson.

Bowlby, J. (1969). *Attachment and loss. Vol. 1: Attachment.* New York: Basic Books.

Bowlby, J. (1973). *Attachment and loss. Vol. 2: Separation: Anxiety and anger.* New York: Basic Books.

Bowlby, J. (1977). The making and breaking of affectionate bonds. *British Journal of Psychiatry, 130,* 201–210.

Bowlby, J. (1980). *Attachment and loss. Vol. 3: Loss.* New York: Basic Books.

Branje, S., van Lieshout, C., Van Aken, M., & Haselager, G. (2004). Perceived support in sibling relationships and adolescent adjustment. *Journal of Child Psychology and Psychiatry, 45,* 1385–1396.

Bratton, S., & Ray, D. (1999). Group puppetry. In D. Sweeney & L. Homeyer (Eds.), *The handbook of group play* (pp. 86–104). San Francisco, CA: Jossey-Bass.

Brody, G. H., Stoneman, Z., & Burke, M. (1987). Child temperaments, maternal differential behavior, and sibling relationships. *Developmental Psychology, 23,* 354–362.

Brody, G. H., Stoneman, Z., & McCoy, J. K. (1992). Parental differential treatment of siblings and sibling differences in negative emotionality. *Journal of Marriage and the Family, 54,* 643–651.

Brody, L. R., Copeland, A. P., Sutton, L. S., Richardson, D. R., & Guyer, M. (1998). Mommy and daddy like you best: Perceived family favoritism in relation to affect, adjustment and family process. *Journal of Family Therapy, 20,* 269–291.

Bronfenbrenner, U. (1972). *Two worlds of childhood: U.S. and U.S.S.R.* New York: Simon and Schuster.

Bronfenbrenner, U. (1979). *The ecology of human development.* Cambridge, MA: Harvard University Press.

Brotman, L., Dawson-McClure, S., Gouley, K., McGuire, K., Burraston, B., & Bank, L. (2005). Older siblings benefit from a family-based preventive intervention for preschoolers at risk for conduct problems. *Journal of Family Psychology, 19,* 581–591.

Bryant, B. K., & Crockenberg, S. (1980). Correlates and dimensions of prosocial behavior: A study of female siblings with their mothers. *Child Development, 51,* 529–544.

Buhrmester, D. (1992). The developmental courses of sibling and peer relationships. In F. Boer & J. Dunn (Eds.), *Children's sibling relationships: Developmental and clinical issues* (pp. 19–40). Hillsdale, NJ: Lawrence Erlbaum Associates.

Buhrmester, D., & Furman, W. (1990). Perceptions of sibling relationships during middle childhood and adolescence. *Child Development, 61,* 1387–1398.

Buist, K. L. (2010). Sibling relationship quality and adolescent delinquency: A latent growth curve approach. *Journal of Family Psychology, 24,* 400–410.

Buist, K. L., Dekovic, M., & Gerris, J. R. M. (2011). Dyadic family relationships and adolescent internalizing and externalizing problem behavior: Effects of positive and negative affect. *Family Science, 2,* 34–42.

Burke, P. (2010). Brothers and sisters of disabled children: The experience of disability by association. *British Journal of Social Work, 40,* 1681–1699.

Butterworth, M. D., & Fulmer, K. A. (1991). The effect of family violence on children: Intervention strategies including bibliotherapy. *Australian Journal of Marriage and Family, 12,* 170–182.

Byng-Hall, J. (2008). The significance of children fulfilling parental roles: Implications for family therapy. *Journal of Family Therapy, 30,* 147–162.

Cabaniss, D. L., Cherry, S., Douglas, C. J., & Schwartz, A. R. (2011). *Psychodynamic psychotherapy: A clinical manual.* New York: Wiley.

Caffaro, J. V., & Conn-Caffaro, A. (2003). Sibling dynamics and group psychotherapy. *International Journal of Group Psychotherapy, 53,* 135–154.

Carroll, J. J., & Robinson, B. E. (2000). Depression and parentification among adults as related to parental workaholism and alchoholism. *The Family Journal: Counseling and Therapy for Couples and Families, 8,* 360–367.

Caughlin, J. P., Koerner, A. F., Schrodt, P., & Fitzpatrick, M. A. (2011). Interpersonal communication in family relationships. In M. L. Knapp & J. A. Daly (Eds.), *The Sage handbook of interpersonal communication* (4th ed., pp. 679–714). Thousand Oaks, CA: Sage.

Chase, N. D., Deming, M. P., & Wells, M. C. (1998). Parentification, parental alcoholism, and academic status among young adults. *The American Journal of Family Therapy, 26,* 105–114.

Chengappa, K., Stokes, J. O., Costello, A. H., Norman, M. A., Travers, R. M., & McNeil, C. B. (2013). Parent–child interaction therapy for severe sibling conflict in young children. *Journal of Communications Research, 5,* 31–47.

Cicirelli, V. G. (1980). A comparison of college women's feelings toward their siblings and parents. *Journal of Marriage and the Family, 42,* 111–118.

Cicirelli, V. G. (1982). Sibling influence throughout the lifespan. In M. E. Lamb & B. Sutton-Smith (Eds.), *Sibling relationships: Their nature and significance across the lifespan* (pp. 267–284). Hillsdale, NJ: Lawrence Erlbaum Associates.

Cicirelli, V. G. (1989). Feelings of attachment to sibling and well-being in later life. *Psychology and Aging, 4,* 211–216.

Cicirelli, V. G. (1991). Sibling relationships in adulthood. *Marriage and Family Review, 16,* 291–310.

Cicirelli, V. G. (1995). *Sibling relationships across the life span.* New York: Plenum Press.

Coale, H. W. (1999). Therapeutic rituals and rites of passage: Helping parentified children and their families. In N. Chase (Ed.), *Burdened children: Theory, research, and treatment of parentification* (pp. 132–140). Thousand Oaks, CA: Sage.

Cole, A., & Kerns, K. A. (2001). Perceptions of sibling qualities and activities of early adolescents. *Journal of Early Adolescence, 21*, 204–226.

Coles, P. (2003). *The importance of sibling relationships in psychoanalysis.* London: Karnac Books.

Coles, P. (2007). Transgenerational conflicts between sisters. *British Journal of Psychotherapy, 23*, 562–574.

Colonna, A., & Newman, L. (1983). Psychoanalytic literature on siblings. *Psychoanalytic Study of the Child, 38*, 285–309.

Conley, D. (2004). *The pecking order: Which siblings succeed and why.* New York: Pantheon Books.

Cornell, D. G. & Grossberg, I. N. (1986). Siblings of children in a gifted program. *Journal for the Education of the Gifted, 9*, 253–264.

Cox, J. E., DuRant, R. H., Emans, S. J., & Woods, E. R. (1995). Early parenthood for the sisters of adolescent mothers: A proposed conceptual model of decision making. *Adolescent and Pediatric Gynecology, 8*, 188–194.

Creek, M. (2009). Mental health strategies to support sibling relationships: Nonverbal interventions to process trauma and maintain the sibling bond. In D. N. Silverstein, S. L. Smith, D. N. Silverstein, & S. L. Smith (Eds.), *Siblings in adoption and foster care: Traumatic separations and honored connections* (pp. 139–152). Westport, CT: Praeger Publishers/Greenwood Publishing Group.

Criss, M., & Shaw, D. (2005). Sibling relationships as contexts for delinquency training in low-income families. *Journal of Family Psychology, 19*, 592–600.

Crumbley, J., & Little, R. L. (1997). *Relatives raising children: An overview of kinship care.* Washington, DC: Child Welfare League of America Press.

Cummings, E. M., & Davies, P. T. (2010). *Marital conflict and children: An emotional security perspective.* New York: Guilford Press.

Cuornos, F. (2003). Lessons for high-risk populations from attachment research and September 11: Helping children in foster care. In S. W. Coates, J. L. Rosenthal, & D. S. Schechter (Eds.), *September 11: Trauma and human bonds* (pp. 255–272). Hillsdale, NJ: Analytic Press.

Dattilio, F. M. (1993). Cognitive techniques with couples and families. *The Family Journal, 1*, 51–65.

Dattilio, F. M. (2013). *Cognitive-behavioral therapy with couples and families: A comprehensive guide for clinicians.* New York: Guilford Press.

David-Ferdon, C., & Hertz, M. F. (2007). Electronic media, violence, and adolescents: An emerging public health problem. *Journal of Adolescent Health, 41*, S1–S5.

Davis, K., & Gavidia-Payne, S. (2009). The impact of child, family, and professional support characteristics on the quality of life in families of young children with disabilities. *Journal of Intellectual and Developmental Disability, 34*, 153–162.

Day, R., & Lamb, M. (2004). Conceptualizing and measuring father involvement: Pathways, problems and progress. In R. Day & M. Lamb (Eds.), *Conceptualizing and measuring father involvement* (pp. 1–15). Hillsdale, NJ: Lawrence Erlbaum Associates.

DeRosier, M. E., & Kupersmidt, J. B. (1991). Costa Rican children's perceptions of their social networks. *Developmental Psychology, 27,* 656–662.

Dew, A., Llewellyn, G., & Balandin, S. (2004). Post-parental care: A new generation of sibling-carers. *Journal of Intellectual and Developmental Disability, 29,* 176–179.

Dishion, T. J., & Stormshak, E. (2007). *Intervening in children's lives: An ecological, family centered approach to mental health care.* Washington, DC: American Psychological Association.

Doherty, W. J., & Beaton, J. M. (2004). Mothers and fathers parenting together. In A. Vangelisti (Ed.), *Handbook of family communication* (pp. 269–286). Mahwah, NJ: Lawrence Erlbaum Associates.

Donley, M. G., & Likins, L. (2010). The multigenerational impact of sibling relationships. *The American Journal of Family Therapy, 38,* 383–396.

Dowling, E., & Gorell-Barnes, G. (2000). *Working with children and parents through separation and divorce.* Basingstoke: Macmillan.

Downey, D. B., & Condron, D. J. (2004). Playing well with others in kindergarten: The benefit of siblings at home. *Journal of Marriage and Family, 66,* 333–350.

Dreikurs, R. (1964). *Children: The challenge.* New York: Hawthorne.

Duhn, L. (2010). The importance of touch in the development of attachment. *Advances in Neonatal Care, 10,* 294–300.

Duncan, G. J., & Yeung, W. J. (1995). Extent and consequences of welfare dependence among America's children. *Children and Youth Services Review, 17,* 157–182.

Dunn, J. (1983). Sibling relations in early childhood. *Child Development, 54,* 787–811.

Dunn, J. (2000). State of the art: Siblings. *Psychologist, 13,* 244–248.

Dunn, J., Brown, J. R., & Maguire, M. (1995). The development of children's moral sensibility: Individual differences and emotional understanding. *Developmental Psychology, 31,* 649–659.

Dunn, J., Brown, J. R., Slomkowski, C., Telsa, C., & Youngblade, L. M. (1991). Young children's understanding of other people's feelings and beliefs: Individual differences and their antecedents. *Child Development, 62,* 1352–1366.

Dunn, J., Deater-Deckard, K., Pickering, K., Golding, J., & the ALSPAC Study Team. (1999). Siblings, parents, and partners: Family relationships within a longitudinal community study. *Journal of Child Psychology and Psychiatry, 40,* 1025–1037.

Dunn, J., & Kendrick, C. (1982). *Sibling: Love, envy, and understanding.* Cambridge, MA: Harvard University Press.

Dunn, J., & McGuire, S. (1994). Young children's nonshared experiences: A summary of studies in Cambridge and Colorado. In E. M. Hetherington, D. Reiss, & R. Plomin (Eds.), *Separate social worlds of siblings: The impact of nonshared environment on development* (pp. 111–128). Hillsdale, NJ: Lawrence Erlbaum Associates.

Dunn, J., & Plomin, R. (1990). *Separate lives: Why siblings are so different.* New York: Basic Books.

Dunn, J., Slomkowski, C., & Beardsall, L. (1994). Sibling relationships from the preschool period through middle childhood and early adolescence. *Developmental Psychology, 30,* 315–324.

Dupuis, S. B. (2007). Examining remarriage: A look at issues affecting remarried couples and the implications towards therapeutic techniques. *Journal of Divorce and Remarriage, 48,* 91–104.

Dusenbury, L., & Falco, M. (1997). Nine critical elements of promising violence prevention programs. *Journal of School Health, 67,* 409–415.

East, P. L. (1998). Impact of adolescent childbearing on families and younger siblings: Effects that increase younger siblings' risk for early pregnancy. *Applied Developmental Science, 2,* 62–74.

East, P. L., & Khoo, S. (2005). Longitudinal pathways linking family factors and sibling relationship qualities to adolescent substance use and sexual risk behaviors. *Journal of Family Psychology, 19,* 571–580.

East, P. L., & Rook, K. S. (1992). Compensatory patterns of support among children's peer relationships: A test using school friends, nonschool friend and siblings. *Developmental Psychology, 28,* 163–172.

Edward, J. (2013). Sibling discord: A force for growth and conflict. *Clinical Social Work Journal, 41,* 77–83.

Eisenberg, A. R. (2004). Grandchildren's perspectives on relationships with grandparents: The influence of gender across generations. *Sex Roles, 19,* 205–217.

Elstein, S. G. (1999). Making decisions about siblings in the child welfare system. *Child Law Practice, 18,* 101–108.

Erel, O., Margoline, G., & John, R. S. (1998). Observed sibling interaction: Links with the marital and the mother–child relationship. *Developmental Psychology, 34,* 288–298.

Evans, J., & Rodger, S. (2008). Routines or rituals: Mealtimes and bedtimes as key family occupations. *Journal of Occupational Science, 15,* 98–104.

Eyberg, S. (1988). Parent–child interaction therapy: Integration of traditional and behavioral concerns. *Child & Family Behavior Therapy, 10,* 33–46.

Faber, A., & Mazlish, E. (2012). *Siblings without rivalry: How to help your children live together so you can live too.* New York: Norton.

Faber, A. J. (2004). Examining remarried couples through a Bowenian family systems lens. *Journal of Divorce and Remarriage, 40,* 121–133.

Falconer, C. W., & Ross, C. A. (1988). The tilted family. In M. D. Kahn & K. G. Lewis (Eds.), *Siblings in therapy: Life span and clinical issues* (pp. 273–296). New York: Norton.

Falconer, C. W., Wilson, K. G., & Falconer, J. (1990). A psychometric investigation of gender-tilted families: Implications for family therapy. *Family Relations, 39,* 8–13.

Falicov, J. C. (1998). The cultural meaning of family triangles. In M. McGoldrick (Ed.), *Revisioning family therapy* (pp. 282–294). New York: Guilford Press.

Feinberg, M. E., & Hetherington, E. M. (2000). Sibling differentiation in adolescence: Implications for behavioral genetic theory. *Child Development, 71,* 1512–1524.

Feinberg, M. E., McHale, S., Crouter, A., & Cumsille, P. (2003). Sibling differentiation: Sibling and parent relationship trajectories in adolescence. *Child Development, 74,* 1261–1274.

Feinberg, M. E., Reiss, D., Neiderhiser, J. M., & Hetherington, E. M. (2005). Differential association of family subsystem negativity on siblings' maladjustment: Using behavior genetic methods to test process theory. *Journal of Family Psychology, 19,* 601–610.

Feinman, S., & Lewis, M. (1983). Social referencing and second order effect in ten-month-old infants. *Child Development, 54,* 878–887.

Felson, R. B. (1983). Aggression and violence between siblings. *Social Psychology Quarterly, 46,* 271–285.

Fiese, B., Hooker, K., Kotary, L., & Schwagler, J. (1993). Family rituals in the early stages of parenthood. *Journal of Marriage and the Family, 55,* 633–642.

Finzi-Dottan, R., & Cohen, O. (2010). Young adult sibling relations: The effects of perceived parental favoritism and narcissism. *The Journal of Psychology: Interdisciplinary and Applied, 145,* 1–22.

Fishman, H. C. (1993). *Intensive structural therapy: Treating families in their social context.* New York: Basic Books.

Floyd, F. J., & Gallagher, E. M. (1997). Parental stress, care demands, and use of support services for school-age children with disabilities and behavior problems. *Family Relations, 46,* 359–371.

Freud, A., & Dann, S. (1951). An experiment in group upbringing. *Psychoanalytic Study of the Child, 6,* 127–168.

Freud, S. (1900). *The interpretation of dreams.* New York: Basic Book (Avon), 1965.

Freud, S. (1938). *An outline of psychoanalysis.* London: Hogarth.

Freud, S. (1955). Group psychology and the analysis of the ego. In J. Strachey (Ed. & Trans.), *The standard edition of the complete psychological works of Sigmund Freud* (Vol. 18, pp. 65–143). London: Hogarth.

Friedberg, R. D., McClure, J. M., & Hillwig-Garcia, J. (2009). *Cognitive therapy techniques for children and adolescents: Tools for enhancing practice.* New York: Guilford Press.

Furman, W., & Buhrmester, D. (1985). Children's perceptions of the personal relationships in their social networks. *Developmental Psychology, 21,* 1016–1024.

Furman, W., & Giberson, R. S. (1995). Identifying the links between parents and their children's sibling relationships. In S. Shulman (Ed.), *Close relationships and socioemotional development* (pp. 95–108). Norwood, NJ: Ablex.

Furman, W., & Lanthier, R. (1996). Personality and sibling relationships. In G. H. Brody (Ed.), *Sibling relationships: Their causes and consequences* (pp. 127–146). Westport, CT: Ablex Publishing.

Gallo, A., Breitmayer, B., Knafl, K., & Zoeller, L. (1991). Stigma in childhood chronic illness: A well siblings perspective. *Pediatric Nursing, 17,* 42–48.

Garcia, M. M., Shaw, D. S., Winslow, E. B., & Yaggi, K. E. (2000). Destructive sibling conflict and the development of conduct problems in young boys. *Developmental Psychology, 36,* 44–53.

Giallo, R., & Gavidia-Payne, S. (2006). Child, parent and family factors as predictors of adjustment for siblings of children with a disability. *Journal of Intellectual Disability Research, 50,* 937–948.

Giallo, R., Gavidia-Payne, S., Minett, B., & Kapoor, A. (2012). Sibling voices: The self-reported mental health of siblings of children with a disability. *Clinical Psychologist, 16,* 36–43.

Gnaulati, E. (2002). Extending the uses of sibling therapy with children and adolescents. *Psychotherapy: Theory, Research, Practice, Training, 39,* 76–87.

Gold, D. T. (1987). Siblings in old age: Something special. *The Canadian Journal on Aging, 6,* 211–227.

Goldenberg, H., & Goldenberg, I. (2012). *Family therapy: An overview.* New York: Cengage Learning.

Goldenthal, P. (2002). *Why can't we get along: Healing adult sibling relationships.* New York: Wiley.

Goleman, D. (2006). *Emotional intelligence.* New York: Bantam Books.

Gonzales, J. (2009). Prefamily counseling: Working with blended families. *Journal of Divorce and Remarriage, 50,* 148–157.

Gonzalez, A., Holbein, M., & Quilter, S. (2002). High school students' goal orientations and their relationship to perceived parenting styles. *Contemporary Educational Psychology, 27,* 450–471.

Goodwin, M., & Roscoe, B. (1990). Sibling violence and agonistic interactions among middle adolescents. *Adolescence, 25,* 451–467.

Gottman, J. M. (1997). *Raising an emotionally intelligent child.* New York: Simon and Schuster.

Gottman, J. M., & Krokoff, L. J. (1989). Marital interaction and satisfaction: A longitudinal view. *Journal of Consulting and Clinical Psychology, 57,* 47–52.

Gottman, J. M., & Levenson, R. W. (2002). A two-factor model for predicting when a couple will divorce: Exploratory analyses using 14-year longitudinal data. *Family Process, 41,* 83–96.

Groenendyk, A. E., & Volling, B. L. (2007). Coparenting and early conscience development in the family. *The Journal of Genetic Psychology, 168,* 201–224.

Grotevant, H. (1978). Sibling constellations and sex-typing of interests in adolescence. *Child Development, 49,* 540–542.

Groza, V., Maschmeier, C., Jamison, C., & Piccola, T. (2003). Siblings and out-of-home placement: Best practices. *Families in Society: The Journal of Contemporary Human Services, 84,* 480–490.

Guite, J., Lobato, D., Kao, B., & Plante, W. (2004). Discordance between sibling and parent reports of the impact of chronic illness and disability on siblings. *Children's Health Care, 33,* 77–92.

Hai-Yahia, M., & Dawud-Noursi, S. (1998). Predicting the use of different conflict tactics among Arab siblings in Israel: A study based on social learning theory. *Journal of Family Violence, 13,* 81–102.

Harmer Cox, A., Marshell, E., Mandlesco, B., & Olsen, S. (2003). Coping responses to daily life stressors of children who have a sibling with a disability. *Journal of Family Nursing, 9*, 397–413.

Harris, K. M., & Morgan, S. P. (1991). Fathers, sons, and daughters. Differential paternal involvement in parenting. *Journal of Marriage and the Family, 53*, 531–544.

Harvey, J. B. (1974). The Abilene paradox: The management of agreement. *Organizational Dynamics, 3*, 63–80.

Hasday, J. E. (2012). Siblings in law. *Vanderbilt Law Review, 65*, 897–931.

Hastings, R. P. (2003). Brief report: Behavioral adjustment of siblings of children with autism. *Journal of Autism and Developmental Disorders, 33*, 99–104.

Healey, M. D., & Ellis, B. J. (2007). Birth order, conscientiousness, and openness to experience: Tests of the family-niche model of personality using a within-family methodology. *Evolution and Human Behavior, 28*, 55–59.

Hequembourg, A., & Brallier, S. (2005). Gendered stories of parental caregiving among siblings. *Journal of Aging Studies, 19*, 53–71.

Hetherington, E. M. (1988). Parents, children and siblings: Six years after divorce. In R. A. Hinde & J. Stevenson-Hinde (Eds.), *Relationships within families: Mutual influences* (pp. 311–331). Oxford: Oxford University Press.

Hetherington, E. M. (1989). Coping with family transition: Winners, losers, and survivors. *Child Development, 60*, 1–14.

Hinde, R. A. (1979). *Towards understanding relationships*. London: Academic Press.

Hooper, L. M., & Doehler, K. (2012). Assessing family caregiving: A comparison of three retrospective parentification measures. *Journal of Marital and Family Therapy, 38*, 653–666.

Hooper, L. M., Marotta, S. A., & Lanthier, R. P. (2008). Predictors of growth and distress following parentification among college students. *Journal of Child and Family Studies, 17*, 693–705.

Hunter, L. (1993). Sibling play therapy with homeless children: An opportunity in the crisis. *Child Welfare, 72*, 65–75.

Ingoldsby, E. M., Shaw, D. S., Owens, E. B., & Winslow, E. B. (1999). A longitudinal study of interparental conflict, emotional and behavioral reactivity, and preschoolers' adjustment problems among low-income families. *Journal of Abnormal Child Psychology, 27*, 343–356.

Jacobson, E. (1964). *The self and the object world*. New York: International Universities Press.

Jenkins, J. (1992). Sibling relationships in disharmonious homes: Potential difficulties and protective effects. In F. Boer & J. Dunn (Eds.), *Children's sibling relationships: Developmental and clinical issues* (pp. 125–138). Hillsdale, NJ: Lawrence Erlbaum Associates.

Jenkins, J., Dunn, J., O'Connor, T., Rasbash, J., & Behnke, P. (2005). Change in maternal perception of sibling negativity: Within- and between-family influences. *Journal of Family Psychology, 19*, 533–541.

Jensen, A. C., Whiteman, S. D., Fingerman, K. L., & Birditt, K. S. (2013). "Life still isn't fair": Parental differential treatment of young adult siblings. *Journal of Marriage and Family, 75*, 438–452.

Johnson, S. M. (2008). Emotionally focused couple therapy. In A. S. Gurman (Ed.), *Clinical handbook of couple therapy* (4th ed., pp. 107–137). New York: Guilford Press.

Jones, R. A., & Wells, M. (1996). An empirical study of parentification and personality. *The American Journal of Family Therapy, 24*, 145–163.

Jurkovic, G. J. (1997) *Lost childhoods: The plight of the parentified child.* New York: Brunner/Mazel.

Jurkovic, G. J., Thirkield, A., & Morrell, R. (2001). Parentification of adult children of divorce: A multidimensional analysis. *Journal of Youth and Adolescence, 30*, 245–157.

Kahn, M. D. (1988). Intense sibling relationships: A self-psychological view. In M. D. Kahn & K. G. Lewis (Eds.), *Siblings in therapy: Life span and clinical issues* (pp. 3–24). New York: Norton.

Kahn, M. D., & Lewis, K. G. (1988). *Siblings in therapy.* New York: Norton.

Kahn, S. (1982). Remembering and reinterpreting sibling bonds. In F. Boer & J. Dunn (Eds.), *Children's sibling relationships: Developmental and clinical issues* (pp. 139–151). Hillsdale, NJ: Lawrence Erlbaum Associates.

Karavasilis, L., Doyle, A., & Markiewicz, D. (2003). Associations between parenting style and attachment to mother in middle childhood and adolescence. *International Journal of Behavioral Development, 27*, 153–164.

Karreman, A., van Tuijl, C., van Aken, M. A., & Dekovic, M. (2008). Parenting, coparenting, and effortful control in preschoolers. *Journal of Family Psychology, 22*, 30–40.

Kauffman, D., Gaston, E., Santa Lucia, R., Salcedo, O., Rendina-Gobioff, G., & Gadd, R. (2000). The relationship between parenting style and children's adjustment: The parents' perspective. *Journal of Child and Family Studies, 9*, 231–245.

Kerr, M. E., & Bowen, M. (1988). *Family evaluation.* New York: Norton.

Khoo, S. T., & Muthén, B. (2000). Longitudinal data on families: Growth modeling alternatives. In J. S. Rose, L. Chassin, C. C. Presson, & S. J. Sherman (Eds.), *Multivariate applications in substance use research: New methods for new questions* (pp. 43–78). Hillsdale, New Jersey: Lawrence Erlbaum Associates.

Kim, J., McHale, S., Osgood, D., & Crouter, A. (2006). Longitudinal course and family correlates of sibling relationships from childhood through adolescence. *Child Development, 77*, 1746–1761.

Kivowitz, A. (1995). Attending to sibling issues and transferences in psychodynamic psychotherapy. *Clinical Social Work Journal, 23*, 37–46.

Klein, N. C., Alexander, J. F., & Parsons, B. V. (1977). Impact of family systems interventions on recidivism and sibling delinquency: A model of primary prevention and program evaluation. *Journal of Consulting and Clinical Psychology, 45*, 469–474.

Knapp, M. L., Vangelisti, A. L., & Caughlin, J. P. (2013) *Interpersonal communication and human relationships* (7th ed.). Boston, MA: Pearson.

Kohut, H. (1971). *Analysis of the self*. New York: International Universities Press.

Kowal, A. K., & Kramer, L. (1997). Children's under-standing of parental differential treatment. *Child Development, 68,* 113–126.

Kowal, A. K., Kramer, L., Krull, J. L., & Crick, N. R. (2002). Children's perceptions of the fairness of parental preferential treatment and their socioemotional well-being. *Journal of Family Psychology, 16,* 297–306.

Kowal, A. K., Krull, J. L., & Kramer, L. (2006). Shared understanding of parental differential treatment in families. *Social Development, 15,* 276–295.

Kramer, L., & Kowal, A. K. (2005) Sibling relationship quality from birth to adolescence: The enduring contributions of friends. *Journal of Family Psychology, 19,* 503–511.

Kramer, L., Perozynski, L. A., & Chung, T. (1999). Parental responses to sibling conflict: The effects of development and parent gender. *Child Development, 70,* 1401–1414.

Ladd, G. W., & Golter, B. S. (1988). Parents' management of preschoolers' peer relations: Is it related to children's social acceptance? *Developmental Psychology, 24,* 109–117.

Lam, C. B., Solmeyer, A. R., & McHale, S. M. (2012). Sibling relationships and empathy across the transition to adolescence. *Journal of Youth and Adolescence, 41,* 1657–1670.

Lamb, M. E. (1986). *The father's role: Applied perspectives*. New York: Wiley.

Lanthier, R., Stocker, C., & Furman, W. (2001). Adult Sibling Relationship Questionnaire. In J. Touliatos, B. F. Perlmutter, & G. W. Holden (Eds.), *Handbook of family measurement techniques* (Vol. 2, pp. 53–54). Thousand Oaks, CA: Sage Publications.

Larson, E. (2006). Caregiving and autism: How does children's propensity for routinization influence participation in family activities? *The Occupational Therapy Journal of Research: Occupation, Participation and Health, 26,* 69–79.

Laursen, B., Finkelstein, B. D., & Betts, N. T. (2001). A developmental meta-analysis of peer conflict resolution. *Developmental Review, 21,* 423–449.

Leahy, R. L. (2003). *Cognitive therapy techniques: A practitioner's guide*. New York: Guilford Press.

Leavit, K. S., Gardner, S. A., Gallagher, M. M., & Schamess, G. (1998). Severely traumatized siblings: A treatment strategy. *Clinical Social Work Journal, 26,* 55–71.

Lesser, R. M. (1978). Sibling transference and countertransference. *Journal of the American Academy of Psychoanalysis, 6,* 37–49.

Levitt, J. A., Levitt, M., & Levitt, J. (2001). *Sibling revelry: 8 steps to successful adult sibling relationships*. New York: Dell Publishing.

Levitt, M. J. (1991). Attachment and close relationships: A life-span perspective. In J. L. Gewirtz & W. M. Kurtines (Eds.), *Intersections with attachment* (pp. 183–205). Hillsdale, NJ: Lawrence Erlbaum Associates.

Levitt, M. J., Guacci, N., & Coffman, S. (1993). Social networks in infancy: An observational study. *Merrill-Palmer Quarterly, 39*, 233–251.

Levitt, M. J., Guacci-Franco, N., & Levitt, J. L. (1993). Convoys of social support in childhood and early adolescence: Structure and function. *Developmental Psychology, 29*, 811–818.

Lewin, V., & Sharp, B. (2009). *Siblings in development: A psychoanalytical view.* London: Karnac Books.

Lewis, K. G. (1988). Young siblings in brief therapy. In M. D. Kahn & K. G. Lewis (Eds.), *Siblings in therapy: Life span and clinical issues* (pp. 93–114). New York: Norton.

Lewis, K. G. (1995). Sibling therapy: One step in breaking the cycle of recidivism in foster care. In L. Combrinck-Graham (Ed.), *Children in families at risk: Maintaining the connections* (pp. 301–325). New York: Guilford Press.

Lewis, M. (1994). Does attachment imply a relationship or multiple relationships? *Psychological Inquiry, 5*, 47–51.

Linares, L. O., Li, M., Shrout, P., Brody, G., & Pettit, G. (2007). Placement shift, sibling relationship quality, and child outcomes in foster care: A controlled study. *Journal of Family Psychology, 21*, 736–743.

Lobato, D., Kao, B., & Plante, W. (2005). Latino sibling knowledge and adjustment to chronic disability. *Journal of Family Psychology, 19*, 625–632.

Lockwood, R. L., Gaylord, N., Kitzmann, K., & Cohen, R. (2002). Family stress and children's rejection by peers: Do siblings provide a buffer? *Journal of Child and Family Studies, 11*, 331–345.

Lockwood, R. L., Kitzmann, K. M., & Cohen, R. (2001). The impact of sibling warmth and conflict on children's social competence with peers. *Child Study Journal, 31*, 47–69.

MacKinnon, C. (1989). An observational investigation of sibling interaction in married and divorced families. *Developmental Psychology, 25*, 36–44.

Macks, R. J., & Reeve, R. E. (2007). The adjustment of non-disabled siblings of children with autism. *Journal of Autism and Developmental Disorders, 37*, 1060–1067.

Maguire-Pavao, J., St. John, M., Ford-Cannole, R., Fischer, T., Maluccio, A., & Peining, S. (2007). Sibling kinnections: A clinical visitation program. *Child Welfare, 86*, 13–30.

Margolin, G., Christensen, A., & John, R. S. (1996). The continuance and spillover of everyday tensions in distressed and nondistressed families. *Journal of Family Psychology, 10*, 304–321.

Margolin, G., Gordis, E. B., & John, R. S. (2001). Coparenting: A link between marital conflict and parenting in two-parent families. *Journal of Family Psychology, 15*, 3–21.

Marks, S. U., Matson, A., & Barraza, L. (2005). The impact of sibling with disabilities on their brothers and sisters pursuing a career in special education. *Research and Practice for Persons with Severe Disabilities, 30*, 205–218.

Marquenie, K., Rodger, S., Mangohig, K., & Cronin, A. (2011). Dinnertime and bedtime routines and rituals in families with a young child with an autism spectrum disorder. *Australian Occupational Therapy Journal, 58*, 145–154.

Martin-Uzzi, M., & Duval-Tsioles, D. (2013). The experience of remarried couples in blended families. *Journal of Divorce and Remarriage, 54,* 43–57.

Maynard, A. E. (2002). Cultural teaching: The development of teaching skills in Maya sibling interactions. *Child Development, 73,* 969–982.

McCubbin, H., McCubbin, M., Thompson, A., Han, S., & Allen, C. (1997). Families under stress: What makes them resilient. *Journal of Family and Consumer Sciences, 89,* 2–11.

McCubbin, H., Thompson, A., & McCubbin, M. (1996). *Family assessment: Resiliency, coping and adaptation.* Madison, WI: University of Wisconsin Publishers.

McElwain, N. L., & Volling, B. L. (2005). Preschool children's interactions with friends and older siblings: Relationship specificity and joint contributions to problem behavior. *Journal of Family Psychology, 19,* 486–496.

McGarvey, T. P., & Haen, C. (2005). Intervention strategies for treating traumatized siblings on a pediatric inpatient unit. *American Journal of Orthopsychiatry, 75,* 395–408.

McGhee, J. L. (1985). The effects of siblings on the life satisfaction of the rural elderly. *Journal of Marriage and the Family, 47,* 85–91.

McHale, S. M., Updegraff, K. A., Helms-Erikson, H., & Crouter, A. C. (2001). Sibling influences on gender development in middle childhood and early adolescence: A longitudinal study. *Developmental Psychology, 37,* 115–125.

McHale, S. M., Updegraff, K. A., Tucker, C. J., & Crouter, A. C. (2000). Step in or stay out? Parents' roles in adolescent siblings' relationships. *Journal of Marriage and the Family, 62,* 746–761.

McKinney, C., Milone, M. C., & Renk, K. (2011). Parenting and late adolescent emotional adjustment: Effects of discipline and gender. *Child Psychiatry and Human Development, 42,* 463–481.

McNeil, C., & Hembree-Kigin, T. L. (2010). *Parent–child interaction therapy* (2nd ed.). New York: Springer Science/Business Media.

Meyer, D. J., & Vadasy, P. F. (2008). *Sibshops: Workshops for siblings of children with special needs.* Baltimore, MD: Brookes Publishing.

Milevsky, A. (2004). Perceived parental marital satisfaction and divorce: Effects on sibling relations in emerging adults. *Journal of Divorce and Remarriage, 41,* 115–128.

Milevsky, A. (2005). Compensatory patterns of sibling support in emerging adulthood: Variations in loneliness, self-esteem, depression and life satisfaction. *Journal of Social and Personal Relationships, 22,* 743–755.

Milevsky, A. (2011). *Sibling relationships in childhood and adolescence: Predictors and outcomes.* New York: Columbia University Press.

Milevsky, A., & Heerwagen, M. (2013). A phenomenological examination of sibling relationships in emerging adulthood. *Marriage and Family Review, 49,* 251–263.

Milevsky, A., & Levitt, M. J. (2005). Sibling support in early adolescence: Buffering and compensation across relationships. *European Journal of Developmental Psychology, 2,* 299–320.

Milevsky, A., & Rodriguez, A. N. (2015, May). *Development of the Parenting Enjoyment Scale (PES)*. Paper presented at the meeting of the Association for Psychological Sciences, New York, NY.

Milevsky, A., Schlechter, M., Klem, L., & Kehl, R. (2008). Constellations of maternal and paternal parenting styles in adolescence: Congruity and adjustment. *Marriage and Family Review, 44*, 81–98.

Milevsky, A., Schlechter, M. J., Klem, L., Edelman, J., Kiphorn, M., & Anrico, H. (2007, March). *Qualitative and quantitative variations in adolescent sibling relationships*. Symposium presented at the meeting of the Eastern Psychological Association, Philadelphia, PA.

Milevsky, A., Schlechter, M. J., & Machlev, M. (2011). Effects of parenting style and involvement in sibling conflict on adolescent sibling relationships. *Journal of Social and Personal Relationships, 28*, 1130–1148.

Milevsky, A., Schlechter, M. J., Netter, S. A., & Keehn, D. (2007). Maternal and paternal parenting styles in adolescents: Associations with self-esteem, depression and life-satisfaction. *Journal of Child and Family Studies, 16*, 39–47.

Milevsky, A., Thudium, K., & Guldin, J. (2014). *The transitory nature of parental, sibling, and romantic partner relationships in emerging adulthood*. Springer Briefs series in Well-Being Research and Quality of Life Studies.

Milevsky, A., Thudium, K., Milevsky, I. M., & Roth, B. (2013, March). *Cross-cultural variations in parenting challenges*. Paper presented at the meeting of the Eastern Psychological Association, New York.

Minnett, A. M., Vandell, D. L., & Santrock, J. W. (1983). The effects of sibling status on sibling interaction: Influence of birth order, age spacing, sex of child, and sex of sibling. *Child Development, 54*, 1064–1072.

Minuchin, S. (1974). *Families and family therapy*. London: Tavistock.

Minuchin, S. (1981). *Family therapy techniques*. Cambridge, MA: Harvard University Press.

Mischel, W. (1966). A social learning view of sex differences in behavior. In E. E. Maccoby (Ed.), *The development of sex differences* (pp. 57–81). Palo Alto, CA: Stanford University Press.

Mitchell, J. (2003). *Siblings. Sex and violence*. Oxford: Blackwell/Polity.

Montague, A. (1995) Animadversions on the development of a theory of touch. In T. Field (Ed.), *Touch in early development* (pp. 1–10). Hillsdale, NJ: Lawrence Erlbaum Associates.

Moorman, J. (1994). My sister's keeper. *Family Therapy Networker, 18*, 41–44.

Moyer, M. S. (1992). Sibling relationships among older adults. *Families and Aging, 52*, 55–58.

Namysłowska, I., & Siewierska, A. (2010). The significance and role of siblings in family therapy. *Archives of Psychiatry and Psychotherapy, 12*, 5–13.

Neaves, R. D., & Crouch, J. G. (1990). Deidentification in two-child families. *Journal of Adolescent Research, 5*, 370–386.

Newman, J. (1991). College students' relationships with siblings. *Journal of Youth and Adolescence, 20*, 629–645.

Newman, J. (1996). The more the merrier? Effects of family size and sibling spacing on sibling relationships. *Child: Care, Health, and Development, 22,* 285–302.

Noland, V. J., Liller, K. D., McDermott, R. J., Coulter, M. L., & Seraphine, A. E. (2004). Is adolescent sibling violence a precursor to college dating violence? *American Journal of Health Behavior, 28,* S13–S23.

Noller, P., Feeney, J., Sheehan, G., Rogers, C., & Darlington, Y. (2008). Conflict in divorcing and continuously married families: A study of marital, parent–child and sibling relationships. *Journal of Divorce and Remarriage, 49,* 1–24.

Norris-Shortle, C., Donohure Colletta, N., Beyer Cohen, M., & McCombs, R. (1995). Sibling play therapy with children under three. *Child and Adolescent Social Work Journal, 12,* 251–261.

Nuttall, A. K., Valentino, K., & Borkowski, J. G. (2012). Maternal history of parentification, maternal warm responsiveness, and children's externalizing behavior. *Journal of Family Psychology, 26,* 767–775.

O'Bryant, S. L. (1988). Sibling support and older widows' well-being. *Journal of Marriage and the Family, 50,* 173–183.

O'Leary, K., O'Leary, S., & Becker, W. C. (1973). Modification of a deviant sibling interaction pattern in the home. In J. M. Stedman, W. F. Patton, K. F. Walton, J. M. Stedman, W. F. Patton, & K. F. Walton (Eds.), *Clinical studies in behavior therapy with children, adolescents and their families* (pp. 265–276). Springfield, IL: Charles C. Thomas Publisher.

Olson, R. L., & Roberts, M. W. (1987). Alternative treatments for sibling aggression. *Behavior Therapy, 18,* 243–250.

Panish, J. B., & Sticker, G. (2001). Parental marital conflict in childhood and influence on adult sibling relationships. *Journal of Psychotherapy in Independent Practice, 2,* 3–16.

Parke, R. D., & O'Neil, R. (1999). Social relationships across contexts: Family-peer linkages. In A. W. Collins & B. Laursen (Eds.), *Relationships as developmental contexts. The Minnesota symposia on child psychology* (Vol. 30, pp. 211–239). Mahwah, NJ: Lawrence Erlbaum Associates.

Parker, J. G., & Asher, S. R. (1993). Friendship and friendship quality in middle childhood: Links with peer group acceptance and feelings of loneliness and social satisfaction. *Developmental Psychology, 29,* 611–621.

Patterson, C., Cohn, D., & Kao, B. (1989). Maternal warmth as a protective factor against risks associated with peer rejection among children. *Development and Psychopathology, 1,* 21–38.

Perlman, M., & Ross, H. S. (1997). The benefits of parent intervention in children's disputes: An examination of concurrent changes in children's fighting styles. *Child Development, 68,* 690–700.

Perlmutter, M. S. (1988). Enchantment of siblings: Effects of birth order and trance on family myth. In M. D. Kahn & K. G. Lewis (Eds.), *Siblings in therapy: Life span and clinical issues* (pp. 25–45). New York: Norton.

Perozynski, L., & Kramer, L. (1999). Parental beliefs about managing sibling conflict. *Developmental Psychology, 35,* 489–500.

Petalas, M. A., Hastings, R. P., Nash, S., Lloyd, T., & Dowey, A. (2009). Emotional and behavioral adjustment in siblings of children with intellectual disability with and without autism. *Autism, 13,* 417–483.

Piaget, J. (1965). *The moral judgment of the child.* New York: Free Press.

Pike, A., Coldwell, J., & Dunn, J. (2005). Sibling relationships in early/middle childhood: Links with individual adjustment. *Journal of Family Psychology, 19,* 523–532.

Pillemer, K., Suitor, J. J., Pardo, S., & Henderson, C. J. (2010). Mothers' differentiation and depressive symptoms among adult children. *Journal of Marriage and Family, 72,* 333–345.

Pomery, E., Gibbons, F., Gerrard, M., Cleveland, M., Brody, G., & Wills, T. (2005). Families and risk: Prospective analyses of familial and social influences on adolescent substance use. *Journal of Family Psychology, 19,* 560–570.

Powell, M. A., & Parcel, T. L. (1997). Effects of family structure on the earnings attainment process: Differences by gender. *Journal of Marriage and the Family, 59,* 419–433.

Purswell, K. E., & Dillman-Taylor, D. (2013). Creative use of sibling play therapy: An example of a blended family. *Journal of Creativity in Mental Health, 8,* 162–174.

Rabin, H. (1989). Peers and siblings: Their neglect in analytic group psychotherapy. *International Journal of Group Psychotherapy, 39,* 209–221.

Rabain-Jamin, J., Maynard, A., & Greenfield, P. (2003). Implications of sibling caregiving for sibling relations and teaching interactions in two cultures. *Ethos, 31,* 204–231.

Rende, R., Slomkowski, C., Lloyd-Richardson, E., & Niaura, R. (2005). Sibling effects on substance use in adolescence: Social contagion and genetic relatedness. *Journal of Family Psychology, 19,* 611–618.

Richmond, M. K., Stocker, C. M., & Rienks, S. L. (2005). Longitudinal associations between sibling relationship quality, parental differential treatment, and children's adjustment. *Journal of Family Psychology, 19,* 550–559.

Riggio, H. R. (2001). Relations between parental divorce and the quality of adult sibling relationships. *Journal of Divorce and Remarriage, 36,* 67–82.

Riggio, H. R. (2006). Relationships in young adulthood: Structural features of sibling dyads and attitudes toward sibling. *Journal of Family Issues, 27,* 1233–1254.

Romero, A. J., Robinson, T. N., Farish-Haydel, K., Mendoza, F., & Killen, J. D. (2004). Associations among familism, language preference, and education in Mexican-American mothers and their children. *Developmental and Behavioral Pediatrics, 25,* 34–40.

Rosenberg, B. G. (1982). Lifespan personality stability in sibling status. In M. E. Lamb & B. Sutton-Smith (Eds.), *Sibling relationships: Their nature and significance across the lifespan* (pp. 167–224). Hillsdale, NJ: Lawrence Erlbaum Associates.

Rosenberg, E. B. (1980). Therapy with siblings in reorganizing families. *International Journal of Family Therapy, 2,* 139–158.

Rosner, S. (1985). On the place of siblings in psychoanalysis. *Psychoanalytic Review, 72*, 457–477.

Ross, C. E., & Mirowsky, J. (1999). Parental divorce, life-course disruption, and adult depression. *Journal of Marriage and the Family, 61*, 1034–1045.

Ross, H., Filyer, R., Lollis, S. P., Perlman, M., & Martin, J. L. (1994). Administering justice in the family. *Journal of Family Psychology, 8*, 254–273.

Ross, P., & Cuskelly, M. (2006). Adjustment, sibling problems and coping strategies of brothers and sisters of children with autistic spectrum disorder. *Journal of Intellectual and Developmental Disability, 31*, 77–86.

Rossiter, L., & Sharpe, D. (2001). The siblings of individuals with mental retardation: A quantitative integration of the literature. *Journal of Child and Family Studies, 10*, 65–84.

Rowe, D. C., & Gulley, B. (1992). Sibling effects on substance abuse and delinquency. *Criminology, 30*, 217–233.

Rowe, D. C., Woulbroun, E. J., & Gulley, B. L. (1994). Peers and friends as nonshared environmental influences. In E. M. Hetherington, D. Reiss, & R. Plomin (Eds.), *Separate social worlds of siblings: The impact of nonshared environment on development* (pp. 159–173). Hillsdale, NJ: Lawrence Erlbaum Associates.

Rutter, M. (1990). Psychosocial resilience and protective mechanisms. In J. Rolf, A. S. Masten, D. Cicchetti, K. H. Nuechterlein, & S. Weintraub (Eds.), *Risk and protective factors in the development of psychopathology* (pp. 181–214). New York: Cambridge University Press.

Safer, J. (2002). *The normal one: Life with a difficult or damaged sibling.* New York: Bantam Dell.

Salovey, P., & Mayer, J. D. (1990). Emotional intelligence. *Imagination, Cognition and Personality, 3*, 185–211.

Sanders, R. (2004). *Sibling relationships: Theory and issues for practice.* New York: Palgrave Macmillan.

Sandler, I. N. (1980). Social support resources, stress, and maladjustment of poor children. *American Journal of Community Psychology, 8*, 41–52.

Satir, V. (1964). *Conjoint family therapy.* Palo Alto, CA: Science and Behavior Books.

Satir, V., & Baldwin, M. (1983). *Satir step by step: A guide to creating change in families.* Palo Alto, CA: Science and Behavior Books.

Saudino, K., McGuire, S., Hetherington, E., Reiss, D., & Plomin, R. (1995). Parent ratings of EAS temperaments in twins, full siblings, half siblings, and step siblings. *Journal of Personality and Social Psychology, 68*, 723–733.

Schachter, F. F., Gilutz, G., Shore, E., & Adler, M. (1978). Sibling deidentification judged by mothers: Cross-validation and developmental studies. *Child Development, 49*, 543–546.

Schachter, F. F., Shore, E., Feldman-Rotman, S., Marquis, R. E., & Campbell, S. (1976). Sibling deidentification. *Developmental Psychology, 12*, 418–427.

Scharf, M., Shulman, S., & Avigad-Spitz, L. (2005). Sibling relationships in emerging adulthood and in adolescence. *Journal of Adolescent Research, 20*, 64–90.

Schermer, V. (2000). Contributions of object relations theory and self psychology to relational psychology and group psychotherapy. *International Journal of Group Psychotherapy, 50,* 199–217.

Schibuk, M. (1989). Treating the sibling subsystem: An adjunct of divorce therapy. *American Journal of Orthopsychiatry, 59,* 226–237.

Schneider, B. H., Smith, A., Poisson, S. E., & Kwan, A. B. (1997). Cultural dimensions of children's peer relations. In S. Duck (Ed.), *Handbook of personal relationships* (pp. 121–146). New York: Wiley.

Scholte, R. H., Engels, R. C. M. E., de Kemp, R. A. T., Harakeh, Z., & Overbeek, G. (2007). Differential parental treatment, sibling relationships and delinquency in adolescence. *Journal of Youth and Adolescence, 36,* 661–671.

Schoppe-Sullivan, S. J., Weldon, A. H., Cook, J. C., Davis, E. F., & Buckley, C. K. (2009). Coparenting behavior moderates longitudinal relations between effortful control and preschool children's externalizing behavior. *Journal of Child Psychology and Psychiatry, 50,* 698–706.

Schulman, G. L. (1999). Siblings revisited: Old conflicts and new opportunities in later life. *Journal of Marital and Family Therapy, 25,* 517–524.

Scott, L., McCoy, H., Munson, M., Snowden, L., & McMillen, J. (2011). Cultural mistrust of mental health professionals among Black males transitioning from foster care. *Journal of Child and Family Studies, 20,* 605–613.

Seaver, W. (1973). Effects of naturally induced teacher expectancies. *Journal of Personality and Social Psychology, 28,* 333–342.

Seginer, R. (1998). Adolescents' perception of relationships with older siblings in the context of other close relationships. *Journal of Research on Adolescence, 8,* 287–308.

Shalash, F. M., Wood, N. D., & Parker, T. S. (2013). Our problems are your sibling's fault: Exploring the connections between conflict styles of siblings during adolescence and later adult committed relationships. *American Journal of Family Therapy, 41,* 288–298.

Shanahan, L., Mchale, S., Crouter, A., & Osgood, D. (2008). Linkages between parents' differential treatment, youth depressive symptoms, and sibling relationships. *Journal of Marriage and Family, 70,* 480–494.

Shapiro, E., & Ginzberg, R. (2001). The persistently neglected sibling relationship and its applicability to group therapy. *International Journal of Group Psychotherapy, 51,* 327–341.

Shebloski, B., Conger, K., & Widaman, K. (2005). Reciprocal links among differential parenting, perceived partiality, and self-worth: A three-wave longitudinal study. *Journal of Family Psychology, 19,* 633–642.

Sherwin-White, S. (2007). Freud on brothers and sisters: A neglected topic. *Journal of Child Psychotherapy, 33,* 4–20.

Simons, L. G., & Conger, R. D. (2007). Linking mother–father differences in parenting to a typology of family parenting styles and adolescent outcomes. *Journal of Family Issues, 28,* 212–241.

Slomkowski, C., Rende, R., Conger, K. J., Simons, R. L., & Conger, R. D. (2001). Sisters, brothers, and delinquency: Evaluating social influence during early and middle adolescence. *Child Development, 72,* 271–283.

Slomkowski, C., Rende, R., Novak, S., Lloyd-Richardson, E., & Niaura, R. (2005). Sibling effects on smoking in adolescence: Evidence for social influence from a genetically informative design. *Addiction, 100*, 430–438.

Smith, J., & Ross, H. (2007). Training parents to mediate sibling disputes affects children's negotiation and conflict understanding. *Child Development, 78*, 790–805.

Smith, T. E. (1993). Growth in academic achievement and teaching younger siblings. *Social Psychology Quarterly, 56*, 77–85.

Snyder, J., Bank, L., & Burraston, B. (2005). The consequences of antisocial behavior in older male siblings for younger brothers and sisters. *Journal of Family Psychology, 19*, 643–653.

Song, J. H., & Volling, B. L. (2015). Coparenting and children's temperament predict firstborns' cooperation in the care of an infant sibling. *Journal of Family Psychology, 29*, 130–135.

Sroufe, L. A., Egeland, B., & Kreutzer, T. (1990). The fate of early experience following developmental change: Longitudinal approaches to individual adaptation in childhood. *Child Development, 61*, 1363–1373.

Steinberg, L., Lamborn, S., Darling, N., Mounts, N., & Dornbusch, S. (1994). Over-time changes in adjustment and competence among adolescents from authoritative, authoritarian, indulgent, and neglectful families. *Child Development, 65*, 754–770.

Stewart, R. B., Kozak, A. L., Tingley, L. M., Goddard, J. M., Blake, E. M, & Cassel, W. A. (2001). Adult sibling relationship: A validation of a typology. *Personal Relationships, 8*, 299–324.

Stocker, C. M. (1994). Children's perceptions of relationships with siblings, friends, and mothers: Compensatory processes and links with adjustment. *Journal of Child Psychology and Psychiatry, 35*, 1447–1459.

Stocker, C. M., & Dunn, J. (1990). Sibling relationships in childhood: Links with friendships and peer relationships. *British Journal of Developmental Psychology, 8*, 227–244.

Stocker, C. M., & Youngblade, L. (1999). Marital conflict and parental hostility: Links with children's sibling and peer relationships. *Journal of Family Psychology, 13*, 598–609.

Straus, M., Gelles, R., & Steinmetz, S. (1980). *Behind closed doors*. New York: Doubleday.

Strickland-Clark, L., Campbell, D., & Dallos, R. (2000). Children and adolescent's views on family therapy. *Journal of Family Therapy, 22*, 324–342.

Sue, D. W. (1990). Culture-specific strategies in counseling: A conceptual framework. *Professional Psychology: Research and Practice, 21*, 424–433.

Suitor, J. J., Sechrist, J., & Pillemer, K. (2007). Within-family differences in mothers' support to adult children in Black and White families. *Research on Aging, 29*, 410–435.

Suitor, J. J., Sechrist, J., Plikuhn, M., Pardo, S. T., Gilligan, M., & Pillemer, K. (2009). The role of perceived maternal favoritism in sibling relations in midlife. *Journal of Marriage and Family, 71*, 1026–1038.

Sullivan, H. S. (1953). *The interpersonal theory of psychiatry*. New York: Norton.

Sulloway, F. J. (1996). *Born to rebel: Birth order, family dynamics, and creative lives.* New York: Pantheon.

Sulloway, F. J. (2007). Birth order. In C. Salmon & T. Shackelford (Eds.), *Evolutionary family psychology* (pp. 162–182). Oxford: Oxford University Press.

Takahashi, K. (1990). Affective relationships and their lifelong development. In P. B. Baltes, D. L. Featherman, & L. R. Sherrod (Eds.), *Life-span development and behavior* (pp. 1–27). Hillsdale, NJ: Lawrence Erlbaum Associates.

Tejerina-Allen, M., Wagner, B., & Cohen, P. (1994). A comparison of across-family and within-family parenting predictors of adolescent psychopathology and suicidal ideation. In E. M. Hetherington, D. Reiss, & R. Plomin (Eds.), *Separate social worlds of siblings: The impact of nonshared environment on development* (pp. 143–158). Hillsdale, NJ: Lawrence Erlbaum Associates.

Tesser, A. (1980). Self-esteem maintenance in family dynamics. *Journal of Personality and Social Psychology, 39,* 77–91.

Teti, D. M. (2002). Retrospect and prospect in the psychological study of sibling relationships. In J. P. McHale & W. S. Grolnick (Eds.), *Retrospect and prospect in the psychological study of families* (pp. 193–224). Mahwah, NJ: Lawrence Erlbaum Associates.

Teti, D. M., & Ablard, K. E. (1989). Security of attachment and infant-sibling relationships: A laboratory study. *Child Development, 60,* 1519–1528.

Tucker, C. J., Barber, B. L., & Eccles, J. S. (1997). Advice about life plans and personal problems in late adolescent sibling relationships. *Journal of Youth and Adolescence, 26,* 63–76.

Tucker, C. J., Updegraff, K. A., McHale, S. M., & Crouter, A. C. (1999). Siblings as socializers of empathy. *Journal of Early Adolescence, 19,* 176–198.

Tyndall-Lind, A., Landreth, G. L., & Giordano, M. A. (2001). Intensive group play therapy with child witnesses of domestic violence. *International Journal of Play Therapy, 10,* 53–83.

Updegraff, K. A., McHale, S. M., & Crouter, A. C. (2002). Adolescents' sibling relationship and friendship experiences: Developmental patterns and relationship linkages. *Social Development, 11,* 182–204.

Updegraff, K., McHale, S., Whiteman, S., Thayer, S., & Delgado, M. (2005). Adolescent sibling relationships in Mexican American families: Exploring the role of familism. *Journal of Family Psychology, 19,* 512–522.

Vaillant, G. E., & Vaillant, C. O. (1990). Natural history of male psychological health, xii: A 45-year study of predictors of successful aging at age 65. *American Journal of Psychiatry, 147,* 31–37.

van Aken, M. A. G., & Asendorpf, J. B. (1997). Support by parents, classmates, friends and siblings in preadolescence: Covariation and compensation across relationships. *Journal of Social and Personal Relationships, 14,* 79–93.

van Beekum, S. (2013). Changing the focus: The impact of sibling issues on group dynamics. *Transactional Analysis Journal, 43,* 347–351.

Van Volkom, M. (2006). Sibling relationships in middle and older adulthood: A review of the literature. *Marriage and Family Review, 40,* 151–170.

Verte, S., Roeyers, H., & Busse, A. (2003). Behavioral problems, social competence and self-concept in siblings of children with autism. *Child: Care, Health and Development, 29*, 193–205.

Visher, E., & Visher, J. (2003). The remarried family: Characteristics and interventions. In E. Visher & J. Visher (Eds.), *Textbook of family and couples therapy: Clinical applications* (pp. 523–538). Washington, DC: American Psychiatric Publishing.

Volling, B. L. (2003). Sibling relationships. In M. H. Bornstein (Ed.), *Well-being: Positive development across the life course* (pp. 205–220). Mahwah, NJ: Lawrence Erlbaum Associates.

Volling, B. L. (2012). Family transitions following the birth of a sibling: An empirical review of changes in the firstborn's adjustment. *Psychological Bulletin, 138*, 497–528.

Vondra, J. I., Shaw, D. S., Swearingen, L., Cohen, M., & Owens, E. B. (1999). Early relationship quality from home to school: A longitudinal study. *Early Education and Development, 10*, 163–190.

Voorpostel, M., & Blieszner, R. (2008). Intergenerational solidarity and support between adult siblings. *Journal of Marriage and Family, 70*, 157–167.

Wagner, M. E., Schubert, H., & Schubert, D. S. (1985). Effects of sibling spacing on intelligence, interfamilial relations, psychosocial characteristics, and mental and physical health. In H. W. Reese (Ed.), *Advances in child development and behavior* (pp. 149–206). Orlando, FL: Academic Press.

Waldinger, R. J., Vaillant, G. E., & Orav, E. J. (2007). Childhood sibling relationships as a predictor of major depression in adulthood: A 30-year prospective study. *American Journal of Psychiatry, 164*, 949–954.

Wallerstein, J. S., & Kelly, J. B. (1980). *Surviving the breakup: How children and parents cope with divorce.* New York: Basic Books.

Wallerstein, J. S., Lewis, J., & Blakeslee, S. (2002). *The unexpected legacy of divorce. A 25-year landmark study.* London: Fusion Press.

Wallin, D. J. (2007). *Attachment in psychotherapy.* New York: The Guilford Press.

Walsh, W. M. (1992). Twenty marriage issues in remarriage families. *Journal of Counseling and Development, 70*, 709–715.

Weisner, T. S. (1982). Sibling interdependence and child caretaking: A cross cultural view. In M. E. Lamb & B. Sutton-Smith (Eds.), *Sibling relationships: Their nature and significance across the lifespan* (pp. 305–327). Hillsdale, NJ: Lawrence Erlbaum Associates.

Weisner, T. S. (1989). Comparing sibling relationships across cultures. In P. G. Zukow (Ed.), *Sibling interaction across cultures: Theoretical and methodological issues* (pp. 11–25). New York: Springer-Verlag.

Weisner, T. S. (1993). Ethnographic and ecocultural perspectives on sibling relationships. In Z. Stoneman & P. W. Berman (Eds.), *The effects of mental retardation, disability, and illness on sibling relationships: Research issues and challenges* (pp. 51–83). Baltimore, MD: Paul H. Brookes Publishing.

Weiss, L., & Schwarz, J. C. (1996). The relationship between parenting types and older adolescents' personality, adjustment, academic achievement, and substance abuse. *Child Development, 67*, 2101–2114.

Weiss, R. S. (1974). The provisions of social relationships. In Z. Rubin (Ed.), *Doing unto others.* Englewood Cliffs, NJ: Prentice-Hall.

Werner DeGrace, B. (2004). The everyday occupations of families with children with autism. *The American Journal of Occupational Therapy, 58,* 543–550.

Whiteman, S. D., Jensen, A. C., & Maggs, J. L. (2013). Similarities in adolescent siblings' substance use: Testing competing pathways of influence. *Journal of Studies on Alcohol and Drugs, 74,* 104–113.

Whiteman, S. D., Jensen, A. C., & Maggs, J. L. (2014). Similarities and differences in adolescent siblings' alcohol-related attitudes, use, and delinquency: Evidence for convergent and divergent influence processes. *Journal of Youth and Adolescence, 43,* 687–697.

Whiteman, S. D., McHale, S. M., & Crouter, A. C. (2007). Competing processes of sibling influence: Observational learning and sibling deidentification. *Social Development, 16,* 642–661.

Wichman, A. L., Rodgers, J. L., & MacCallum, R. C. (2006). A multilevel approach to the relationship between birth order and intelligence. *Personality and Social Psychology Bulletin, 32,* 117–127.

Wiehe, V. R. (2000). Sibling abuse. In H. Henderson (Ed.), *Domestic violence and child abuse source book* (pp. 409–492). Detroit, MI: Omnigraphics.

Wittenberg, E. E. (2009). Siblings as selfobjects in childhood: An interview study of factors and consequences. *Psychoanalytic Social Work, 16,* 31–57.

Wolf, E. S. (1988). *Treating the self: Elements of clinical self psychology.* New York: Guilford Press.

Wood, L. J., Sherman, E. M., Hamiwka, L. D., Blackman, M. A., & Wirrell, E. C. (2008). Maternal depression: The cost of caring for a child with intractable epilepsy. *Pediatric Neurology, 39,* 418–422.

Yeh, H., & Lempers, J. (2004). Perceived sibling relationships and adolescent development. *Journal of Youth and Adolescence, 33,* 133–147.

Youniss, J. (1980). *Parents and peers in social development.* Chicago: University of Chicago Press.

Zukow, P. G. (1989). *Sibling interaction across cultures: Theoretical and methodological issues.* New York: Springer-Verlag.

Zukow, P. G. (1995). Sibling caregiving. In M. H. Bornstein (Ed.), *Handbook of parenting: Vol. 3: Being and becoming a parent* (pp. 177–208). Mahwah, NJ: Lawrence Erlbaum Associates.

Zukow, P. G. (2002). Sibling caregiving. In M. H. Bornstein (Ed.), *Handbook of parenting: Vol. 3: Being and becoming a parent* (2nd ed., pp. 253–286). Hillsdale, NJ: Lawrence Erlbaum Associates.

Index

CPSIA information can be obtained
at www.ICGtesting.com
Printed in the USA
LVOW04s2037130516

488158LV00010B/220/P